IE4 Administration

The Cram Sheet

This Cram Sheet contains the distilled, key facts about IE4 administration. Review this information last thing before you enter the test room, paying special attention to those areas where you feel you need the most review. You can transfer any of these facts from your head onto a blank sheet of paper before beginning the exam.

Planning

1. The IEAK licensing agreement requires you to report your usage on a quarterly basis. A 10-digit code is assigned, based on your role. Know the differences between the three roles:
   - **Corporate Administrator** Can import and define channels (including software distribution channels), Auto-configuration settings, Security Zone settings, proxy settings, content rating settings, Certificate Authorities, and Authenticode information.
   - **Internet Service Provider** Can add one channel and one custom desktop component, use single floppy distribution, delete competing channels, define an Internet Sign-up Server method, add custom sign-up files, and define DUN parameters.
   - **Internet Content Provider/Developer** Can add one channel, delete competing channels, and add one desktop component.
2. Besides a download site, IE distribution methods are: CD-ROM, floppy disks, and single floppy. Single floppy is for ISPs only!
3. The minimum hardware requirements for the IEAK are:
   - 486/66 processor
   - 8MB RAM on Windows 95 or 16MB RAM on NT 4
   - 40MB disk space to install
   - 40MB—100MB per custom package
4. The amount of disk space needed for installing IE varies with the components included in the package:
   - **Minimal Installation** 39MB
   - **Standard Installation** 51MB
   - **Full Installation** 70MB
5. If Corporate Administrators choose silent install, they have to choose whether to install Active Desktop. They also can specify only one installation option and one download site.

Installation And Configuration

6. IE is available for the following platforms: Windows 3.x (including Windows For Workgroups), Mac, Unix, NT 4, and Windows 95.
7. Know the stages of the IEAK Wizard:
   - **Stage 1** Gathering Information
   - **Stage 2** Specifying Active Setup Parameters
   - **Stage 3** Customizing Active Setup
   - **Stage 4** Customizing The Browser
   - **Stage 5** Customizing Components

   Corporate Administrators have an additional System Policies And Restrictions screen, which makes up Stage 6.
8. As you move through Stage 3, you can customize items, such as your own channel in the Channel Guide and custom help files to be used by IE4.
9. IEAK users can include up to 10 custom components and can specify up to 10 download sites, unless a Corporate Administrator is using silent mode, in which case it's 1 component and 1 download site.
10. History is a collection of shortcuts to recently visited Web sites. By default, history files are kept in the C:\Windows\History folder. The History folder is purged every 20 days.
11. Cache is a collection of recently downloaded items, such as Web pages and images. Cached files are kept in the C:\Windows\Temporary Internet Files folder.
12. NetMeeting is for one-to-one collaboration. NetShow is for one-to-many broadcasts.
13. Using NetMeeting through a firewall requires opening ports 389, 522, 1503, 1720, 1730, and two dynamic UDP ports.
14. IEAK can be configured to change the InfoPane to point to either a customized HTML file on the user's local machine or to a URL on the Internet or intranet. When using a URL, offline users receive a blank InfoPane.
15. IE4 supports Automatic Version Synchronization, which ensures that you have the latest versions of all IE components before proceeding with a build. This is done by connecting to the download site you select and comparing file dates and times.
16. Default corporate disclaimers that are locked into place can be used to meet legal notification requirements.

Configuring And Managing Resource Access

17. The four main Security Zones and their default security levels are:
    - **Local Intranet Zone** Medium
    - **Trusted Sites Zone** Low
    - **Internet Zone** Medium
    - **Restricted Sites Zone** High
18. A fifth Security Zone—the Local PC Zone—is only configurable through the Registry.
19. An Auto-proxy file contains JavaScript that can remotely define and update users' proxy settings. Valid Auto-proxy file extensions are .JS, .JVS, and .PAC. These files can be created with a configuration file for a user or a group.
20. An Auto-configuration file contains Internet Explorer and Active Setup information and can be used to remotely define and update users' IE settings. The IEAK Profile Manager is used to update these INS (Internet Setup) files.
21. ADM files are policy templates used to create INF files for IE policies. There are ADM files for:
    - Chat
    - NetMeeting
    - Internet restrictions
    - Internet settings
    - Outlook Express
    - Web Desktop
    - Subscriptions

    After creating INF files with the Profile Manager, they are immediately packaged into

Are You Certifiable?

That's the question that's probably on your mind. The answer is: You bet! But if you've tried and failed or you've been frustrated by the complexity of the MCSE program and the maze of study materials available, you've come to the right place. We've created our new publishing and training program, *Certification Insider Press*, to help you accomplish one important goal: to ace an MCSE exam without having to spend the rest of your life studying for it.

The book you have in your hands is part of our *Exam Cram* series. Each book is especially designed not only to help you study for an exam but also to help you understand what the exam is all about. Inside these covers you'll find hundreds of test-taking tips, insights, and strategies that simply cannot be found anyplace else. In creating our guides, we've assembled the very best team of certified trainers, MCSE professionals, and networking course developers.

Our commitment is to ensure that the *Exam Cram* guides offer proven training and active-learning techniques not found in other study guides. We provide unique study tips and techniques, memory joggers, custom quizzes, insights about trick questions, a sample test, and much more. In a nutshell, each *Exam Cram* guide is closely organized like the exam it is tied to.

To help us continue to provide the very best certification study materials, we'd like to hear from you. Write or email us (craminfo@coriolis.com) and let us know how our *Exam Cram* guides have helped you study, or tell us about new features you'd like us to add. If you send us a story about how an *Exam Cram* guide has helped you ace an exam and we use it in one of our guides, we'll send you an official *Exam Cram* shirt for your efforts.

Good luck with your certification exam, and thanks for allowing us to help you achieve your goals.

Keith Weiskamp

Keith Weiskamp
Publisher, Certification Insider Press

IE4 Administration

Exam # 70-079

Microsoft Certified Systems Engineer

David Johnson
Tim Catura-Houser

MCSE IE4 Administration Exam Cram

The Coriolis Group, Inc.
An International Thomson Publishing Company
14455 N. Hayden Road, Suite 220
Scottsdale, Arizona 85260

602/483-0192
FAX 602/483-0193
http://www.coriolis.com

Library of Congress Cataloging-in-Publication Data
Johnson, David, 1970-
MCSE IE4 administration exam cram/by David Johnson and Tim Catura-Houser.
p. cm.
Includes index.
ISBN 1-57610-286-6
1. Electronic data processing personnel--Certification. 2. Microsoft software--Examinations--Study guides. 3. Microsoft Internet Explorer. I. Catura-Houser, Tim. II. Title.
QA76.3.J6397 1998
005.7'13769--dc21 98-25773
CIP

Printed in the United States of America
10 9 8 7 6 5 4 3 2 1

Publisher
Keith Weiskamp

Acquisitions
Shari Jo Hehr

Project Editor
Meredith Brittain

Production Coordinator
Jon Gabriel

Cover Design
Anthony Stock

Layout Design
April Nielsen

an International Thomson Publishing company

Albany, NY • Belmont, CA • Bonn • Boston • Cincinnati • Detroit • Johannesburg • London • Madrid Melbourne • Mexico City • New York • Paris • Singapore • Tokyo • Toronto • Washington

About The Authors

David Johnson (a.k.a. DJ)

DJ has worked in the networking trenches as a network administrator, manager, and trainer for eight years. Working for large corporations such as Pharmaco and GTECH, he learned his way around LAN and WAN technologies in exotic locations that range from Trinidad, to the United Kingdom, to Austin, TX, to Belo Horizonte, Brazil, to Warwick, RI. He has contributed to numerous NT- and MCSE-focused courses and books, on subjects that include Networking Essentials, Windows NT Server 4.0, Workstation 4.0, Windows NT Server 4.0 in the Enterprise, and TCP/IP. He hopes to complete his MCSE and ECNE in the very near future, as well as to spend more time in the classroom training while working on a series of exam preparation and MCSE study guide books. You can reach DJ at count0@worldnet.att.net.

Tim Catura-Houser

Tim began his digital journey with C/PM computers for Office Solutions, and Point of Sale systems. His certifications include MCSE +I and MCT. With his first love being hardware, he carries certifications from Artisoft to Cisco and IBM. When Tim isn't writing, he is either teaching technical courses or leading CTT/MCT trainer classes. His single favorite toy is his battery-powered Ricochet wireless modem. He has so much fun with computers that he has no time for anything else. Tim reads all his email, so you can question, pan or praise him by email at Tcat@usa.net.

Acknowledgments

David Johnson

First, I'd like to thank my co-author, Tim. I must say, my friend, this has definitely been an adventure. I'd like to thank the staff at Coriolis—Meredith, Jon, Wendy, Cynthia, and Tony—for all their hard work on this project. I'd especially like to thank Meredith for dealing with us in all our harried glory. Not bad for our first project together. Ready for the next one? As always, thank you to the staff at LANWrights for supporting me. Thanks to Ed for giving me this wonderful opportunity. Thanks to Michael, Natanya, and Bill for understanding when I didn't return their calls. And, of course, thanks to Dawn and Mary for wading through the drafts and making it all sound good. Finally, and most importantly, a resounding thank you to the countless technical experts who helped me understand the ins and outs of this interesting product—you know who you are.

Tim Catura-Houser

Without the fantastic assistance of several super people, I couldn't have gotten the concepts presented to print. Somehow, a mere mega-thanks doesn't seem enough for Marilyn, for letting me stack servers like firewood in the living room; Compaq Computer, for helping build the stack of servers; and most important of all, the people at LANWrights. A very special thanks to Dawn, DJ, Mary, and Ed for the patience in converting me (regardless of the pain and suffering it caused them) from a writer of newsletters to technical manuals. Without the invaluable assistance of all of these grand folks, I never would have made it.

Table Of Contents

Introduction

Welcome to the *MCSE IE4 Administration Exam Cram*! This book aims to help you get ready to take—and pass—the Microsoft certification test numbered "Exam 70-079," titled "Implementing and Supporting Microsoft Internet Explorer 4.0 by Using the Internet Explorer Administration Kit." This Introduction explains Microsoft's certification programs in general and talks about how the Exam Cram series can help you prepare for Microsoft's certification exams.

Exam Cram books help you understand and appreciate the subjects and materials you need to pass Microsoft certification exams. Exam Cram books are aimed strictly at test preparation and review. They do not teach you everything you need to know about a topic (such as the ins and outs of managing an Internet Explorer implementation). Instead, we (the authors) present and dissect the questions and problems we've found that you're likely to encounter on a test. We've worked from Microsoft's own training materials, preparation guides, and tests, and from a battery of third-party test preparation tools. Our aim is to bring together as much information as possible about Microsoft certification exams.

Nevertheless, to completely prepare yourself for any Microsoft test, we recommend that you begin your studies with some classroom training, or that you pick up and read one of the many study guides available from Microsoft or third-party vendors, including The Coriolis Group's Exam Prep series. We also strongly recommend that you install, configure, and fool around with the software or environment that you'll be tested on, because nothing beats hands-on experience and familiarity when it comes to understanding the questions you're likely to encounter on a certification test. Book learning is essential, but hands-on experience is the best teacher of all!

The Microsoft Certified Professional (MCP) Program

The MCP Program currently includes seven separate tracks, each of which boasts its own special acronym (as a would-be certificant, you need to have a high tolerance for alphabet soup of all kinds):

- **MCP (Microsoft Certified Professional)** This is the least prestigious of all the certification tracks from Microsoft. Attaining MCP status requires an individual to pass one exam. Passing any of the major Microsoft exams (except the Networking Essentials Exam) qualifies an individual for MCP credentials. Individuals can demonstrate proficiency with additional Microsoft products by passing additional certification exams.
- **MCP + I (Microsoft Certified Professional plus Internet)** This mid-level certification is attained by completing three core exams: Windows NT Server, TCP/IP, and Internet Information Server.
- **MCP + SB (Microsoft Certified Professional + Site Building)** This new certification program is designed for individuals who are planning, building, managing, and maintaining Web sites. Individuals with the MCP + SB credential will have demonstrated the ability to develop Web sites that include multimedia and searchable content and Web sites that connect to and communicate with a back-end database. It requires one MCP exam, plus two of these three exams: Designing and Implementing Commerce Solutions with Microsoft Site Server 3.0 Commerce Edition, Designing and Implementing Web Sites with Microsoft FrontPage 98, and Designing and Implementing Web Solutions with Microsoft Visual InterDev 6.0.
- **MCSD (Microsoft Certified Solution Developer)** The new MCSD credential reflects the new skills required to create multitier, distributed, and COM-based solutions, in addition to desktop and Internet applications, using new technologies. To obtain an MCSD, an individual must demonstrate the ability to analyze and interpret user requirements; select and integrate products, platforms, tools, and technologies; design and implement code and customize applications; and perform necessary software tests and quality assurance operations.

  To become an MCSD, you must pass a total of four exams: three core exams (available fall 1998) and one elective exam. The required exam is Analyzing Requirements and Defining Solution Architectures (Exam 70-100). Each candidate must also choose one of these two desktop application exams—Designing and Implementing Desktop Applications with Microsoft Visual C++ 6.0 (Exam 70-016) or Visual Basic 6.0 (Exam 70-176)—PLUS one of these two distributed application exams—Designing and Implementing Distributed Applications with Visual C++ 6.0 (Exam 70-015) or Visual Basic 6.0 (Exam 70-175).

  Elective exams cover specific Microsoft applications and languages, including Visual Basic, C++, the Microsoft Foundation Classes, Access, SQL Server, Excel, and more. If you are on your way to becoming an

MCSD and have already taken some exams, visit **Microsoft.com/ train_cert** for information about how to proceed with your MCSD certification under this new track.

- **MCSE (Microsoft Certified Systems Engineer)** Anyone who has a current MCSE is warranted to possess a high level of expertise with Windows NT (either version 3.51 or 4) and other Microsoft operating systems and products. This credential is designed to prepare individuals to plan, implement, maintain, and support information systems and networks built around Microsoft Windows NT and its BackOffice family of products.

  To obtain an MCSE, an individual must pass four core operating system exams, plus two elective exams. The operating system exams require individuals to demonstrate competence with desktop and server operating systems and with networking components.

  You must pass at least two Windows NT-related exams to obtain an MCSE: one on Implementing and Supporting Windows NT Server (version 3.51 or 4) and the other on Implementing and Supporting Windows NT Server in the Enterprise (version 3.51 or 4). These tests are intended to indicate an individual's knowledge of Windows NT in smaller, simpler networks and in larger, more complex, and heterogeneous networks, respectively.

  You must pass two additional tests as well. These tests are networking and desktop operating system related. At present, the networking requirement can only be satisfied by passing the Networking Essentials test. The desktop operating system test can be satisfied by passing a Windows 95, Windows NT Workstation (the version must match whichever core curriculum is pursued), or Windows 98 test.

  The two remaining exams are elective exams. An elective exam may fall in any number of subject or product areas, primarily BackOffice components. These include tests on IE4, SQL Server, IIS, SNA Server, Exchange Server, Systems Management Server, and the like. However, it is also possible to test out on electives by taking advanced networking topics like Internetworking with Microsoft TCP/IP (but here again, the version of Windows NT involved must match the version for the core requirements taken).

  Whatever mix of tests is completed toward MCSE certification, individuals must pass six tests to meet the MCSE requirements. It's not uncommon for the entire process to take a year or so, and many individuals find that they must take a test more than once to pass. Our primary goal with the Exam Cram series is to make it possible, given proper study and preparation, to pass all of the MCSE tests on the first try.

- **MCSE + Internet (Microsoft Certified Systems Engineer + Internet)** This is a newer Microsoft certification and focuses not just on Microsoft operating systems, but also on Microsoft's Internet servers and TCP/IP.

  To obtain this certification, an individual must pass seven core exams, plus two elective exams. The core exams include not only the server operating systems (NT Server and Server in the Enterprise) and a desktop OS (Windows 95, Windows 98, or Windows NT Workstation), but also include Networking Essentials, TCP/IP, Internet Information Server (IIS), and the Internet Explorer Administration Kit (IEAK).

  The two remaining exams are elective exams. These elective exams can be in any of four product areas: SQL Server, SNA Server, Exchange Server, or Proxy Server.

- **MCT (Microsoft Certified Trainer)** Microsoft Certified Trainers are individuals who are deemed capable of delivering elements of the official Microsoft training curriculum, based on technical knowledge and instructional ability. Thus, it is necessary for an individual seeking MCT credentials (which are granted on a course-by-course basis) to pass the related certification exam for a course and successfully complete the official Microsoft training in the subject area, as well as demonstrate an ability to teach.

  This latter criterion may be satisfied by proving that one has already attained training certification from Novell, Banyan, Lotus, the Santa Cruz Operation, or Cisco, or by taking a Microsoft-sanctioned workshop on instruction. Microsoft makes it clear that MCTs are important cogs in the Microsoft training channels. Instructors must be MCTs before Microsoft will allow them to teach in any of its official training channels, including Microsoft's affiliated Authorized Technical Education Centers (ATECs), Authorized Academic Training Programs (AATPs), and the Microsoft Online Institute (MOLI).

Certification is an ongoing activity. Once a Microsoft product becomes obsolete, MCSEs (and other MCPs) typically have 12 to 18 months in which they may recertify on current product versions. (If individuals do not recertify within the specified time period, their certification becomes invalid.) Because technology keeps changing and new products continually supplant old ones, this should come as no surprise.

The best place to keep tabs on the MCP Program and its various certifications is on the Microsoft Web site. The current root URL for the MCP program is titled "Microsoft Certified Professional Web site" at **www.microsoft.com/mcp**. But Microsoft's Web site changes frequently, so if this URL doesn't work, try using the Search tool on Microsoft's site with either "MCP" or the quoted phrase "Microsoft Certified Professional Program" as the search string. This will help you find the latest and most accurate information about the company's certification programs.

You can also obtain a special CD from Microsoft that contains a copy of the Microsoft Education And Certification Roadmap. The Roadmap covers much of the same information as the Web site, and it is updated quarterly. To obtain your copy of the CD, call Microsoft at 1 (800) 636-7544, Monday through Friday, 6:30 A.M. through 7:30 A.M. Pacific Time.

Taking A Certification Exam

Alas, testing is not free. You'll be charged $100 for each test you take, whether you pass or fail. In the U.S. and Canada, tests are administered by Sylvan Prometric. Sylvan Prometric can be reached at 1 (800) 755-3926 or 1 (800) 755-EXAM, any time from 7:00 A.M. to 6:00 P.M., Central Time, Monday through Friday. If this number doesn't work, please try (612) 896-7000 or (612) 820-5707.

To schedule an exam, call at least one day in advance. To cancel or reschedule an exam, you must call at least 12 hours before the scheduled test time (or you may be charged regardless). When calling Sylvan Prometric, please have the following information ready for the telesales staffer who handles your call:

- Your name, organization, and mailing address.
- Your Microsoft Test ID. (For most U.S. citizens, this will be your social security number. Citizens of other nations can use their taxpayer IDs or make other arrangements with the order taker.)
- The name and number of the exam you wish to take. (For this book, the exam number is 70-079, and the exam name is "Implementing and Supporting Microsoft Internet Explorer 4.0 by Using the Internet Explorer Administration Kit.")
- A method of payment must be arranged. (The most convenient approach is to supply a valid credit card number with sufficient available credit. Otherwise, payments by check, money order, or purchase order must be received before a test can be scheduled. If the latter methods are required, ask you order taker for more details.)

When you show up to take a test, try to arrive at least 15 minutes before the scheduled time slot. You must bring and supply two forms of identification, one of which must be a photo ID.

All exams are completely closed-book. In fact, you will not be permitted to take anything with you into the testing area, but you will be furnished with a blank sheet of paper and a pen. We suggest that you immediately write down on that sheet of paper all the information you've memorized for the test.

In Exam Cram books, this information appears on a tear-out sheet inside the front cover of each book. You will have some time to compose yourself, to record this information, and even to take a sample orientation exam before you must begin the real thing. We suggest you take the orientation test before taking your first exam, but because they're all more or less identical in layout, behavior, and controls, you probably won't need to do this more than once.

When you complete a Microsoft certification exam, the software will tell you whether you've passed or failed. All tests are scored on a basis of 1,000 points, and results are broken into several topic areas. Even if you fail, we suggest you ask for—and keep—the detailed report that the test administrator should print for you. You can use this report to help you prepare for another go-round, if needed.

If you need to retake an exam, you'll have to call Sylvan Prometric, schedule a new test date, and pay another $100 to take it again. Microsoft has recently implemented a new policy regarding failed tests. The first time you fail a test, you are able to retake the test the next day. However, if you fail a second time, you must wait 14 days before retaking that test. The 14-day waiting period is in effect for all tests after the first failure.

Tracking MCP Status

As soon as you pass any Microsoft exam other than Networking Essentials, you'll attain Microsoft Certified Professional (MCP) status. Microsoft also generates transcripts that indicate which exams you have passed and your corresponding test scores. You can order a transcript by email at any time by sending an email addressed to **mcp@msprograms.com**. You can also obtain a copy of your transcript by downloading the latest version of the MCT Guide from the Web site and consulting the section titled "Key Contacts" for a list of telephone numbers and related contacts.

Once you pass the necessary set of exams (six for MCSE or nine for MCSE + Internet), you'll be certified. Official certification normally takes anywhere from four to six weeks, so don't expect to get your credentials overnight. When the package arrives, it will include a Welcome Kit that contains a number of elements, including:

- An MCSE or MCSE + I certificate, suitable for framing, along with a Professional Program Membership card and lapel pin.
- A license to use the MCP logo, thereby allowing you to use the logo in advertisements, promotions, and documents, and on letterhead, business cards, and so on. Along with the license comes an MCP logo sheet, which includes camera-ready artwork. (Note: before using any of the artwork, individuals must sign and return a licensing agreement that indicates they'll abide by its terms and conditions.)
- A one-year subscription to TechNet, a collection of CDs that includes software, documentation, service packs, databases, and more technical information than you can possibly ever read. In our opinion, this is the best and most tangible benefit of attaining MCSE or MCSE + I status.
- A subscription to *Microsoft Certified Professional Magazine*, which provides ongoing data about testing and certification activities, requirements, and changes to the program.
- A free Priority Comprehensive 10-pack with Microsoft Product Support, and a 25 percent discount on additional Priority Comprehensive 10-packs. This lets you place up to 10 free calls to Microsoft's technical support operation at a higher-than-normal priority level.
- A one-year subscription to the Microsoft Beta Evaluation program. This subscription will get you all beta products from Microsoft for the next year. (This does not include developer products. You must join the MSDN program or become an MCSD to qualify for developer beta products.)

Many people believe that the benefits of MCP certification go well beyond the perks that Microsoft provides to newly anointed members of this elite group. We're starting to see more job listings that request or require applicants to have an MCSE, MCSE + I, MCSD, etc., and many individuals who complete the program can qualify for increases in pay or responsibility. As an official recognition of hard work and broad knowledge, one of the MCP credentials is a badge of honor in many IT organizations.

How To Prepare For An Exam

Preparing for any Windows NT Server-related test (including IEAK) requires that you obtain and study materials designed to provide comprehensive information about NT Server and the specific exam for which you are preparing. The following list of materials will help you study and prepare:

- The Microsoft Windows NT Server 4 manuals (or online documentation and help files, which ship on the CD with the product and also appear on the TechNet CDs).

- *The Microsoft Windows NT Server 4 Resource Kit*, published by Microsoft Press, Redmond, WA, 1996. ISBN: 1-57231-343-9. Even though it costs a whopping $149.95 (list price), it's worth every penny—not just for the documentation, but also for the utilities and other software included (which add considerably to the base functionality of Windows NT Server 4).
- The exam prep materials, practice tests, and self-assessment exams on the Microsoft Training And Certification Download page (**www.microsoft.com/Train_Cert/download/downld.htm**). Find the materials, download them, and use them!

In addition, you'll probably find any or all of the following materials useful in your quest for Windows NT Server expertise:

- **Microsoft Training Kits** Although there's no training kit currently available from Microsoft Press for the Internet Explorer Administration Kit, many other topics have such kits. It's worthwhile to check to see if Microsoft has come out with anything by the time you need this information. In place of a training kit for IEAK, we recommend the *Internet Explorer Resource Kit* from Microsoft Press. It contains information not only on IE, but on IEAK as well.
- **Study Guides** Publishers like Certification Insider and Sybex offer MCSE study guides of one kind or another. We've reviewed them and found the Certification Insider Press and Sybex titles to be informative and helpful for learning the materials necessary to pass the tests. The Certification Insider Press series includes:

  - **The Exam Cram series** These books give you information about the material you need to know to pass the tests.

  - **The Exam Prep series** These books provide a greater level of detail than the Exam Crams.

  Together, the two series make a perfect pair.
- **Classroom Training** ATECs, AATPs, MOLI, and unlicensed third-party training companies (like Wave Technologies, American Research Group, Learning Tree, Data-Tech, and others) all offer or will soon be offering classroom training on Exchange Server 5.5. These companies aim to help prepare network administrators to run Windows NT-based networks and pass the MCSE tests. While such training runs upwards of $350 per day in class, most of the individuals lucky enough to partake (including your humble authors, who've even taught such courses) find them to be quite worthwhile.

- **Other Publications** You'll find direct references to other publications and resources in this text, but there's no shortage of materials available about Internet Explorer and IEAK. To help you sift through some of the publications out there, we end each chapter with a "Need To Know More?" section that provides pointers to more complete and exhaustive resources covering the chapter's information. This should give you an idea of where we think you should look for further discussion.

- **The TechNet CD** TechNet is a monthly CD subscription available from Microsoft. TechNet includes all the Windows NT BackOffice Resource Kits and their product documentation. In addition, TechNet provides the contents of the Microsoft Knowledge Base and many kinds of software, white papers, training materials, and other good stuff. TechNet also contains all service packs, interim release patches, and supplemental driver software released since the last major version for most Microsoft programs and all Microsoft operating systems. A one-year subscription costs $299—worth every penny, even if only for the download time it saves.

By far, this set of required and recommended materials represents a nonpareil collection of sources and resources for Windows NT Server, Internet Explorer, and IEAK topics and software. We anticipate that you'll find that this book belongs in this company. In the section that follows, we explain how this book works, and we give you some good reasons why this book counts as a member of the required and recommended materials list.

About This Book

Each topical Exam Cram chapter follows a regular structure, along with graphical cues about important or useful information. Here's the structure of a typical chapter:

- **Opening Hotlists** Each chapter begins with a list of the terms, tools, and techniques that you must learn and understand before you can be fully conversant with that chapter's subject matter. We follow the hotlists with one or two introductory paragraphs to set the stage for the rest of the chapter.

- **Topical Coverage** After the opening hotlists, each chapter covers a series of at least four topics related to the chapter's subject title. Throughout this section, we highlight topics or concepts likely to appear on a test using a special Study Alert layout, like this:

This is what a Study Alert looks like. Normally, a Study Alert stresses concepts, terms, software, or activities that are likely to relate to one or more certification test questions. For that reason, we think any information found offset in Study Alert format is worthy of unusual attentiveness on your part. Indeed, most of the information that appears on the Cram Sheet appears as Study Alerts within the text.

Occasionally, you'll see tables called "Vital Statistics." The contents of Vital Statistics tables are worthy of an extra once-over. These tables usually contain informational tidbits that might show up in a test question, but they're not quite as important as Study Alerts.

Pay close attention to material flagged as a Study Alert; although all the information in this book pertains to what you need to know to pass the exam, we flag certain items that are really important. You'll find what appears in the meat of each chapter to be worth knowing, too, when preparing for the test. Because this book's material is very condensed, we recommend that you use this book along with other resources to achieve the maximum benefit.

In addition to the Study Alerts and Vital Statistics tables, we have provided tips that will help build a better foundation for IE knowledge. Although the information may not be on the exam, it is certainly related and will help you become a better test taker.

This is how tips are formatted. Keep your eyes open for these, and you'll become an Internet Explorer guru in no time!

- **Exam Prep Questions** Although we talk about test questions and topics throughout each chapter, this section presents a series of mock test questions and explanations of both correct and incorrect answers. We also try to point out especially tricky questions by using a special icon, like this:

Ordinarily, this icon flags the presence of a particularly devious inquiry, if not an outright trick question. Trick questions are calculated to be answered incorrectly if not read more than once, and carefully, at that. Although they're not ubiquitous, such questions make regular appearances on the Microsoft exams. That's why we say exam questions are as much about reading comprehension as they are about knowing your material inside out and backwards.

- **Details And Resources** Every chapter ends with a section titled "Need To Know More?", which provides direct pointers to Microsoft and third-party resources offering more details on the chapter's subject. In addition, this section tries to rank or at least rate the quality and thoroughness of the topic's coverage by each resource. If you find a resource you like in this collection, use it, but don't feel compelled to use all the resources. On the other hand, we only recommend resources we use on a regular basis, so none of our recommendations will be a waste of your time or money (but purchasing them all at once probably represents an expense that many network administrators and would-be MCSEs might find hard to justify).

The bulk of the book follows this chapter structure slavishly, but there are a few other elements that we'd like to point out. Chapter 10 is a sample test that provides a good review of the material presented throughout the book to ensure you're ready for the exam. Chapter 11 is an answer key to the sample test that appears in Chapter 10. The appendix provides a detailed outline of all available options when creating a custom build of Internet Explorer. Additionally, you'll find a glossary that explains terms and an index that you can use to track down terms as they appear in the text.

Finally, the tear-out Cram Sheet attached next to the inside front cover of this Exam Cram book represents a condensed and compiled collection of facts, figures, and tips that we think you should memorize before taking the test. Because you can dump this information out of your head onto a piece of paper before answering any exam questions, you can master this information by brute force—you only need to remember it long enough to write it down when you walk into the test room. You might even want to look at it in the car or in the lobby of the testing center just before you walk in to take the test.

How To Use This Book

If you're prepping for a first-time test, we've structured the topics in this book to build on one another. Therefore, some topics in later chapters make more sense after you've read earlier chapters. That's why we suggest you read this book from front to back for your initial test preparation. If you need to brush up on a topic or you have to bone up for a second try, use the index or table of contents to go straight to the topics and questions that you need to study. Beyond the tests, we think you'll find this book useful as a tightly focused reference to some of the most important aspects of Internet Explorer and IEAK.

Given all the book's elements and its specialized focus, we've tried to create a tool that will help you prepare for—and pass—Microsoft Certification Exam 70-079, "Implementing and Supporting Microsoft Internet Explorer by Using the Internet Explorer Administration Kit." Please share your feedback on the book with us, especially if you have ideas about how we can improve it for future test-takers. We'll consider everything you say carefully, and we'll respond to all suggestions.

Please send your questions or comments to our series editor, Ed Tittel, via email at **etittel@lanw.com**. He coordinates our efforts and ensures that all questions get answered. You can also contact David ("DJ") Johnson directly via email at **count0@worldnet.att.net**. Please remember to include the title of the book in your message; otherwise, we'll be forced to guess which book you're writing about. And we don't like to guess—we want to KNOW! Also, be sure to check out the Web pages at **http://www.examcram.com** and **http://www.lanw.com/examcram**; where you'll find information updates, commentary, and clarifications on documents for each book that you can either read online or download for use later on.

Thanks, and enjoy the book!

Microsoft Certification Exams

Terms and concepts you'll need to understand:

- √ Radio button
- √ Checkbox
- √ Exhibit
- √ Multiple-choice question formats
- √ Careful reading
- √ Process of elimination

Techniques you'll need to master:

- √ Preparing to take a certification exam
- √ Practicing (to make perfect)
- √ Making the best use of the testing software
- √ Budgeting your time
- √ Saving the hardest questions until last
- √ Guessing (as a last resort)

Exam taking is not something that most people anticipate eagerly, no matter how well prepared they may be. In most cases, familiarity helps ameliorate test anxiety. In plain English, this means you probably won't be as nervous when you take your fourth or fifth Microsoft certification exam as you'll be when you take your first one.

Whether it's your first exam or your tenth, understanding the details of exam taking (how much time to spend on questions, the environment you'll be in, and so on) and the exam software will help you concentrate on the material rather than on the setting. Likewise, mastering a few basic exam-taking skills should help you recognize—and perhaps even outfox—some of the tricks and gotchas you're bound to find in some of the exam questions.

This chapter, besides explaining the exam environment and software, describes some proven exam-taking strategies that you should be able to use to your advantage.

The Exam Situation

When you arrive at the testing center where you scheduled your exam, you'll need to sign in with an exam coordinator. He or she will ask you to show two forms of identification, one of which must be a photo ID. After you've signed in and your time slot arrives, you'll be asked to deposit any books, bags, or other items you brought with you. Then, you'll be escorted into a closed room. Typically, the room will be furnished with anywhere from one to half a dozen computers, and each workstation will be separated from the others by dividers designed to keep you from seeing what's happening on someone else's computer.

You'll be furnished with a pen or pencil and a blank sheet of paper, or, in some cases, an erasable plastic sheet and an erasable felt-tip pen. You're allowed to write down any information you want on both sides of this sheet. Before the exam, you should memorize as much of the material that appears on The Cram Sheet (inside the front cover of this book) as you can so you can write that information on the blank sheet as soon as you are seated in front of the computer. You can refer to your rendition of The Cram Sheet anytime you like during the test, but you'll have to surrender the sheet when you leave the room.

Most test rooms feature a wall with a large picture window. This permits the exam coordinator standing behind it to monitor the room, to prevent exam takers from talking to one another, and to observe anything out of the ordinary that might go on. The exam coordinator will have preloaded the appropriate Microsoft certification exam—for this book, that's Exam 70-079—and you'll be permitted to start as soon as you're seated in front of the computer.

All Microsoft certification exams allow a certain maximum amount of time in which to complete your work (this time is indicated on the exam by an onscreen counter/clock, so you can check the time remaining whenever you like). Exam

70-079 consists of 70 randomly selected questions. You may take up to 90 minutes to complete the exam.

All Microsoft certification exams are computer generated and use a multiple-choice format. Although this may sound quite simple, the questions are constructed not only to check your mastery of basic facts and figures about Internet Explorer 4 and the Internet Explorer Administration Kit, but they also require you to evaluate one or more sets of circumstances or requirements. Often, you'll be asked to give more than one answer to a question. Likewise, you might be asked to select the best or most effective solution to a problem from a range of choices, all of which technically are correct. Taking the exam is quite an adventure, and it involves real thinking. This book shows you what to expect and how to deal with the potential problems, puzzles, and predicaments.

Exam Layout And Design

Some exam questions require you to select a single answer, whereas others ask you to select multiple correct answers. The following multiple-choice question requires you to select a single correct answer. Following the question is a brief summary of each potential answer and why it is either right or wrong.

Question 1

Which of the following files can be added to a standard Web site to create an Active Channel?

❍ a. JavaScript

❍ b. HTML

❍ c. XML

❍ d. CDF

The correct answer to this question is d. A CDF file can be added to an existing site to create an Active Channel. Whereas Active Channels can contain both JavaScript and HTML documents, they have no role in creating the channel. Therefore, answers a and b are incorrect. Although CDF is a subset of XML, XML itself does not have the ability to create an Active Channel. Therefore, answer c is incorrect.

This sample question format corresponds closely to the Microsoft certification exam format—the only difference on the exam is that questions are not followed by answer keys. To select an answer, position the cursor over the radio button next to the answer. Then, click the mouse button to select the answer.

Let's examine a question that requires choosing multiple answers. This type of question provides checkboxes rather than radio buttons for marking all appropriate selections.

Question 2

Which of the following applications can be used by administrators to manage access to Active Channels?

- ❑ a. IEAK Configuration Wizard
- ❑ b. Internet Explorer Management System
- ❑ c. IEAK Channel Administrator
- ❑ d. IEAK Profile Manager

The correct answers to this question are a and d. The IEAK Configuration Wizard and IEAK Profile Manager can be used to control access to Active Channels. Both answers b and c are fictitious; therefore, they are incorrect.

For this type of question, more than one answer is required. As far as the authors can tell (and Microsoft won't comment), such questions are scored as wrong unless all the required selections are chosen. In other words, a partially correct answer does not result in partial credit when the test is scored. For Question 2, you have to check the boxes next to items a and d to obtain credit for a correct answer. Notice that picking the right answers also means knowing why the other answers are wrong!

Although these two basic types of questions can appear in many forms, they constitute the foundation on which all the Microsoft certification exam questions rest. More complex questions include so-called exhibits, which are usually screenshots of Internet Explorer or the Internet Explorer Administration Kit. For some of these questions, you'll be asked to make a selection by clicking on a checkbox or radio button on the screenshot itself. For others, you'll be expected to use the information displayed therein to guide your answer to the question. Familiarity with the underlying utility is your key to choosing the correct answer(s).

Other questions involving exhibits use charts or network diagrams to help document a workplace scenario that you'll be asked to troubleshoot or configure. Careful attention to such exhibits is the key to success. Be prepared to toggle frequently between the exhibit and the question as you work.

Using Microsoft's Exam Software Effectively

A well-known principle when taking exams is to first read over the entire exam from start to finish while answering only those questions you feel absolutely sure of. On subsequent passes, you can dive into more complex questions more deeply, knowing how many such questions you have left.

Fortunately, Microsoft exam software makes this approach easy to implement. At the top-left corner of each question is a checkbox that permits you to mark that question for a later visit. (Note: Marking questions makes review easier, but you can return to any question if you are willing to click the Forward or Back button repeatedly.) As you read each question, if you answer only those you're sure of and mark for review those that you're not sure of, you can keep working through a decreasing list of questions as you answer the trickier ones in order.

There's at least one potential benefit to reading the exam over completely before answering the trickier questions: Sometimes, you can find information in later questions that sheds more light on earlier questions. Other times, information you read on later questions might jog your memory about IEAK facts, figures, or behavior that also will help with earlier questions. Either way, you'll come out ahead if you defer those questions about which you're not absolutely sure.

Keep working on the questions until you're certain of all your answers or until you know you'll run out of time. If questions remain unanswered, you'll want to zip through them and guess. Not answering a question guarantees you won't receive credit for it, and a guess has at least a chance of being correct.

At the very end of your exam period, you're better off guessing than leaving questions unanswered.

Exam-Taking Basics

The most important advice about taking any exam is this: Read each question carefully. Some questions are deliberately ambiguous, some use double negatives, and others use terminology in incredibly precise ways. The authors have taken numerous exams—both practice and live—and in nearly every one have missed at least one question because they didn't read it closely or carefully enough.

Here are some suggestions on how to deal with the tendency to jump to an answer too quickly:

- Make sure you read every word in the question. If you find yourself jumping ahead impatiently, go back and start over.
- As you read, try to restate the question in your own terms. If you can do this, you should be able to pick the correct answer(s) much more easily.
- When returning to a question after your initial read-through, read every word again—otherwise, your mind can fall quickly into a rut. Sometimes, revisiting a question after turning your attention elsewhere lets you see something you missed, but the strong tendency is to see what you've seen before. Try to avoid that tendency at all costs.
- If you return to a question more than twice, try to articulate to yourself what you don't understand about the question, why the answers don't appear to make sense, or what appears to be missing. If you chew on the subject for awhile, your subconscious might provide the details that are lacking or you might notice a "trick" that will point to the right answer.

Above all, try to deal with each question by thinking through what you know about Internet Explorer and the Administration Kit—the characteristics, behaviors, facts, and figures involved. By reviewing what you know (and what you've written down on your information sheet), you'll often recall or understand things sufficiently to determine the answer to the question.

Question-Handling Strategies

Based on exams the authors have taken, some interesting trends have become apparent. For those questions that take only a single answer, usually two or three of the answers will be obviously incorrect, and two of the answers will be plausible—of course, only one can be correct. Unless the answer leaps out at you (if it does, reread the question to look for a trick; sometimes those are the ones you're most likely to get wrong), begin the process of answering by eliminating those answers that are most obviously wrong.

Things to look for in obviously wrong answers include spurious menu choices or utility names, nonexistent software options, and terminology you've never seen. If you've done your homework for an exam, no valid information should be completely new to you. In that case, unfamiliar or bizarre terminology probably indicates a totally bogus answer.

Numerous questions assume that the default behavior of a particular utility is in effect. If you know the defaults and understand what they mean, this knowledge will help you cut through many Gordian knots.

As you work your way through the exam, another counter that Microsoft thankfully provides will come in handy—the number of questions completed and questions outstanding. Budget your time by making sure that you've completed one-quarter of the questions one-quarter of the way through the exam period (or the first 17 or 18 questions in the first 22 or 23 minutes) and three-quarters of them three-quarters of the way through (52 or 53 questions in the first 66 to 69 minutes).

If you're not finished when 85 minutes have elapsed, use the last 5 minutes to guess your way through the remaining questions. Remember, guessing is potentially more valuable than not answering, because blank answers are always wrong, but a guess may turn out to be right. If you don't have a clue about any of the remaining questions, pick answers at random, or choose all a's, b's, and so on. The important thing is to submit an exam for scoring that has an answer for every question.

Mastering The Inner Game

In the final analysis, knowledge breeds confidence, and confidence breeds success. If you study the materials in this book carefully and review all the exam prep questions at the end of each chapter, you should become aware of those areas where additional learning and study are required.

Next, follow up by reading some or all of the materials recommended in the "Need To Know More?" section at the end of each chapter. The idea is to become familiar enough with the concepts and situations you find in the sample questions that you can reason your way through similar situations on a real exam. If you know the material, you have every right to be confident that you can pass the exam.

After you've worked your way through the book, take the practice exam in Chapter 10. This will provide a reality check and help you identify areas you need to study further. Make sure you follow up and review materials related to the questions you miss on the practice exam before scheduling a real exam. Only when you've covered all the ground and feel comfortable with the whole scope of the practice exam should you take a real one.

If you take the practice exam and don't score at least 75 percent correct, you'll want to practice further. Though one is not available for the Internet Explorer Administration Kit yet, Microsoft usually provides free Personal Exam Prep (PEP) exams and the self-assessment exams from the Microsoft Certified Professional Web site's download page (its location appears in the next section). If you're more ambitious or better funded, you might want to purchase a practice exam from a third-party vendor.

Armed with the information in this book and with the determination to augment your knowledge, you should be able to pass the certification exam. However, you need to work at it, or you'll spend the exam fee more than once before you finally pass. If you prepare seriously, you should do well. Good luck!

Additional Resources

A good source of information about Microsoft certification exams comes from Microsoft itself. Because its products and technologies—and the exams that go with them—change frequently, the best place to go for exam-related information is online.

If you haven't already visited the Microsoft Certified Professional site, do so right now. The MCP home page resides at **www.microsoft.com/mcp** (see Figure 1.1).

> *Note: This page might not be there by the time you read this, or it might have been replaced by something new and different, because things change regularly on the Microsoft site. Should this happen, please read the sidebar titled "Coping With Change On The Web."*

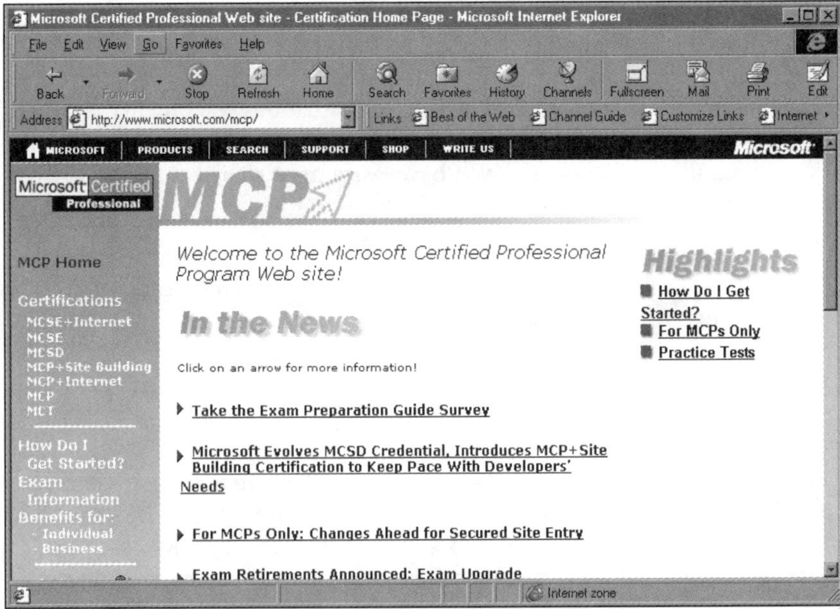

Figure 1.1 The Microsoft Certified Professional home page.

The menu options in the left column of the home page point to the most important sources of information in the MCP pages. Here's what to check out:

- **Certification Choices** Use this menu entry to read about the various certification programs that Microsoft offers.
- **Search/Find An Exam** Use this menu entry to pull up a search tool that lets you list all Microsoft exams and locate all exams relevant to any Microsoft certification (MCPS, MCSE, MCT, and so on) or those exams that cover a particular product. This tool is quite useful not only to examine the options but also to obtain specific exam preparation information, because each exam has its own associated preparation guide. This is Exam 70-079.
- **Downloads** Use this menu entry to find a list of the files and practice exams that Microsoft makes available to the public. These include several items worth downloading, especially the Certification Update, the Personal Exam Prep (PEP) exams, various assessment exams, and a general exam study guide. Try to make time to peruse these materials before taking your first exam.

These are just the high points of what's available in the Microsoft Certified Professional pages. As you browse through them—and we strongly recommend that you do—you'll probably find other informational tidbits mentioned that are every bit as interesting and compelling.

Coping With Change On The Web

Sooner or later, all the information we've shared with you about the Microsoft Certified Professional pages and the other Web-based resources mentioned throughout the rest of this book will go stale or be replaced by newer information. In some cases, the URLs you find here might lead you to their replacements; in other cases, the URLs will go nowhere, leaving you with the dreaded "404 File not found" error message. When that happens, don't give up.

There's always a way to find what you want on the Web if you're willing to invest some time and energy. Most large or complex Web sites—and Microsoft's qualifies on both counts—offer a search engine. Looking back at Figure 1.1, you can see that a Search button appears along the top edge of the page. As long as you can get to Microsoft's site (it should stay at **www.microsoft.com** for a long while yet), you can use this tool to help you find what you need.

The more focused you can make a search request, the more likely the results will include information you can use. For example, you can search for the string "training and certification" to produce a lot of data about the subject in general, but if you're looking for the preparation guide for Exam 70-079, "Implementing and Supporting Microsoft Internet Explorer 4.0 by Using the Internet Explorer Administration Kit," you'll be more likely to get there quickly if you use a search string similar to the following:

```
"Exam 70-079" AND "preparation guide"
```

Likewise, if you want to find the Training and Certification downloads, try a search string such as this:

```
"training and certification" AND "download page"
```

Finally, feel free to use general search tools—such as **www.search.com**, **www.altavista.com**, and **www.excite.com**—to search for related information. Although Microsoft offers the best information about its certification exams online, there are plenty of third-party sources of information, training, and assistance in this area that need not follow Microsoft's party line. The bottom line is this: If you can't find something where the book says it lives, start looking around. If worse comes to worst, you can always email us. We just might have a clue.)

Need More Practice?

LANWrights, Inc., the company behind this book, also offers practice tests for sale. You can order practice exam diskettes via snail mail, email, or through our Web site (**http://www.lanw.com/books/examcram/order.htm**). Because we wrote these tests ourselves, we don't feel comfortable telling you how great they are—but they surely are a good deal! (See the end of the book for detailed information on these tests.)

2

Introduction To IE4 And The IE Administration Kit

Terms you'll need to understand:

- ActiveX
- Active Desktop
- Active Setup
- ASP (Active Server Pages)
- AutoComplete
- CDF (Channel Definition Format)
- Dynamic HTML
- FrontPage Express
- IMAP4 (Internet Message Access Protocol version 4)
- LDAP (Lightweight Directory Access Protocol)
- NetMeeting
- NetShow
- Outlook Express
- PICS (Platform for Internet Content)
- POP3 (Post Office Protocol Version 3)
- Smart Recovery
- SMTP (Simple Mail Transfer Protocol)
- SoftBoot
- URL (Uniform Resource Locator)
- Webcasting
- Web Crawling
- Windows Desktop Update

Techniques you'll need to master:

- Examining the options available when downloading Internet Explorer 4 and related components
- Understanding Active Setup
- Understanding Active Desktop
- Examining the minimum requirements for each type of installation
- Understanding the different types of licensing and the licensing requirements
- Examining the key features of Outlook Express, NetShow, NetMeeting, Personal Web Server, FrontPage Express, and Internet Explorer 4
- Understanding migration issues

As you no doubt know, Internet Explorer 4 (IE4) is the latest in a long line of Web browsers available from Microsoft. In an effort to distribute Internet Explorer more easily, for both Internet Service Providers (ISPs) and corporate administrators, Microsoft has created the Internet Explorer Administration Kit (IEAK). In this chapter, you'll look at a number of details required for the IEAK 4 exam. You'll review the options available when downloading Internet Explorer 4 and related components, and you'll get an overview of how to customize installation using the Internet Explorer 4 Administration Kit (the IEAK is discussed in detail in Chapter 6). You'll also look at the purpose and function of many of the components and features of Internet Explorer 4.

Internet Explorer 4 Overview

As mentioned, Microsoft introduced the IEAK to provide a simple means of distributing customized versions of Internet Explorer 4, referred to as *builds*. Each of the components of IE can be configured and used in the builds, which provides the ISP or corporate administrator a wide variety of installation options. Before we delve into the IEAK, it is important to understand the installation process for Internet Explorer.

Installing Internet Explorer

Active Setup is a new program in IE4. This small program (about 400 bytes) can be downloaded and saved for use with network installs or used during the initial download. The purpose of Active Setup (IE4SETUP.EXE) is to check the system for installed components, which prevents you from downloading unneeded files. Furthermore, if a download should fail (perhaps due to net congestion), Active Setup switches to another download site. Active Setup also picks up at the point of a download failure, rather than performing a complete restart.

IE4 is language dependent. This means that if you are creating a custom build of IE4, you have to create one for each language you plan to use and store each version in a separate subdirectory. You should know about the use of different language versions and their placement in separate folders. The Active Desktop does not check for correct use of a language. If you configure this incorrectly, some functions, such as Active Desktop, will fail.

When you install IE4, it replaces Internet Explorer 3. If you are using Netscape, it will not be replaced, but information, such as bookmarks and Favorites, is imported into IE4. See Chapter 3 for more information on converting to IE4 from Netscape and Internet Explorer 3.

Besides the infinite variety of custom builds, there are three standard Installation options: Browser, Standard, and Full. Table 2.1 describes each type of installation.

Internet Explorer 4 is available for:

- Windows 3.x
- Windows 9x
- Macintosh
- NT 4
- Unix (not all platforms)

If you install IE4 on Windows NT 4, which requires SP3 or greater, your emergency repair disk (ERD) should be updated. To update your ERD, run Rdisk.exe. Use Rdisk.exe /s to update more than administrator access. (Note that IE4 will not install on NT 3.x.)

IE4 has many extensions to the operating system (OS). For example, let's say your OS is on logical drive C. You tell Active Setup to install on logical drive D, using a normal install. The end result will be about 40MB of IE4 installed on logical drive C, with about 1MB installed on logical drive D. Also, many newer programs require these IE4 files to be installed on the target computer before they will run. NT Option Pack 1 and Outlook 98 are two examples. You are not required to use IE4 as your browser to use these newer programs.

Upon completion of the installation of IE4, you might experience a SoftBoot. SoftBoot takes note of what programs are open, then closes them, updates the

Table 2.1 IE4 installation options.

Option	Disk Space	Components
Browser	40MB	IE4, JavaVM, DirectShow, DirectX, Direct Draw, Direct Animation, and Active Movie
Standard	51MB	IE4, JavaVM, Outlook Express, Connection Manager, Internet Connection Wizard, Interactive Music Control, DirectShow, ActiveMovie, VDO Player, Microsoft Wallet, and Web Fonts
Full	64MB	IE4, Outlook Express, NetMeeting, NetShow, FrontPage Express, Web Publishing Wizard, Chat 2, Connection Manager, Internet Connection Wizard, JavaVM, Interactive Music Control, DirectShow, ActiveMovie, VDO Player, RealPlayer, Indeo, Visual Basic runtime, Microsoft Wallet, and Web Fonts

Registry, and reopens the programs that were open. At the present time, SoftBoot works only with Windows 9x operating systems. SoftBoot is also used to verify that Smart Recovery is required if a download has failed.

Internet Explorer Features

Internet Explorer includes a number of features that work closely with the operating system to provide users a dynamic and configurable browser. The following sections discuss a few of these features.

Profiles

When you have multiple users on a single machine, each user has a unique profile. These entries are kept in the Registry and in a subfolder—*X*:\Windows\Profiles. Roaming profiles are supported. Keep in mind that the differences between Windows 95 and NT 4 must be honored.

AutoComplete

When you start to type a URL into IE4's Address box, the AutoComplete feature offers you a complete URL. As you continue to type the rest of the URL, AutoComplete continues to look for matches from the History folder. If your History folder is empty, this feature does not work.

AutoComplete gets its data from the Windows\History folder.

In addition to standard AutoComplete, IE4 can enter standard Web address information for you. For example, if you type "microsoft" in the Address box and press Ctrl+Enter, "http://www." is automatically added to the front of the address, ".com" is added to the end, and you are immediately taken to the site.

A function similar to AutoComplete is AutoDomain searching. If you enter only part of a URL, AutoDomain attempts to correct it. For example, if you type "microsoft" and the DNS entry can't be resolved, it adds the "www." prefix and attempts various suffixes, such as ".com", ".edu", and ".org" . Regedit can be used to customize this feature.

By default, information is held in the Windows\History folder for 20 days.

Explorer Bar And Favorites

When you click on an Explorer bar icon (such as the Search, History, or Favorites button) in the Standard toolbar, a pane opens on the left side of the window. This window stays open until you close it, and it displays the information you requested in the right window. If you need more screen area, close the Explorer bar and click on the Full Screen button in the Standard toolbar. The Full Screen button displays a small toolbar across the top of the window and maximizes the browser's viewing area. To revert to IE4's default view, click on the Full Screen button again.

Favorites are shortcuts that are identical to the system shortcuts in Windows 9x, NT 4, and NT 5. Because favorites are the same as system shortcuts, you have greater control over how shortcuts are used. You can cut and paste Favorites throughout your system. One nice feature of favorites in Internet Explorer is that they provide an easy way to access not only Internet resources, but also local or intranet resources.

As mentioned, clicking on the Search button on the Standard toolbar opens a pane on the left side of the window, in which your search results are displayed. By default, selecting Search points to **http://home.microsoft.com/search/search.asp**, though this can be changed using the Administration Kit.

When adding a Favorite, you have three options. These options are accessed by clicking on Favorites|Add To Favorites. Figure 2.1 shows the options.

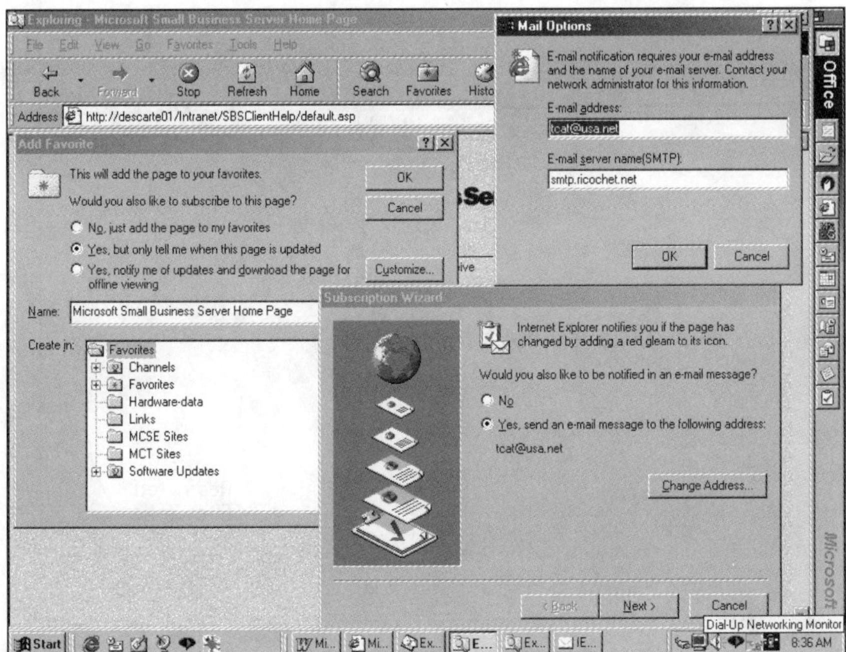

Figure 2.1 The Add Favorite, Subscription Wizard, and Mail Options dialog boxes.

Internet Explorer Security

The security structure, specifically the Security Zone architecture, is different in IE4 from Internet Explorer 3.

A change in how Security Zones are designed means that IE3 security policies will not import into IE4 when upgrading.

IE4 has five Security Zones; however, only four of them are configurable (see Figure 2.2). The fifth zone, Local Machine, is not configurable via a user interface, but it can be changed in the Registry. The Local Machine Zone is a completely trusted zone. Security in the local zone is just about zero.

There are three major levels of security: Low, Medium, and High. In addition, there is a fourth, minor level called Custom. Custom is configurable. Internet Explorer works with each zone as follows:

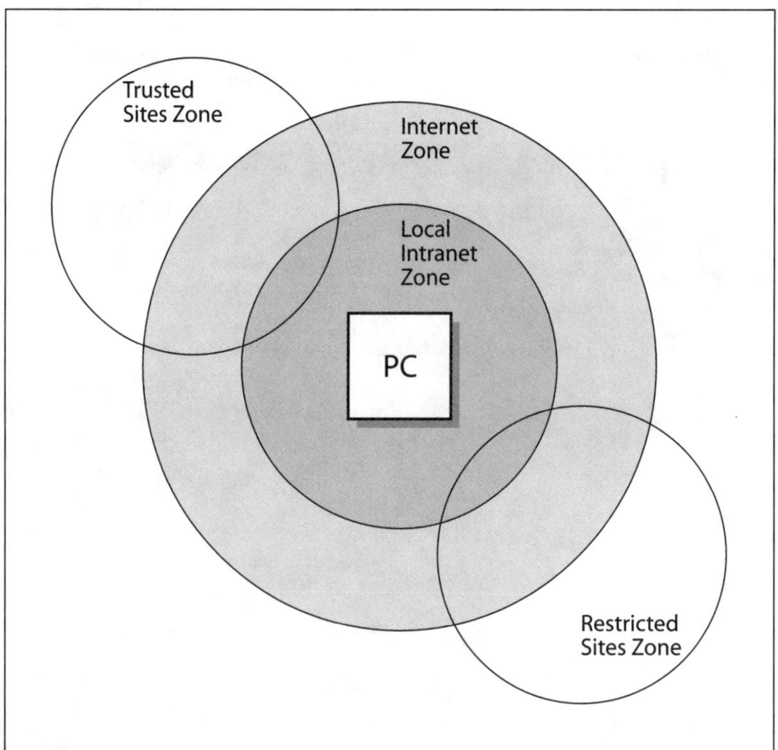

Figure 2.2 IE4's configurable Security Zones.

- **Local Intranet Zone** Moving out from the local PC level, the first zone is the Local Intranet Zone. This is the local LAN, as well as any Web applications that require the local hard drive. The default setting for this zone is medium security.
- **Trusted Sites Zone** This zone contains any sites you declare safe. The default security for this section is low. Often, the Trusted Sites Zone is used for other sites within a company.
- **Restricted Sites Zone** This is any site you have specifically included to not trust. The default security for these sites is high.
- **Internet Zone** This zone contains any site that has not been expressly granted higher access (via the Trusted Sites Zone) or any site placed in the Restricted Sites Zone. The default security is medium.

Chapter 8 discusses each of these zones in greater detail. In addition, IE4 supports customized security settings, digital certificates, Authenticode, and Java security—all of which are discussed in upcoming chapters.

Content Advisor

IE4 reads tags placed inside HTML code to determine if the content is suitable. Currently, the most common rating standard is PICS, or Platform for Internet Content. For more information, visit **www.w3.org/PICS**.

The Recreational Software Advisory Council (RSAC) uses a 0 to 4 rating in areas of violence, nudity, sex, and language. All content ratings are set to 0 by default. To set the Content Advisor, select View|Internet Options|Content. The first time Content Advisor is invoked, a supervisor's password must be selected. This password must be used to effect any changes, including disabling the Content Advisor. Also, it is possible to update the Content Advisor on Internet Explorer browsers that have already been deployed to users.

Windows Desktop Update

The purpose of the Windows Desktop Update is to create one common view of the local machine or network and the Internet. If you are comfortable using the Start button, the Windows Desktop Update adds your Favorites folder to the first pane. The Find button has a People offering, and the Settings now offer an Active Desktop option that will cascade to options, such as View As Web Page, Customize My Desktop, and Update Now. Also, a Quick Launch toolbar (see Figure 2.3) has been placed next to the Start bar. More information on Windows Desktop Update can be found in Chapter 4.

Figure 2.3 The Quick Launch toolbar includes Internet Explorer 4, Outlook or Outlook Express, and the desktop and channels.

It is very easy to add a desktop shortcut to the Quick Launch toolbar—simply drag it over and release. If the Quick Launch area is not large enough, hover your mouse over the edge of the Quick Launch area until the double-headed arrow (↔) displays; then, drag your mouse to the right to give yourself more room. Figure 2.4 shows that the Real Audio icon has been added to the toolbar.

Subscribing To Sites

Site subscriptions, which are discussed in Chapter 4, allow the user to check Web sites automatically for new content at regular intervals. Subscriptions are part of the Favorites area of Internet Explorer and can be established when a Favorite is created.

Active Channels

Channels use the Channel Definition Format (CDF), which is a method used to perform managed Webcasting. Creating Active Channels employs products such as Dynamic HTML, ActiveX, Visual Basic, and so forth.

You can create your own publishing Channel for your Web site. From a programming standpoint, the Active Desktop also works with the same development tools. We'll further examine Subscriptions and Active Channels in Chapter 4.

Adding Channel Screen Savers

You can create a screen saver provided by a subscribed Active Channel, even if it is not specified in the Active Channel CDF file.

You should know that you can display data in realtime to either an Active Channel screen saver or to an Active Desktop.

Figure 2.4 The Real Audio icon is now available for quick launching.

CDF files for Active Desktop require, at a minimum, one ITEM element under the top-level CHANNEL element. Please see Chapter 4 for more information on Active Channels.

IE4 Components

In addition to the features of IE4 discussed in the previous sections, IE4 includes a number of components and separate applications that can be used with IE4 or independently. Some of these components are discussed in the following sections.

Active Desktop

Active Desktop is one of the most-discussed topics in our industry since IE4's beta release. The bad news about Active Desktop is that it requires more resources than a standard desktop. Therefore, if you run Active Desktop on an underpowered machine, the end user's experience will not be positive. On the flip side, Active Desktop enables a user to have the more advanced features of IE4, such as the Active Channels, displayed on the desktop. This means that, for example, you can have active news feeds from the Internet or an intranet. The *Active Desktop* is basically a Web page layered on top of the desktop. That's it! We will delve deeper into the Active Desktop in Chapter 4. Figure 2.5 shows a desktop in normal mode, and Figure 2.6 shows a desktop in Active Desktop mode.

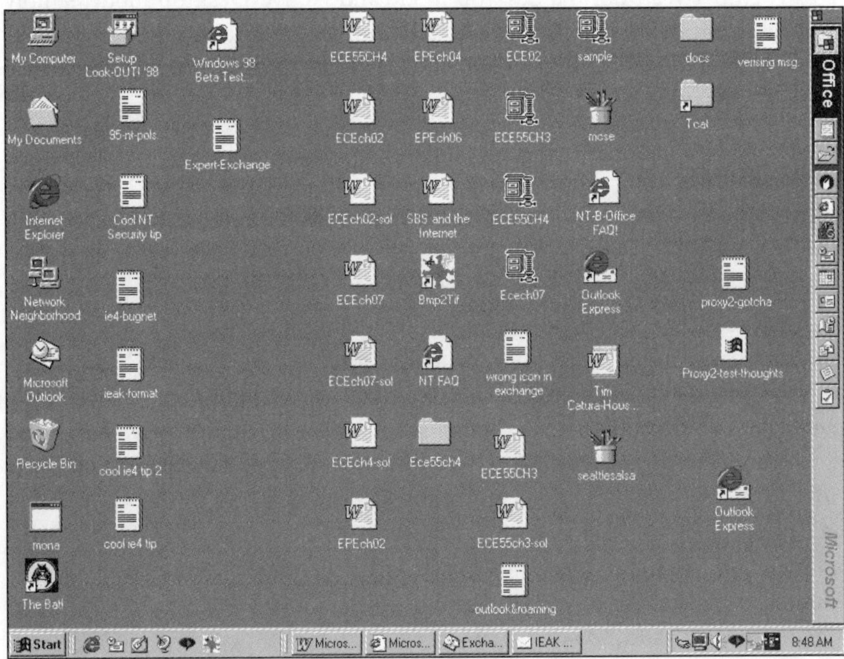

Figure 2.5 A desktop in normal mode.

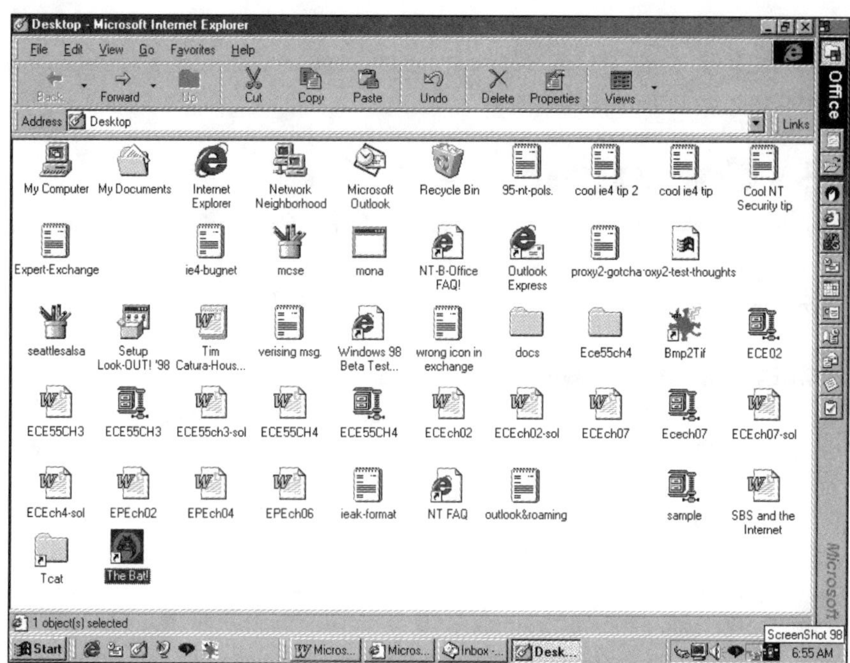

Figure 2.6 A desktop in Active Desktop mode.

To switch between normal desktop mode and Active Desktop mode, simply right-click on the desktop, select Active Desktop, and then select or deselect View As Web page. Depending on the power of your machine, it takes only a moment or two to switch back and forth.

NetMeeting

Chapter 5 presents a more detailed review of NetMeeting. Briefly, NetMeeting allows realtime communication between two or more people. More than two users can collaborate using a text-based chat window or an electronic whiteboard. It is also possible to share programs. A shared program needs to be installed on only one computer. This has proven to be a great method for troubleshooting calls via long distance. No longer are we reliant on the judgment of the usually panicked caller. In addition to the chat and whiteboard features, audio and video connections are possible between two people for one-to-one collaboration. Audio will perform on a connection as slow as a 14.4 modem, and video will perform on as little as a 28.8 connection. File transfer capability is also possible. For high-bandwidth use, such as video, a faster bandwidth connection is strongly suggested. All communications are based on international standards, such as H.323 or T.120.

FrontPage Express

FrontPage Express is a wizard-based method for creating Web sites. The program is a scaled-down version of Microsoft's FrontPage HTML editor. The beauty of FrontPage and FrontPage Express is that the end user doesn't need to know anything about HTML coding to design a Web page. The major difference is that the Express version does not include the ability to create Active Server Pages, and it excludes some WebBot components.

Outlook Express

Chapter 3 covers Outlook Express in detail. The important points of Outlook Express are presented here. First, using Outlook Express allows you to access and manage multiple email and news accounts from a single client. The address book is stored on a per-user basis, if profiles are used.

Outlook Express monitors the accounts from which an email has come. This allows two or more users of a single machine to use one Outlook Express program.

Furthermore, OE is capable of using a spellchecker, such as the one supplied with MS Office, if it is installed. OE also supports HTML formatting in email messages, including support for using stationery (when you use stationery in an email message, you are basically adding a background to your message).

You should know that you can customize the look of email messages by using HTML to create custom stationery.

A signature file can be created, and its use is enforced with the Administration Kit. There may be instances in which a particular company's policies dictate that a standard signature file be included with all email correspondence. It is important to remember that this is managed through the Administration Kit.

Outlook Express supports the Lightweight Directory Access Protocol (LDAP). This protocol gives you the ability to check names against a company-wide address book (similar to the GAL in Exchange) or to check names against public directories, such as BigFoot or Four11. Be sure to know which programs Microsoft has provided for migration. Review Chapter 3 for more details.

Outlook Express will import mail and address books from:

- Eudora Light or Pro
- Microsoft Internet Mail and News

- Netscape v2 or v3
- Netscape Communicator
- Microsoft Exchange
- Microsoft Outlook
- Microsoft Windows Messaging

Addresses can also be imported from text files (comma delimited) or LDAP.

Mail is supported in POP3 or IMAP4. Newsgroups are supported with NNTP. Outlook Express also supports configuration of Security Zones, defined in IE4.

Outlook Express sends mail with the SMTP standard. S/MIME provides the user with a way to send email with a digital signature and encryption.

Personal Web Server

The Personal Web Server is a scaled-down version of Internet Information Server (IIS). The largest difference is that the Personal Web Server can be run on Windows 9x.

Because Personal Web Server can run on Windows 9x, it is possible for an employee to perform tasks, such as data mining or updating an Excel spreadsheet and posting the information for co-workers to obtain the results.

Personal Web Server is not intended to be a replacement for IIS. The number of connections it can support is limited. It does, however, support Microsoft Challenge Handshake Authentication Protocol (MS-CHAP) with NT Workstation.

NetShow

NetShow is similar to NetMeeting; however, it is designed for a one-to-many broadcast of information. The use of NetShow requires a NetShow server broadcasting information.

By using NetShow's sever and clients, a company can have a full multimedia feed. This would allow a company CEO to broadcast a general meeting over the company's LAN or WAN.

Wallet

Microsoft Wallet is a method to store private information, such as credit card account data, on a drive in an encrypted fashion. MS Wallet supports SSL (Secure Sockets Layer) and SET (Secure Electronic Transaction). There are two areas in which you can configure MS Wallet—Address Options and Payment Options.

Until the Profile Assistant is configured with a Security Certificate, the Addresses and Payments buttons will be grayed out.

IEAK Overview

Now that you've had a glimpse of Internet Explorer and many of its components, it's time to take a look at the Internet Explorer Administration Kit (IEAK). As its name implies, the IEAK is used to manage the functionality of Internet Explorer, both in a corporate environment and as an ISP. You can download the Internet Explorer Administration Kit from the Web, or you can order the CD from Microsoft. You can save a lot of download and study time by ordering the CD. In addition, it has been reported that the download version goes through the motions of creating a custom build of Internet Explorer 4, only to have the custom build fail to install.

Before you can begin to work with the IEAK, you must have all the components of Internet Explorer 4 that you plan to use to create custom builds installed on your system. You can perform your first-time install of IE4 by downloading it from the Web or by CD. The download time for the full installation of IE4, using a 28.8 modem, is approximately five to six hours.

Before you can begin creating custom builds of IE4, you need an installation key number, which is provided by Microsoft. You also need the Administration Kit. Each of these can be acquired from Microsoft's IEAK Web site at **http://www.microsoft.com/ie/ieak**. You will need the following items to begin your studies of the Administration Kit:

- Internet Explorer 4 (a full install is recommended)
- Internet Explorer 4 Administration Kit
- Installation Key

The hardware requirements for the IEAK are:

- **Processor** At least 486-66
- **O/S** Windows 9x or NT 4 or greater
- **Memory** 8MB with Windows 95 and 16MB for NT 4
- **Disk Space** 40MB to 60MB for installation and 40MB+ per custom package
- **Connection** An Internet connection is required the first time the wizard is run

It is very important to remember that an Internet connection is required the first time the setup wizard is run.

Disk space for your custom builds will vary significantly, depending on whether you are creating the custom build for downloading or distribution with the programs installed.

Licensing

Simply put, three license types are available. They are:

- Content Provider/Developer
- Service Provider (ISP)
- Corporate Administrator

In each case, you need a 10-digit customization code. Let's say, for example, that you are heading an IS team for a national ISP and you wish to deploy IE4 for your clients and the employees of your firm. You will need two customization keys—one for your role in distributing IE4 to clients and a second for internal use custom builds of IE4.

In any event, part of the licensing agreement requires you to report the number of browsers distributed per customization code on a quarterly basis.

Reporting of the number of browsers distributed is the only requirement for reporting. Microsoft doesn't care who you distributed the browser to, just how many.

Using IEAK For Distribution

Depending on the role you are deploying to, you have different options for distribution. They are:

- CD-ROM
- Floppy
- Download

The CD-ROM and download options are available to all three types of licenses. The floppy option is a little different. All three license types allow for distribution on multiple floppies. Only the ISP role is permitted to distribute by single floppy. If your customization key is not for the ISP role, the single floppy option is grayed out.

Automatic Version Synchronization

The first time the Administration Kit is run, Automatic Version Synchronization (AVS) is required. If you did not follow the suggestion earlier in this chapter to get IE4 by CD, AVS requires a download of the IE4 components you wish to install. Selecting a full installation and having a 28.8 modem delays your next step for many hours. If you have the current versions of these components, the delay is only as long as it takes to check that your versions are indeed current.

AVS uses three symbols to inform you of the status of your components. They are:

- **Red X** Not Installed
- **Yellow !** Installed, but out of date
- **Green OK** Current

Be sure to know the meanings of the three status symbols.

Options

Chapter 6 covers IE4 options in more detail. As a simple summary, it seems that for the most part, the number 10 occurs frequently. For example: You can choose up to 10 download sites to be displayed. You can choose up to 10 optional custom programs to be included. The only place that the number 10 becomes the digit 1 is with Silent Downloads. In this case, there are no options, because the deployment happens "automagically" for the user.

TCP/IP Review

Although not specifically a part of IE, TCP/IP is used to communicate over the Internet and ties closely to IE (and, in fact, nearly all Microsoft products). Because TCP/IP is so integral to a successful implementation of Internet Explorer, a short review is in order.

Although TCP/IP is not required for use in a local area network (LAN), it is used frequently, so we should address this transport type. For any of the IE4 components to function over the Internet, TCP/IP is required. It might not be covered heavily on the test, but a quick review is necessary. For more detailed information on TCP/IP, refer to the *MCSE TCP/IP Exam Cram* (ISBN: 1-57610-195-9), published by The Coriolis Group.

TCP/IP is a cross-platform standard for communication between computer systems. When setting up this protocol, the computer must have two entries. The first one is an address. Addresses come in three classes: A, B, and C. The second required entry is a subnet mask. Both the address and the subnet mask must be in a format of four fields, with each field containing a number from 0 through 255. An example of a Class A address is: 10.0.0.1. A subnet mask for this address would be 255.0.0.0.

There are a number of utilities for TCP/IP used to measure performance, perform troubleshooting, or review configuration. Whereas many of the tools have the same name for both Windows 9x and NT, there is one exception.

NT ships with a command-line tool called IPCONFIG.EXE. This utility displays an IP address, subnet mask, and default gateway for each adapter that uses TCP/IP.

Windows 9x comes with a graphic-based utility called WINIPCFG.EXE, not a character-based version, as found in NT. Both of these display characteristics are part of your TCP/IP configuration. If you prefer the graphical version, a WINIPCFG.EXE for NT is available in the NT Resource Kit.

Know when to use IPCONFIG.EXE and when to use WINIPCFG.EXE. Windows 9x uses WINIPCFG.EXE, and NT uses IPCONFIG.EXE.

Exam Prep Questions

Question 1

IE4 is available for which operating systems?

- ❑ a. Windows 3.x
- ❑ b. Windows 9x
- ❑ c. Macintosh
- ❑ d. NT 4
- ❑ e. Unix

All of these answers are correct. Microsoft has made a version available for each of these platforms.

Question 2

Outlook Express will import mail from which programs?

- ❑ a. Eudora Light or Eudora Pro
- ❑ b. Microsoft Internet Mail and News
- ❑ c. The Bat!
- ❑ d. Netscape Communicator
- ❑ e. Microsoft Exchange

The correct answers to this question are a, b, d, and e. However, this is only a partial list of the programs that Outlook Express will import. The Bat! is a very good shareware email application from Europe, but it was not available when Outlook Express was released. Therefore, answer c is incorrect.

Question 3

Which of the following accurately describes NetMeeting and NetShow?

- ❍ a. NetMeeting is for one-to-many broadcasts. NetShow is for one-to-one collaboration.
- ❍ b. NetMeeting works for one-to-many or one-to-one collaboration. NetShow is for one-to-one collaboration only.
- ❍ c. NetShow is for one-to-many or one-to-one collaboration. NetMeeting is for one-to-many distribution.
- ❍ d. NetMeeting is for one-to-one collaboration. NetShow is for one-to-many broadcasts.
- ❍ e. None of the above.

The correct answer to this question is d. NetMeeting is for one-to-one collaboration, and NetShow is for one-to-many broadcasts. NetMeeting can have more than a one-to-one collaboration; however, this does not apply to audio or video. Therefore, answers a and b are incorrect. The use of audio or video is limited to a one-to-one interface. Text, chat, and whiteboard allow more than two users. NetShow is a one-way multimedia broadcast, for a one-to-many delivery of information. Therefore, answer c is incorrect.

Question 4

You can test IE4 on a trial basis, in a separate folder, while continuing to use Internet Explorer version 3.

- ❍ a. True
- ❍ b. False

This statement is False. Therefore, answer b is correct. IE4 replaces Internet Explorer 3 during an install. The only way to have both programs on the same computer is with different operating systems, such as Windows 98 and NT. Therefore, answer a is incorrect.

Question 5

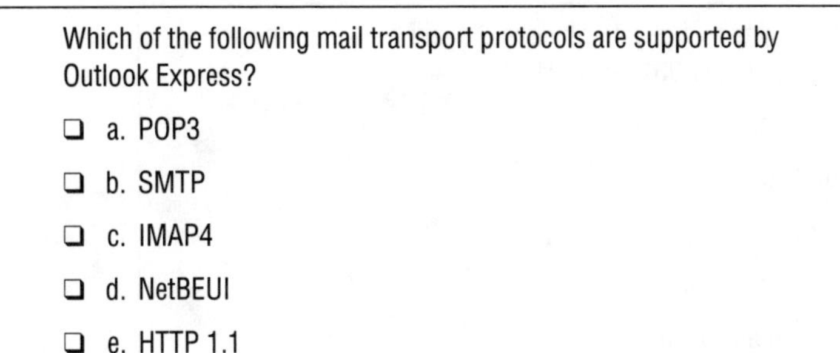
Which of the following mail transport protocols are supported by Outlook Express?

- ❑ a. POP3
- ❑ b. SMTP
- ❑ c. IMAP4
- ❑ d. NetBEUI
- ❑ e. HTTP 1.1

The correct answers to this question are a, b, and c. POP3 and IMAP4 are both standards for incoming mail. SMTP (Simple Mail Transport Protocol) is for outgoing mail. NetBEUI is a LAN protocol, whereas HTTP is used for Web browsers. Therefore, answers d and e are incorrect.

Question 6

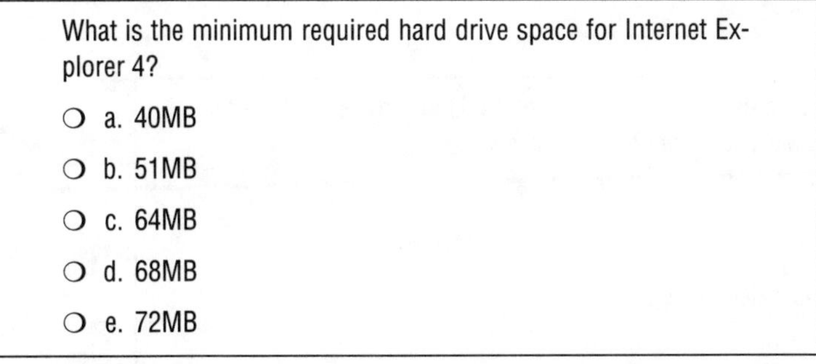
What is the minimum required hard drive space for Internet Explorer 4?

- ❍ a. 40MB
- ❍ b. 51MB
- ❍ c. 64MB
- ❍ d. 68MB
- ❍ e. 72MB

The correct answer to this question is a. 40MB is required for a minimum install. 51MB is required for a standard install. Therefore, answer b is incorrect. 64MB is required for a full install. Therefore, answer c is incorrect. Answers d and e are not indicative of any Internet Explorer requirements. Therefore, they are incorrect.

Question 7

What is the ability to type a few characters and have the browser window complete the URL known as?

- ❍ a. AutoConfigure
- ❍ b. AutoSearch
- ❍ c. AutoRun
- ❍ d. All of the above
- ❍ e. None of the above

The correct answer to this question is e. If provided, the correct answer would be AutoComplete. AutoConfigure is used to create custom builds of IE4. Therefore, answer a is incorrect. AutoSearch is the feature that searches for .com, .org, .edu, and so forth, when you do not give a Fully Qualified Domain Name. Therefore, answer b is incorrect. AutoRun automatically starts a program or music on a CD when it is inserted. Therefore, answer c is incorrect.

Question 8

Where does the data come from that fills in the URL entry after typing a few characters?

- ❍ a. Favorites
- ❍ b. Profiles
- ❍ c. User-defined list
- ❍ d. History
- ❍ e. Temporary Internet files

The correct answer is d. The History folder is found in the Windows\History folder. Favorites are used as shortcuts. Therefore, answer a is incorrect. Profiles are optional and contain user settings. Therefore, answer b is incorrect. There is no such thing as a user-defined list for this question. Therefore, answer c is incorrect. Temporary Internet files are used as a local cache. Therefore, answer e is incorrect.

Question 9

By default, how long is a history for Internet browsing held?

- ❍ a. 7 days
- ❍ b. 15 days
- ❍ c. 20 days
- ❍ d. 30 days
- ❍ e. None of the above

The correct answer is c. A history for Internet browsing is held for 20 days. All other answers could be used; however, this is not the default. You can change this setting by clicking on View|Internet Options under the General tab. Therefore, answers a, b, d, and e are incorrect.

Question 10

An NT server with IIS is required for any documents that you wish to present in HTTP.

- ❍ a. True
- ❍ b. False

The correct answer is False. IE4 has an option for FrontPage Express. This runs on Windows 9x, and it is suitable for testing or very light HTTP access. It does not offer the security of NT, nor does it have the scalability of IIS. It is quite suitable as a low-end solution to publishing personal production work to an intranet.

Question 11

When upgrading from Internet Explorer 3, which of the following would be migrated successfully?

- ❑ a. Favorites
- ❑ b. Security
- ❑ c. History
- ❑ d. Connection
- ❑ e. Proxy Server Settings

The correct answers are a, c, d, and e. Most user settings are brought forward during a migration from either Internet Explorer 3 or Netscape. Due to a change in the method of how security is handled, it does not migrate when installing IE4. Therefore, answer b is incorrect.

Question 12

Authenticode version 1 was used to sign your custom code. You have not upgraded to Aunthenticode version 2. A user makes a request to download your custom code using IE4. What is the result?

- ❍ a. The user cannot download the code until you upgrade to Authenticode version 2.
- ❍ b. No problem. Version 2 simply uses new features that you are not using, so the download is transparent.
- ❍ c. Depending on security settings, the user might get an expiration warning, and the download might be aborted.
- ❍ d. None of the above

The correct answer is c. Depending on security settings, the user might get an expiration warning, and the download might be aborted. The user might simply get a warning, or, if security is set high enough, the download will be prevented. Answer a is incorrect, because security might be set low enough, for example, in the Local Intranet Zone, that the download will not be stopped. Answer b is incorrect, because Authenticode version 1 expired in June 1997.

Question 13

How many Security Zones are there in IE4?

- ❍ a. one
- ❍ b. two
- ❍ c. three
- ❍ d. four
- ❍ e. five

The correct answer is e. Only four zones are user configurable, but there are five zones. The configurable zones are the Local Intranet Zone, Internet Zone, Trusted Sites Zone, and Restricted Sites Zone. The fifth zone is the local PC.

Little to no security is provided with Internet Explorer for the local PC. Security for the local PC is configured through Profiles.

Question 14

When working with another company you do business with frequently, you create a Trusted Site Zone. What is the most common name for this?

- ❍ a. Intranet
- ❍ b. Internet
- ❍ c. Domain
- ❍ d. Extranet
- ❍ e. None of the above

The correct answer is d. An extranet is a trusted site, usually provided by another company. Choice a is incorrect because an intranet is within your firm only. It behaves very similar to a LAN; however, one or more Web servers are used internally. The Internet does not have the security levels set for trusted sites. Therefore, answer b is incorrect. In answer c, domain is a Microsoft NT concept for establishing common security parameters for user groups. This has no direct meaning to IE4, so this is an invalid answer.

Question 15

While working with the Administration Kit, you notice a yellow exclamation point next to NetMeeting while setting up to create your first custom build of IE4. What does this mean?

- ❍ a. You must update your version of NetMeeting.
- ❍ b. You may wish to update your version of NetMeeting.
- ❍ c. NetMeeting is not installed and cannot be included in a custom build.
- ❍ d. None of the above.

The correct answer is b. You may wish to update your version of NetMeeting. You are not required to have the latest and greatest version for each part of Internet Explorer. Therefore, answer a is incorrect. A green symbol means your component is current. A yellow symbol informs you that your version is not the latest. A red symbol is telling you that the component is not installed. Therefore, answer c is invalid because the symbol is yellow, not red.

Question 16

When working with Security Zones, you can choose Low, Medium, High, or Custom to be applied to all Security Zones.

❍ a. True

❍ b. False

The correct answer is False. The choices of Low, Medium, High, or Custom are correct. What makes the statement incorrect is applying them to all Security Zones. Each of the four configurable zones can be customized with one of the three preset options or as you see fit on a zone-by-zone basis. Therefore, answer a is incorrect.

Question 17

What does a user need to have for Microsoft Wallet to be enabled?

❍ a. Content Advisor installed

❍ b. Java scripting

❍ c. Security Certificate

❍ d. All of the above

The correct answer is c. A personal Security Certificate is used to both encrypt the data held in the Wallet and to ensure that the person requesting a credit card purchase is the person who placed the order. The Content Advisor is used in connection with site ratings. Therefore, answer a is incorrect. Java scripts can be used like ActiveX scripts. Neither of these programs is required for MS Wallet. Therefore, answer b is incorrect.

Question 18

You are preparing a custom build of IE4. You see a red X next to NetShow. What does this mean?

❍ a. Your version of NetShow is out of date.

❍ b. Your version of NetShow is not operational.

❍ c. Your version of NetShow doesn't exist.

❍ d. Your version of NetShow is fine.

❍ e. None of the above.

The correct answer is c. In this case, a red X means that you have not installed NetShow. Green indicates that Automatic Version Synchronization has been checked and is current, which would make answer d incorrect. Answer b would not be checked by AVS for a lack of corruption, so this would never be a valid choice. A yellow exclamation point indicates the program is available, but it is not the most recent version.

Need To Know More?

Microsoft Press: *Microsoft Internet Explorer 4 Resource Kit*. Redmond, Washington, 1998. ISBN 1-57231-842-2. An excellent Resource for both the IEAK and IE4.

Microsoft Press: *Microsoft Internet Explorer 4 Technical Support Training*. Redmond, Washington, 1998. ISBN 1-57231-828-7. Adapted from the Microsoft Official Curriculum, complete with labs.

The **microsoft.public.internetexplorer.ieak** newsgroup is the best single source for interactive questions and understanding the IEAK.

The **microsoft.public.internetexplorer.IE4** newsgroup is a good, general source for IE4 information.

Using IEAK For Upgrades

Terms you'll need to understand:

- √ POP3 (Post Office Protocol version 3)
- √ IMAP4 (Internet Message Access Protocol version 4)
- √ SMTP (Simple Mail Transfer Protocol)
- √ LDAP (Lightweight Directory Access Protocol)
- √ BINHEX
- √ UUENCODE
- √ MIME (Multipurpose Internet Mail Extensions), MIME HTML, and S/MIME (Secure MIME)
- √ InfoPane
- √ Preview pane
- √ Outlook bar
- √ Inbox Assistant and Rules
- √ Stationery

Techniques you'll need to master:

- √ Creating a strategy for upgrading a browser
- √ Understanding which features of Internet Explorer 3.x migrate to IE4
- √ Understanding which features of Netscape Navigator migrate to IE4
- √ Understanding key concepts of email
- √ Working with key features of Outlook Express
- √ Understanding which settings, email messages, and address books can be imported to Outlook Express

This chapter looks at a number of Internet Explorer compatibility and upgrade issues. We'll discuss how to create an upgrade strategy, review the top migration issues, cover email terminology and the key features of Outlook Express, and examine how various content and settings can be migrated to Outlook Express.

Upgrading From Other Clients

The various new features of Internet Explorer 4 (IE4) allow end users to be more productive in their everyday activities. IE4 gives Web developers much more flexibility in writing code, and end users reap the benefits of access to more interactive and creative content. IE4 also includes security fixes that help protect end users from attacks. New browser security holes seem to crop up on a regular basis, and once a new version of Internet Explorer is available, Microsoft stops providing patches to previous versions. Instead, users are expected to upgrade their browsers. Fortunately, Microsoft's Internet Explorer Administration Kit (IEAK) enables administrators to easily distribute the newest browser to existing clients. The following sections outline the steps for using IEAK to migrate from other clients.

Creating A Migration Strategy

The first step toward a successful migration of existing systems is research. Depending on the size of your environment, you should either use network asset survey software, such as Microsoft's Systems Management Server (SMS), or send out a questionnaire to identify existing end-user hardware and software configurations.

Based on existing hardware and software information you gather, you can identify most typical configurations, so any proposed migration process can be tested in a lab environment. Your deployment plan should include hardware and software upgrade solutions, as needed.

Chapter 2 discusses hardware and software requirements for IE4. In general, installing IE4 on top of IE3 requires about 10MB less disk space than normal. Whether the system already has Netscape Navigator, however, does not impact software or hardware requirements.

You might want to consider requiring your users to delete Navigator before installing IE4 to buy back some disk space. However, deleting IE3 is not recommended, because IE4 installs directly on top of it and uses some of the same files.

IE3 and IE4 cannot exist on the same machine unless the machine is set to dual-boot between different operating systems. With a dual-boot system, Internet Explorer 3 can be installed under one operating system and IE4 under the other. However, IE4 can coexist with Netscape Navigator on the same machine without a dual boot.

After the testing phase is complete, it is good practice to conduct a pilot test. Finally, once the migration plan is complete, Microsoft recommends that administrators document frequently asked questions (FAQs) about the upgrade and provide training for their end users.

Understanding Migration Issues

Netscape Navigator and Internet Explorer 3.x are the most typical browsers that you'll find on your users' desktops. Fortunately, IE4 Setup includes the ability to import some of the settings from these browsers. The following definitions explain some of the most important Internet settings that users might want to migrate to their new browsers:

- **Proxy settings** Settings that tell Internet Explorer how it should access the Internet—either directly or through a proxy server. A *proxy server* is a program that provides Internet access from an isolated or private network. To view the options available for proxy settings, choose View|Options and click on the Connection tab.
- **Favorites** A folder that maintains a list of links—typically to a user's favorite Web sites or files.

  Note: In Internet Explorer 3.x, Favorites can only be stored alphabetically. With IE4's drag-and-drop functionality, users can now organize their entries in any way they wish. (See Figure 3.1 for an example.)

- **Cookies** Text files that sit on users' machines with personalized information. Web sites use cookies to maintain users' preferences, to maintain state in an application so that the user can return to a specific location on the site, and to gather information and store other specific data for future reuse.
- **QuickLinks** Quick access buttons with shortcuts to frequently used Web sites.
- **Plug-ins** A general term used in this discussion for ActiveX controls, Java applets, and all other client-side applications needed to view and run Web applications.

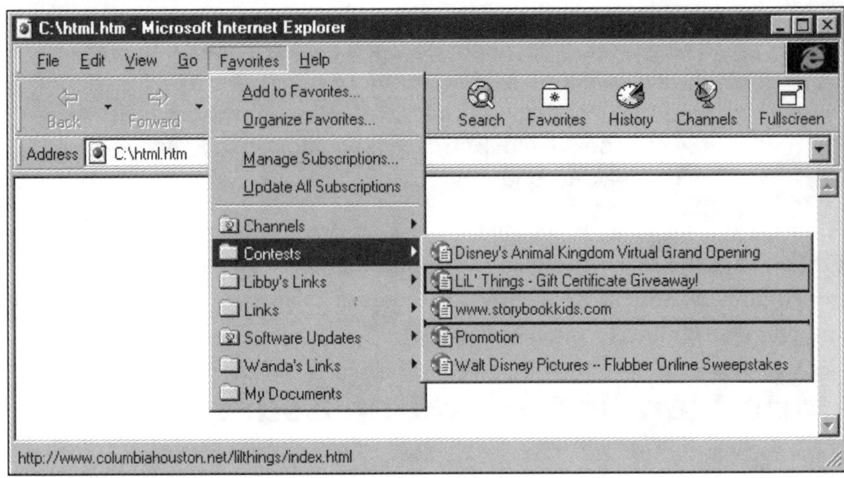

Figure 3.1 Users can sort IE4 Favorites however they like.

Each of the different browsers has its own caveats during migration. The following sections discuss some of these caveats to fully prepare you to perform your migration.

Migrating From Internet Explorer 3.x

IE4 Setup installs over an existing installation of Internet Explorer 3.x, and it imports Internet Explorer 3.x's proxy settings, Favorites, and cookies.

Because the security model and other Internet settings in IE4 differ from Internet Explorer 3.x's settings, they cannot be imported.

When a user imports a collection of Favorites, IEAK imports the contents of the folder but not the folder itself. To include the folder along with its contents, select the parent folder of whatever folder you wish to import.

Even though Internet Explorer 3.x Favorites are maintained, the links in the QuickLinks bar are not. Users need to restore those links manually. Pre-migration notification (probably via email) about this limitation should help avoid too many cases of "user upset."

Migrating From Netscape Navigator 3.x

IE4 Setup imports proxy settings, bookmarks, and cookies from Netscape Navigator 3.x.

After upgrading Navigator clients to IE, a new folder appears under IE's Favorites menu called *Imported Bookmarks*. This folder contains those bookmarks that were used with Navigator. Even when uninstalling Netscape Navigator using Add/Remove Programs, these bookmarks are not deleted from the file system.

There is a plethora of import and export tools for Favorites. Most of them can be downloaded from **www.download.com** under the category Internet Browsing Companions.

Table 3.1 provides a helpful list of Netscape terms and their IE counterparts.

Using Previously Existing Browser Plug-ins

After an upgrade from either IE or Navigator, all browser plug-ins must be reinstalled. To minimize this effort, include the most often-used plug-ins and helper applications as custom components with the IEAK. Whereas some Navigator plug-ins may be compatible with IE4, it is important to note that some might not. Often, patches, updates, or replacements to old plug-ins must be obtained for newer browser versions.

Table 3.1 Internet Explorer's equivalents to Netscape Navigator features.

Navigator Feature	IE Equivalent	Purpose
Bookmarks	Favorites	Maintains a list of favorite Web sites for quick access.
Location field	Address bar	Allows users to view a page or directory by typing in a location.
Reload	Refresh	Downloads the latest version of the page from the Internet.
Personal toolbar	QuickLinks bar	Quick access buttons with shortcuts to favorite Web sites.

For a list of popular Internet plug-ins, refer to the Internet Plug-ins section at **www.download.com**.

For a Netscape helper application to run in tandem with IE4, users must add the application's file extensions to the list of Windows file type associations. Here's how:

1. Double-click on the My Computer icon on your desktop.
2. Choose View|Folder Options.
3. Click on the File Types tab.
4. Click on the New Type button.
5. Enter a description of the file type, the file extension (for example, .HTM, which is a typical file extension for Web pages), and the appropriate MIME type.
6. Click on the New button. In the Action field, type "Open".
7. Click on the Browse button and browse to the appropriate application. Click on OK when finished.
8. Click on OK, and click on OK again, to exit.

Internet Explorer 3.x plug-ins are kept in the occache directory of the C:\Windows default directory, and even though they are no longer used with IE4, they are not deleted automatically during the upgrade. The reason is that if IE4 is uninstalled, IE3 becomes functional and utilizes the occache directory. Plug-ins used by IE4 are stored in the Downloaded Program Files directory in the C:\Windows default directory.

Using Other Email And News Programs

IE4 can be configured to work with existing email and news applications. For example, organizations that already use the Microsoft Office suite might want to build a package that uses Microsoft Outlook instead of Outlook Express to read and send mail. An administrator might also choose to include a new mail or news client as a Custom Component using the Express Configuration Wizard and IEAK. Chapter 6 discusses the steps necessary to specify what's required in more detail. Step 5 of the IEAK allows administrators to specify which programs should be used in conjunction with IE4.

To add an email or news application association manually from within IE4, choose Internet Options from the View menu, then choose the Programs tab. Select the application you wish to use from the drop-down boxes, as shown in Figure 3.2.

Dealing With Compatibility Problems

Web pages and applications developed prior to the introduction of IE4 are sometimes incompatible with IE4. Some Web pages that use browser-specific HTML and scripting might not display correctly, or they might produce scripting errors.

For third-party applications, you can usually obtain patches or upgrades that make these applications compatible with IE4. However, homegrown or custom applications or Web pages might need to be rewritten to make them compatible with IE4.

For the most up-to-date information on HTML standards, refer to the information at the World Wide Web Consortium at **www.wc3.org/MarkUp**.

Quite often, Dynamic HTML (DHTML) is recommended as a replacement for interactive scripting and Web applications. DHTML allows authors to create interactive pages that change dynamically on the client side, so they are usually quicker and more flexible. Both Netscape Navigator 4.x and Internet Explorer 4.x support DHTML, but their implementations differ.

Email And News Basics

Outlook Express (OE) is Microsoft's newest Internet email and news client. It replaces the Internet Mail and News 1 client that shipped with IE3. OE is geared toward standalone clients that use simple dial-up connections. This

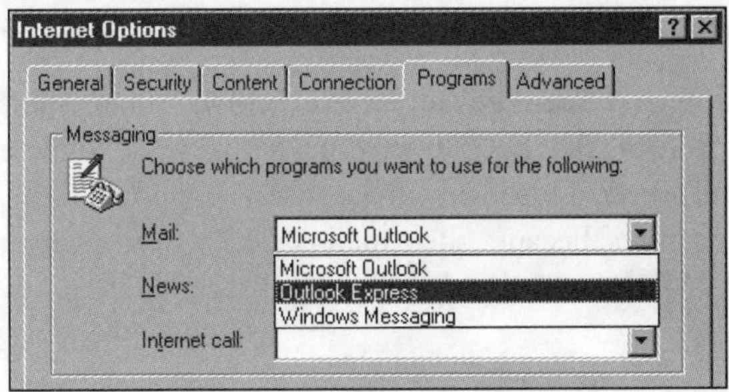

Figure 3.2 Mail and news programs options.

section provides an overview of common email terminology that should help you understand Outlook Express's feature set:

- **Simple Mail Transfer Protocol (SMTP)** A protocol typically used to communicate with an email server for outgoing mail. SMTP also defines the syntax for email addresses including domain names (**user@domainname**), the type and amount of content a message can contain, and how messages move from one email server to another.
- **UUENCODE and BINHEX** Processes used to convert nontextual data into an encoded form that uses plain text characters only. UUENCODE and BINHEX help to avoid introducing control characters or special character sequences that might otherwise signal unwanted end-of-message or message formatting data. When an encoded text file is delivered, the email recipient's client must convert the encoded text back into its original format to make it readable. These tools are used primarily to handle email attachments rather than email messages.
- **Multipurpose Internet Mail Extensions (MIME)** Introduced in 1992, an extension that uses the same approach as UUENCODE, but with more flexibility. When you send an email message with a MIME attachment, the receiving email client automatically knows which icon it should use to display the attachment and what software should be used to open it.

Outlook Express users can *send* and *receive* MIME and UUENCODE attachments, and they can *receive* BINHEX attachments.

- **POP3 (Post Office Protocol 3)** The most common protocol used to grab incoming mail from an email server. POP3 collects any new mail messages from your mail server's computer. When you access a POP3 mailbox, your email client automatically downloads all pending mail onto your hard disk and deletes it from the server (although you can configure your client to leave the original copy on the server).
- **IMAP4 (Internet Message Access Protocol 4)** A new message-handling protocol that permits incoming mail to be collected and held at your mail server. This is beneficial for users who read their mail from multiple locations, because their mail is always in the same place—on the server. IMAP4 can also download messages to local drives whenever users choose.
- **NNTP (Network News Transfer Protocol)** The transport protocol used for Usenet newsgroups and for many private newsgroups (such as Microsoft's **msnews.microsoft.com**).

- **Usenet** A communication medium for groups of messages on the Internet called *newsgroups*. There are three types of newsgroups:
    - **Standard** All Usenet sites are expected to carry these basic newsgroups. Table 3.2 lists the top-level hierarchies that fall into the Standard newsgroups category and their general subject matter.
    - **Alternative** Usenet sites do not have to carry these newsgroups, but most do.
    - **Local** These newsgroups are used by organizations or small communities to communicate among themselves.
- **vCards** A popular standard for electronic business cards, often used with LDAP servers and address books.

Outlook Express Features

Outlook Express includes a number of features that work closely with IE4 to provide users with a powerful email client that is simple to learn and use. Some of the major areas of enhancement in Outlook Express are:

- Accessibility and ease of use
- Security and standards support
- Multiuser support

Table 3.2 The most common newsgroup hierarchies.

Hierarchy Name	Category	Subject Area
alt	Alternative	Wide variety of subjects
biz	Business	Business-related news
comp	Computers	Computers and computer applications
misc	Miscellaneous	Information that doesn't fit any of the other categories
news	News	News about Usenet newsgroups in general
rec	Recreational	Hobbies and activities
sci	Scientific	Science and research
soc	Social	Social and cultural issues
talk	Talk	Discussions and debates on a variety of topics

The best way to learn about the features of Outlook Express is to install and use it. Familiarize yourself with the various options available from the File menu.

Accessibility And Ease Of Use

Microsoft tools are known for their ease of use and their tight integration with one another, and Outlook Express is no exception. Like Microsoft's other products, Outlook Express includes:

- Drag-and-drop functionality
- AutoHyperlinking, where OE automatically recognizes when a user types a hyperlink and makes the link active
- Multiple levels of undo and redo
- Spellchecking, by utilizing Microsoft Office's spellchecker

Other features of Outlook Express that make it easy to use are:

- An Outlook bar for easy folder navigation
- A preview pane that allows the user to preview messages before fully opening them (see Figure 3.3)

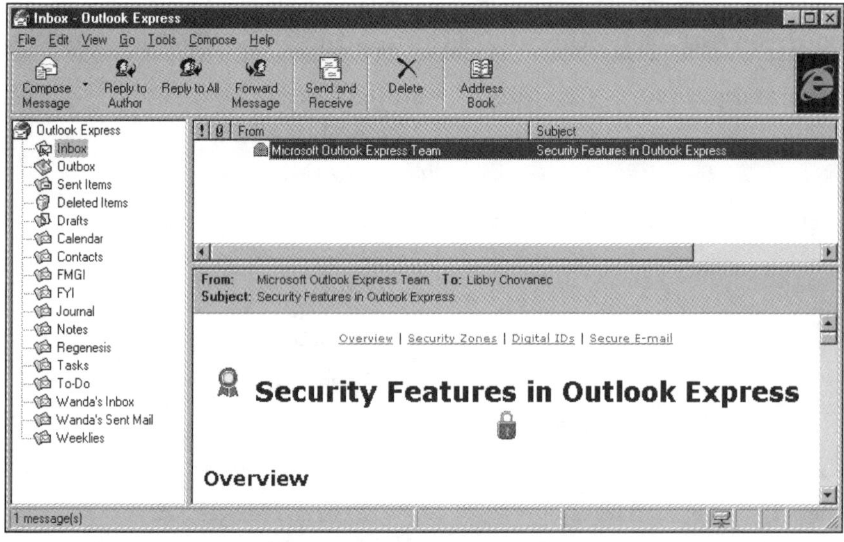

Figure 3.3 The right-hand pane of Outlook Express includes a list of email messages and a preview pane that allows you to preview any message without having to open it.

- A Drafts folder, where unfinished messages are automatically kept for easy access
- An AutoSignature feature that lets users create personalized signatures or attach vCards to all their outgoing mail
- A Find feature that allows users to run queries from within Outlook Express to find specific mail items

Outlook Express also makes it easy to be aware of new messages because:

- It displays the number of unread messages.
- It bolds unread messages and folders that contain unread messages.
- Users can choose to be notified when a new message arrives.

Outlook Express even has a Start Page called the *InfoPane* (see Figure 3.4) that allows users to jump quickly to the task of their choice:

- Read Mail
- Read News
- Compose A Message
- Address Book

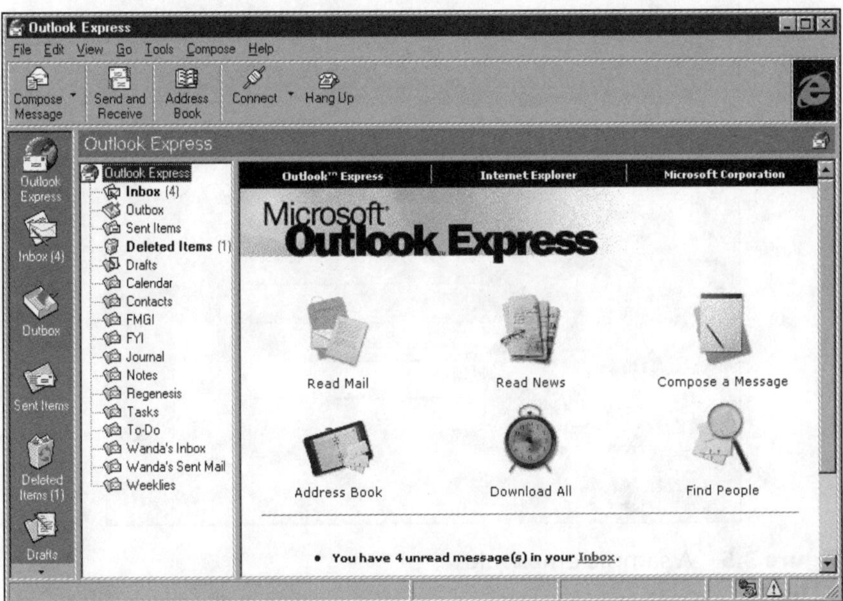

Figure 3.4 The default InfoPane.

- Download All
- Find People

The InfoPane also provides a Tip Of The Day and a summary of the Inbox and Drafts folders.

IEAK can be used to change the InfoPane to point to either a customized HTML file on the user's local machine or to a URL on the Internet or intranet. This page can be used to provide links to frequently used Web sites or other locations. When using a URL, offline users will receive a blank InfoPane. Users have the option of turning off the InfoPane.

Also, to help organize email messages, the Outlook Express Inbox Assistant allows users to create rules for each email account. A rule can be created to forward, move, or copy messages automatically based on predefined criteria (see Figure 3.5).

Other convenient features of OE are its newsgroup filters, which allow users to automatically ignore newsgroup postings based on sender, subject, date posted, or length of message.

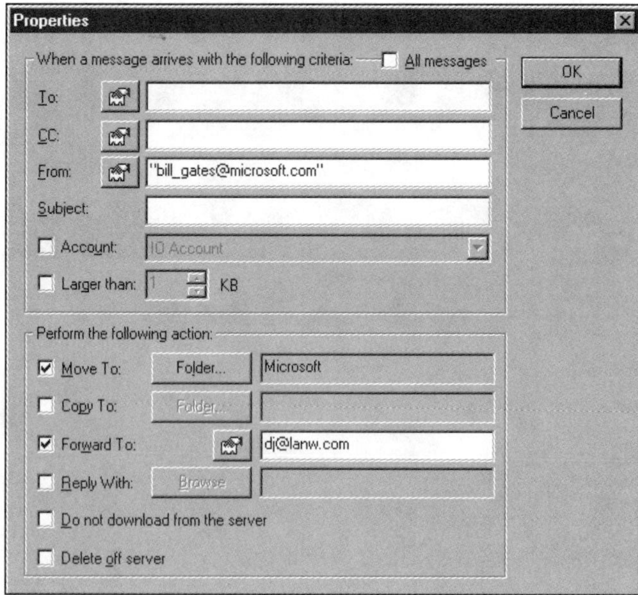

Figure 3.5 A sample email rule.

Security And Standards Support

As with most email programs, Outlook Express supports SMTP and POP3 mail servers, and NNTP news servers. In addition, it also supports newer,more capable standards and protocols (discussed next), which make OE a more powerful and secure email program. The Server Properties dialog box, shown in Figure 3.6, is where the names of the mail servers, as well as logon information, appear.

IMAP4 (Internet Message Access Protocol Version 4) Support

IMAP4 enables users to access email from multiple locations and computers, and they can choose to download headers only. Because users do not have to download their mail every time they access it, IMAP4 also helps to improve bandwidth utilization.

LDAP (Lightweight Directory Access Protocol) Support

LDAP provides access to the most popular Internet directories, such as Four11, InfoSpace, Bigfoot, and SwitchBoard, to locate anyone on the Internet. Think of these servers as online white pages. When users click on the Contact icon in the To line of a message, the Find People dialog box that appears allows users to look up names in their local address books or on an LDAP server (see Figure 3.7).

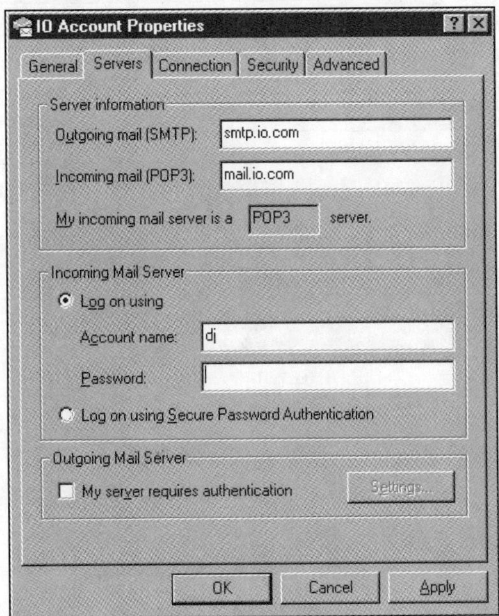

Figure 3.6 The Server Properties dialog box.

Figure 3.7 The OE Find People dialog box has a list of the most popular LDAP servers.

Users can add other LDAP servers at their discretion. In addition, once an address is located, the dialog box changes to allow users to store chosen email names in their address books for quick access later (see Figure 3.8).

> *Note: When a user partially or completely types a name on the To line of a message, OE automatically searches the selected directory service to resolve an appropriate email name.*

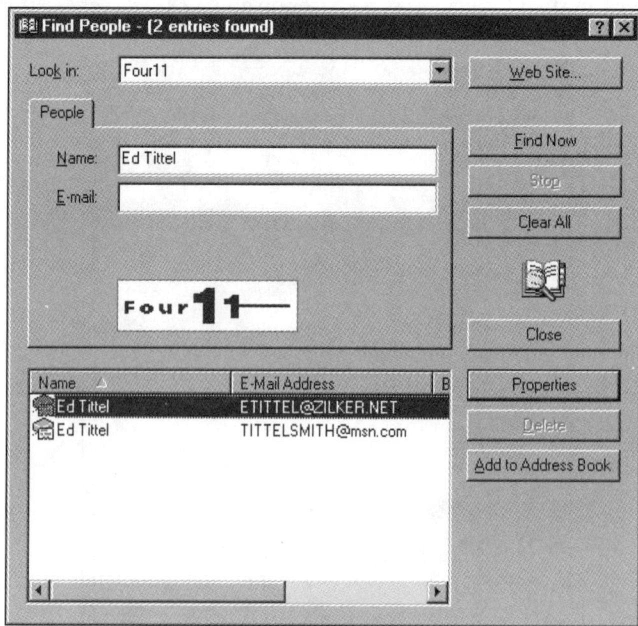

Figure 3.8 Users can store email names in their address books for quick access later.

MIME (Multipurpose Internet Mail Extensions) HTML

The MIME HTML standard allows OE users to encode email messages using HTML and to send full Web pages from the Internet to each other using the Insert HTML command.

On the receiving end, if the client doesn't support MIME, text-based information appears at the top of the message and the raw HTML appears at the bottom. If the recipient supports regular MIME, the message contains the text-based information first, and the HTML is included as an attachment. Finally, if the recipient supports MIME HTML, the email message is displayed like a Web page within the email client itself.

OE can reply automatically to messages in the same format in which they were sent, so if you receive HTML mail, OE responds with HTML. This feature is called Smart Reply.

MIME HTML also enables OE users to take advantage of HTML-based stationery (see Figure 3.9).

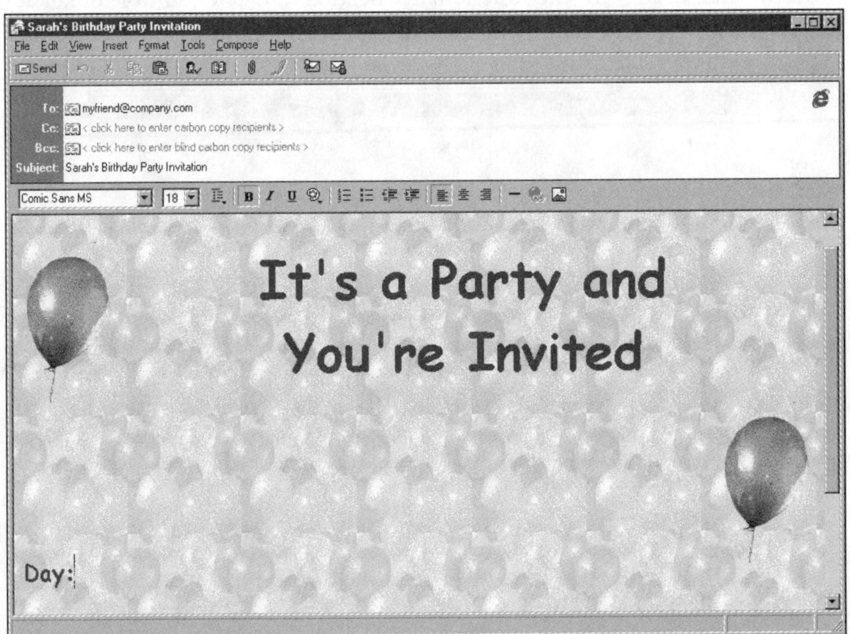

Figure 3.9 An example of using HTML stationery as a background for email.

S/MIME (Secure MIME) Support

Secure MIME provides a level of security that uses public key encryption and certificates. Using a certificate (also called a *digital ID*) as a wrapper, you can share your public key with the people you communicate with most often (see Figure 3.10). This allows them to validate that a message originates from your computer, and only those users who have a copy of your public key can read your messages.

You typically keep your private key to yourself, and when a user encrypts a message using your public key, the only key that can decrypt it is your private key. Therefore, you are the only person who is able to read such an encrypted message.

> *Note: To obtain a digital ID so you can send and receive S/MIME encrypted messages, visit VeriSign's Web site at* ***http://digitalid.verisign.com.***

Multiuser Support

It is not uncommon for users to have multiple Internet accounts, or for multiple users to share the same machine. In either of these cases, Outlook Express provides such users with the functionality needed to create multiple email accounts within a single client. Outlook Express can maintain separate mail stores

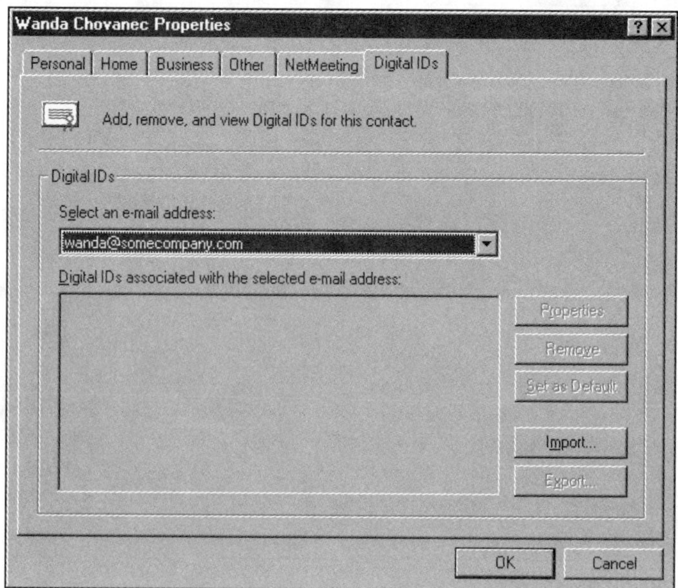

Figure 3.10 Outlook Express users can import digital IDs for their contacts.

and address books for each individual user. OE also supports multiple News Server Accounts in much the same way.

When users log onto a machine, they obtain a Windows profile, which contains their personal settings, such as display settings and Outlook Express settings. To switch from one user profile to another, a user can do any one of the following:

- Select File|Logoff User from within Outlook Express.
- Click on the Windows Start button and choose Logoff User.
- Restart Windows.

To manually install additional email accounts, users can perform the following steps:

1. Within Outlook Express, click on Tools|Accounts. The Internet Accounts window should appear, showing a list of installed mail and news accounts.
2. Click on the Mail tab.
3. Click on the Add button and choose Mail. The Internet Connection Wizard will prompt you for new account information.
4. Enter your account name, mail server address, and password.
5. When finished entering your information, click on Finish.
6. To make this account your default, highlight it and choose Set As Default.

Upgrading From Other Mail Clients

In the first section of this chapter, you learned that one of the steps toward creating a migration strategy is to gather information about your user base. That data, along with a sound email foundation and understanding of the standards that Outlook Express supports, should allow you to define users' Internet mail and news settings using IEAK.

Despite presetting the majority of users' Internet mail and news settings, the Internet Connection Wizard still runs the first time any user attempts to run Outlook Express. To stop the Internet Connection Wizard from running, include a Custom Component in your IE Package that obtains the user's email address and logon information and automatically populates the Windows Registry with the appropriate information.

The Specify Internet Mail Servers, Domain, And News Server dialog box (see Figure 3.11) is where the following Internet mail and news options are specified:

- Internet mail servers, domain servers, and news servers
- Whether Outlook Express should be the default mail client
- Whether Outlook Express should be the default news client
- Secure Password Authentication (SPA), used to authenticate users when they log on
- Lightweight Directory Access Protocol (LDAP) settings:
  - Friendly Name
  - Directory Service
  - Home Page
  - Search Base
  - Service Bitmap
  - An option to check names against the LDAP server when sending mail
  - Authentication Type
- InfoPane and welcome message for Outlook Express
- Default signature files for email and news messages

Finally, as the administrator, you can lock down mail and news features in the System Policies And Restrictions section of the IEAK Configuration Wizard (see Figure 3.12) or the IEAK Profile Manager (discussed in detail in Chapter 6). You must choose whether to:

- Place mail and news in the Restricted Sites Zone.
- Make plain text message composition the default for mail messages and news posts.
- Turn on the Outlook bar.
- Turn off the folder list (tree view of folders).
- Turn on the Folder bar (horizontal line displaying folder names).
- Turn off the Tip Of The Day.

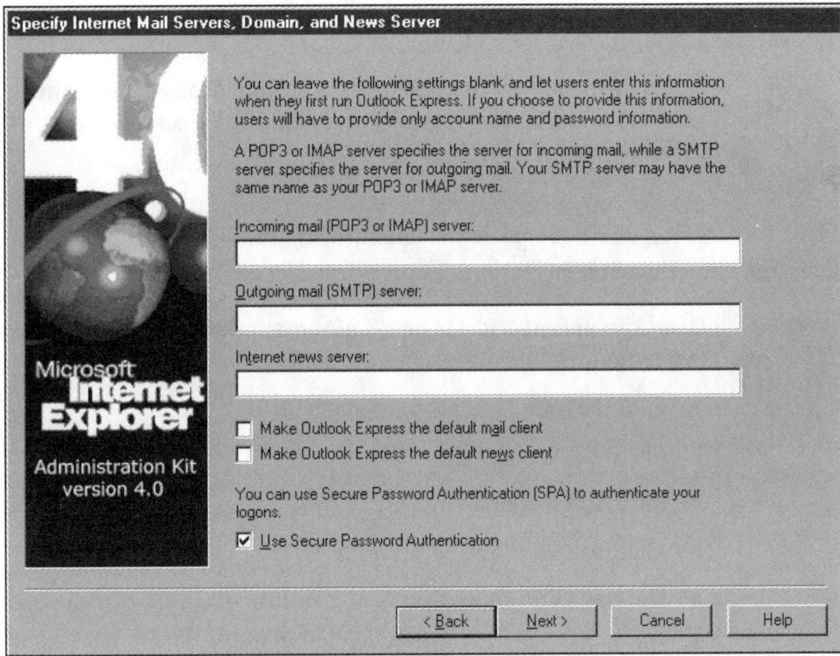

Figure 3.11 The Specify Internet Mail Servers, Domain, And News Server dialog box is the first of four mail and news customization screens.

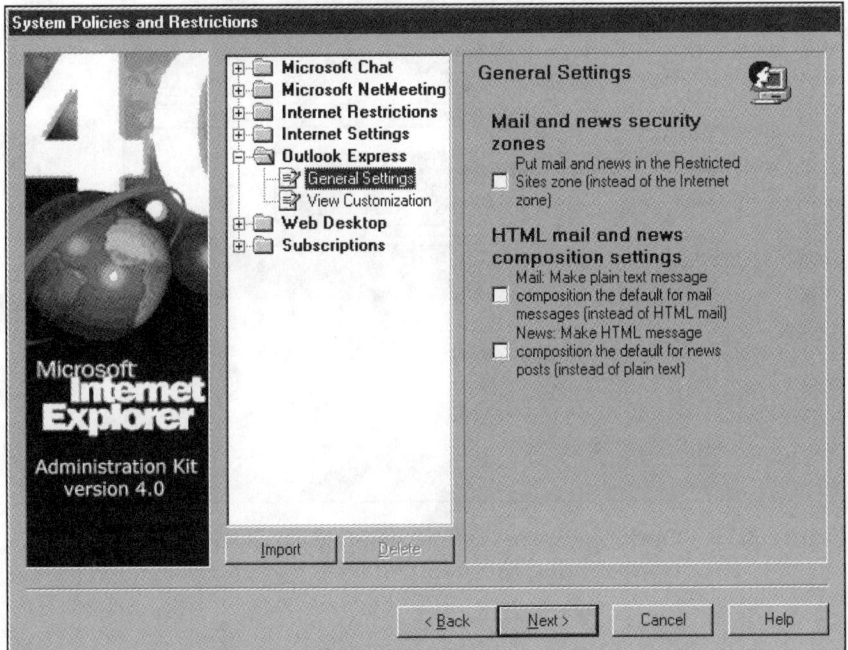

Figure 3.12 The IEAK System Policies And Restrictions dialog box.

Migration From Other Mail Clients

Upon the first boot, Outlook Express automatically detects and offers to import address books, messages, and mail settings from other clients.

These settings can also be imported manually using the Import feature, available from the File menu in Outlook Express (see Figure 3.13).

Users can import address books automatically from the following programs:

- Eudora Pro or Light (through version 3)
- Microsoft Exchange
- Microsoft Outlook
- Microsoft Windows Messaging
- Netscape Communicator
- Netscape Mail (version 2 or 3)

Imported email messages appear in the Outlook Express folders list.

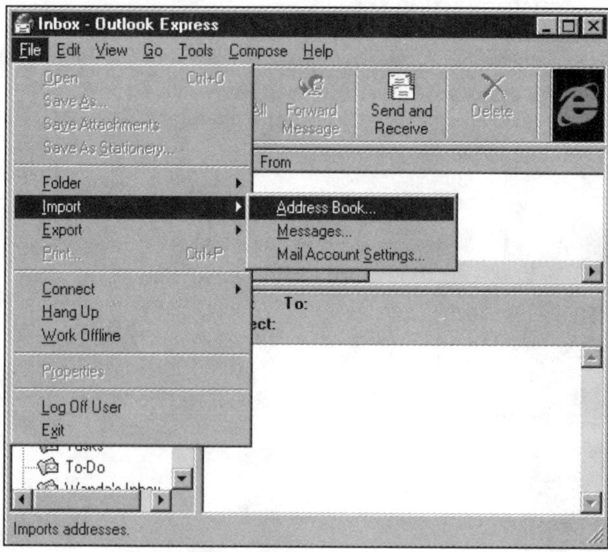

Figure 3.13 Outlook Express offers the ability to import information from existing programs.

Users can import address books manually from the following sources:

- Eudora Pro or Light (through version 3) Address Book
- LDIF-LDAP Data Interchange Format
- Microsoft Exchange Personal Address Book
- Microsoft Internet Mail for Windows 3.1 Address Book
- Netscape Address Book (version 2 or 3)
- Netscape Communicator Address Book (version 4)
- Text Files (comma-separated values)

Note: Any data that can be exported from a product in a comma- or tab-delimited text file can be imported into Outlook Express.

Imported address book entries appear in Outlook Express's Contacts program.

Users can import Internet Mail account settings manually from the following sources:

- Microsoft Windows Messaging
- Microsoft Exchange
- Microsoft Outlook

Exam Prep Questions

Question 1

Which of the following are supported by Outlook Express?

- ❍ a. POP3
- ❍ b. SMTP
- ❍ c. IMAP4
- ❍ d. NNTP
- ❍ e. MIME
- ❍ f. All of the above

The correct answer to this question is f. POP3 and IMAP4 are both standards for incoming mail. SMTP (Simple Mail Transfer Protocol) is used for outgoing mail. Outlook Express uses NNTP as the protocol for newsgroups. MIME is used to encode mail attachments for delivery over the Internet.

Question 2

Outlook Express can import mail from which of the following clients?

- ❑ a. Eudora Light or Pro
- ❑ b. Internet Mail And News
- ❑ c. Netscape Communicator
- ❑ d. Microsoft Exchange
- ❑ e. Microsoft Outlook
- ❑ f. Microsoft Windows Messaging

The correct answers are a, b, c, d, e, and f. All of these clients have mail that can be imported to Outlook Express.

Question 3

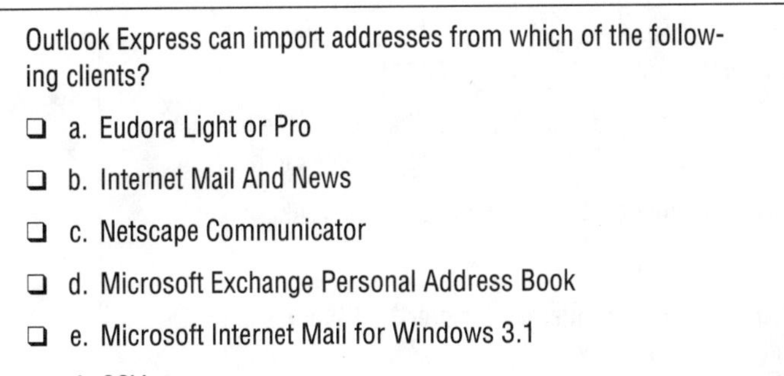

Outlook Express can import addresses from which of the following clients?

- ❑ a. Eudora Light or Pro
- ❑ b. Internet Mail And News
- ❑ c. Netscape Communicator
- ❑ d. Microsoft Exchange Personal Address Book
- ❑ e. Microsoft Internet Mail for Windows 3.1
- ❑ f. CSVs

The correct answers are a, b, c, d, e, and f. Address books from all the clients mentioned can be imported to Outlook Express.

Question 4

Which of the following options are automatically imported to IE4 during an upgrade?

- ❑ a. Cookies
- ❑ b. Plug-ins
- ❑ c. Proxy settings
- ❑ d. Favorites
- ❑ e. QuickLinks

The correct answers to this question are a, c, and d. Cookies, proxy settings, and Favorites are automatically migrated to IE4 during an upgrade. Plug-ins and QuickLinks must be reinstalled manually. Therefore, answers b and e are incorrect.

Question 5

How do you migrate an Internet Explorer 3.x end user's Favorites folder to Internet Explorer 4 using the IEAK?

- ❍ a. Include a batch file in the package that copies the Internet Explorer 3.x Favorites folder to IE4's Favorites folder.
- ❍ b. Check the Import Bookmarks option in the IEAK.
- ❍ c. Migration is automatic.
- ❍ d. You cannot import Internet Explorer 3.x Favorites into Internet Explorer 4.x.

The correct answer to this question is c. The Internet Explorer 3.x Favorites folder is automatically used by IE4. IE4 supports none of the other options mentioned.

Question 6

Which of the following mail settings can be populated using IEAK?

- ❑ a. Default mail client
- ❑ b. Secure Password Authentication
- ❑ c. LDAP settings
- ❑ d. Customizable InfoPane and welcome message
- ❑ e. A default signature file

Answers a, b, c, d, and e are correct. All of these options can be set using IEAK.

Question 7

Which of the following is the location of plug-ins downloaded with IE4?

- ❍ a. C:\Windows\Downloaded Program Files
- ❍ b. C:\Windows\occache
- ❍ c. C:\Program Files\Internet Explorer\Download Internet Files
- ❍ d. C:\Windows\Temporary Internet Files

The correct answer to this question is a. IE4 plug-ins are installed in the default C:\Windows directory under Downloaded Program Files. IE3 stores its plug-ins in the C:\Windows\occache directory. Therefore, answer b is incorrect. C:\Program Files\Internet Explorer\Downloaded Internet Files is a fictitious directory in this case, and C:\Windows\Temporary Internet Files is the directory where the IE4 cache is stored. Therefore, answers c and d are incorrect.

Question 8

Which of the following protocols define the syntax for email addresses?

- ❍ a. IMAP4
- ❍ b. POP3
- ❍ c. SMTP
- ❍ d. TCP/IP

The correct answer to this question is c. The Simple Mail Transfer Protocol is not only used typically for outgoing mail, but it also defines how email addresses should be written. IMAP4, POP3, and TCP/IP do not define syntax for email addresses. Therefore, answers a, b, and d are incorrect.

Question 9

Internet Explorer 3.x and IE4 can coexist on the same operating system.

- ❍ a. True
- ❍ b. False

The correct answer to this question is b. IE3 and IE4 cannot coexist unless they are on separate operating systems via a dual-boot machine.

Question 10

Which of the following settings can be imported from the Mosaic browser?

- ❍ a. Proxy settings
- ❍ b. Plug-ins
- ❍ c. Cookies
- ❍ d. Favorites
- ❍ e. All of the above
- ❍ f. None of the above

The correct answer to this question is f. When you install IE4 over a browser program other than Netscape Navigator or Internet Explorer 3.x, no settings are automatically imported into IE4. Therefore, answers a, b, c, d, and e are all incorrect.

Question 11

Which of the following Outlook Express settings can be preset using IEAK?

- ❑ a. A customized InfoPane
- ❑ b. Email address and username
- ❑ c. NNTP server
- ❑ d. LDAP settings
- ❑ e. A default signature

Answers a, c, d, and e are correct. A customized InfoPane, the NNTP server, LDAP settings, and a default signature can all be specified with the IEAK. Answer b is incorrect because the IEAK cannot specify a user's email address and username.

Need To Know More?

Bott, Ed, Dick Cravens, and Jerry Cox. *Special Edition Using Microsoft Internet Explorer 4*. Que Education & Training, Indianapolis, IN, 1998. ISBN 0-7897-1046-3. Chapters 8 and 10 provide an excellent source for detailed information about IE4 and Outlook Express.

Microsoft Press: *Microsoft Internet Explorer 4 Resource Kit*. Redmond, WA, 1998. ISBN 1-57231-842-2. Another excellent resource for IE4 from Microsoft.

Microsoft Press: *Official Microsoft Internet Explorer 4 Book*. Redmond, WA, 1997. ISBN 1-57231-576-8. A comprehensive guide to Internet Explorer and all its components and features. Chapter 13 explains how to use Outlook Express to your best advantage.

Search the TechNet CD (or its online version at **www.microsoft.com**) using the keywords *Outlook Express*, *Internet Explorer deployment*, and *email*. The TechNet CD also includes a copy of the *IEAK Corporate Deployment Guide*. This is excellent reading to learn more about creating an upgrade strategy.

For more detailed information on Outlook Express and its features, refer to the Microsoft Outlook Express Web site at **www.microsoft.com/ie/ie40/oe**.

The Internet Explorer Deployment Guide includes a wealth of valuable information on IE and using IEAK for Upgrades. It is available for free download at **www.microsoft.com/ie/corp/docs/deploymnt.zip**.

Webcasting Using IE4

Terms you'll need to understand:

- √ Push technology
- √ Pull technology
- √ Webcasting
- √ Basic, managed, and true Webcasting
- √ Site subscription
- √ Gleam
- √ Link crawl
- √ Web crawl
- √ Active Channel
- √ Channel Definition Format (CDF)
- √ Extensible Markup Language (XML)
- √ Channel screen saver
- √ Lightweight Directory Access Protocol (LDAP)
- √ Web View

Techniques you'll need to master:

- √ Subscribing to Web sites
- √ Configuring site subscriptions
- √ Restricting site subscriptions
- √ Subscribing to and configuring Active Channels, Active Desktop items, and channel screen savers
- √ Understanding the role of CDF files
- √ Understanding the options available through the Integrated Start menu and Taskbar
- √ Understanding the Web views available for folders
- √ Customizing and configuring Web views

Webcasting is the term used to describe the technologies used to automatically deliver information to a client's desktop using push and pull technologies. Typically, Web site documents are downloaded from the Internet in realtime. Pull technologies allow the Web browser, in this case Internet Explorer, to automatically request information from a Web site. Push technologies send the information automatically from the server, without client browser intervention.

Webcasting And IE4

With Microsoft Internet Explorer (IE), there are three main types of Webcasting: basic, managed, and true. In basic Webcasting, the user subscribes to a Web site that is periodically checked for new content by the browser. This type of Webcasting is often referred to as *smart pull* technology, because the browser controls the interaction with the Web sites. One drawback to this configuration is that the user generally has no information regarding how often the Web site is updated. For example, users might configure their browsers to check a stock information site once a day at 3:00 p.m. when the market closes, thinking they are getting the closing numbers. But, if the information on the Web site is not updated until 3:30 p.m. each day, they will be downloading the previous day's information.

In managed Webcasting environments, users still subscribe to a particular Web site, but the site has been configured to participate as an Active Channel. In this type of Web site configuration, the Web site publisher provides a predefined update schedule that the browser uses to retrieve the most up-to-date information. In addition, the user can configure the channel to retrieve only specific types of information from the site. Because there is greater control over which content is retrieved, both on the client and server sides, this is sometimes referred to as *programmed pull* technology.

Finally, servers in true Webcasting environments push the information to a user's desktop without user or browser intervention. This type of Webcasting uses multicast protocols to disseminate the same information to all users and is often used on corporate intranets. True Webcasting provides the greatest level of control on the host side and is facilitated in the Microsoft environment by NetShow.

Basic Webcasting Through Subscriptions

As mentioned previously, basic Webcasting is achieved by using IE4's subscription function. After a user subscribes to a particular Web site, the browser automatically checks the site at regular intervals to determine if new content exists. If so, the browser downloads the new data and notifies the user that new data exists or it simply notifies the user. By downloading the new data automatically and storing it in cache, the user is able to view the Web site without being connected to the Internet.

This is one of the benefits of using Webcasting—the ability to download information for offline viewing. This is particularly beneficial to mobile users. It enables them to connect to the Internet, automatically download new information from a number of sites, then disconnect and view the information. In addition, networked computers can be configured to update information to users during off-peak hours, which reduces the stress Internet traffic places on the network.

A user is notified that new data is on the Web site in one of two ways. When IE discovers that a site has been updated, a "gleam" (a red dot) appears on the site's Favorites icon. In addition, the user can configure IE to send an email message to a particular address when a site has been updated. This is a more active approach to notification and ensures the user is made aware of the change immediately after it has been detected.

A nice feature of the basic Webcasting available through IE is that users can subscribe to almost any Internet site. There is no configuration on the server end to enable Webcasting or define download parameters. From the host's point of view, subscription requests are the same as any other Internet requests.

When a user subscribes to a particular site, there are a number of options available to determine how sites are checked. How often the site is checked and how many levels are checked are just two of the available options.

How Does It Work?

IE uses a link crawl, also referred to as Web crawl, process to determine if there is new content on a particular Web site. If configured to do so, IE periodically connects to a site and "crawls" each link on the starting page and subsequent pages. During the crawl, IE determines whether the information has changed by comparing the date of the file in the Temporary Internet Files folder to the date of the file on the server.

This information is included in a special header in the HTTP response. The **GET** request to the server contains a header with an **If_Modified_Since** field. For example, a request might be **GET CORE.HTML If_Modified_Since:Sat, 18 Apr 1998 12:14:31 GMT**. The server will then either respond with the updated **CORE.HTML** file or a not modified message.

This system allows the browser to quickly and easily update the user's cache with only the new information on the site. One caveat to this type of operation is that the server is responsible for interpreting the **If_Modified_Since** requests, and its clock might not be synchronized with the client's clock, which could cause information to be updated incorrectly.

> *Note: Not all Web sites are enabled for Web crawls. Some sites disable this feature for one page or for the entire site. Subscriptions do not work on sites that have Web crawling disabled.*

Subscribing To Web Sites

The process of actually subscribing to a Web site is very straightforward, and it's a function of Internet Explorer Favorites. While browsing a site, select Add To Favorites from the Favorites menu to invoke the Add Favorite dialog box (shown in Figure 4.1).

As shown in Figure 4.1, there are three subscription options available when creating a Favorite:

- **No, Just Add The Page To My Favorites** This option does just what it says. This does not create a subscription, but rather, it creates a shortcut to the site.
- **Yes, But Only Tell Me When The Page Is Updated** This option creates a subscription to the site and checks it periodically, but only places the gleam on the Favorite icon and sends a notification email if the browser has been configured to do so.
- **Yes, Notify Me Of Updates And Download The Page For Offline Viewing** This option subscribes to the page, downloads all new files to the cache, and notifies the user that the site has been updated.

You can also subscribe to an existing Favorite. To do this, right-click on the Favorite you want to subscribe to and select Properties from the shortcut menu. The Properties dialog box for the Favorite should appear, as shown in Figure 4.2.

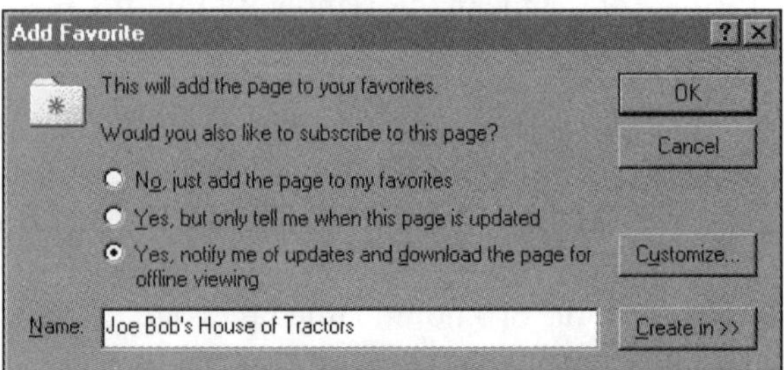

Figure 4.1 A subscription is created using the Add Favorite dialog box.

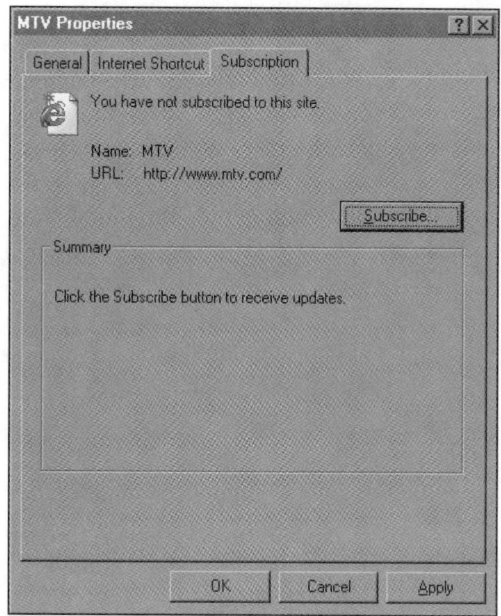

Figure 4.2 Subscribe to an existing Favorite through the Favorite's Properties dialog box.

Click on Subscribe to initiate the subscription. The Subscribe Favorite dialog box should open, and you must decide whether to download the new files or to receive notification when the site is updated. When you click on OK, two new tabs are added to the Properties dialog box—Receiving and Schedule. They are used to customize the subscription configuration.

The Receiving tab is used to determine whether updated files are downloaded and whether an email message is sent for notification. In addition, the Logon option is used to provide an automatic logon and password to sites that require them. Clicking on Advanced invokes the Advanced Download Options dialog box, shown in Figure 4.3.

The user can configure the browser to check pages that are linked to the original page up to three levels deep. This is configured by increasing the value in the Download Linked Pages Within A Depth Of box. By default, this value is set to zero. Selecting the Follow Links Outside Of This Page's Web Site box configures the browser to check linked sites for updated information as well. To decrease connection time, the user can choose not to download specific types of files, such as images, sounds, videos, ActiveX Controls, and Java applets. However, as the note states in the dialog box, choosing these options might omit important content from the pages, which can affect their appearance and operation. Lastly, the user can configure the browser to limit the amount of

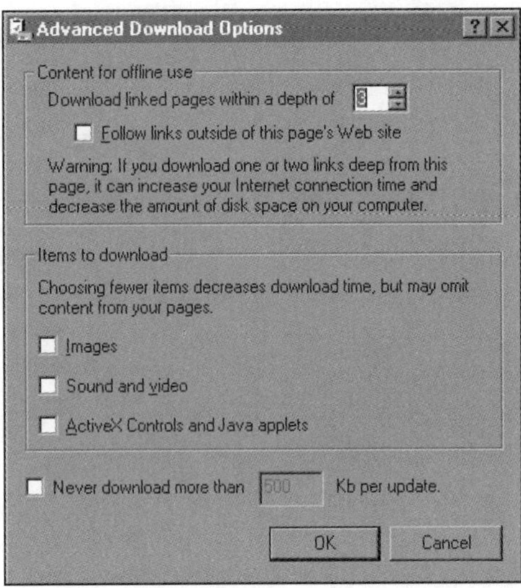

Figure 4.3 The subscription's Advanced Download Options dialog box.

information, in kilobytes, retrieved per session. This can be used to ensure that cached files do not consume a user's hard drive.

As you might imagine, the Schedule tab is used to define how often the browser checks for new information on the site. Three schedules are included by default with Internet Explorer:

- **Daily** Checks the Web site every day at 4:30 a.m.
- **Weekly** Checks the Web site every Monday at 3:30 a.m.
- **Monthly** Checks the Web site the first day of every month at 4:00 a.m.

To change these options, click on Edit. To add a new custom schedule type, click on New, which invokes the Custom Schedule dialog box, shown in Figure 4.4.

Four options remain on the Schedule tab. The first option gives the user the ability to configure the browser to automatically dial up a network connection, if necessary. The second option only updates the site's information manually when the Update All Subscriptions option of the Favorites menu is selected. The third option doesn't update the site's information if the computer is in use. Finally, the Update Now button initiates an immediate update process for the subscription.

You can unsubscribe from a Web site in two ways. You can click on the Favorite's Subscription tab, then click on Unsubscribe. Or, you can display the Favorites menu, right-click on a subscription, and select Unsubscribe from the shortcut list.

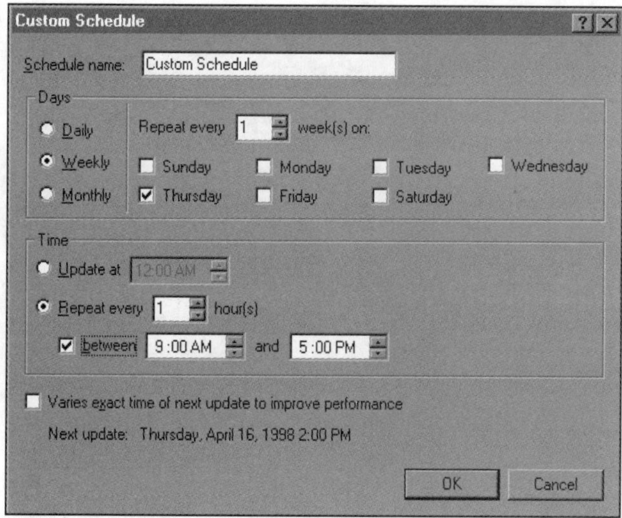

Figure 4.4 The Custom Schedule dialog box is used to create a new schedule type.

Controlling Client Subscriptions

The IEAK Configuration Wizard and Profile Manager are used to control client subscriptions. Though they are used at stages in IE deployment, the Configuration Wizard and the Profile Manager operate in much the same way in regard to subscriptions. Note that the examples shown in this chapter use the Profile Manager. For more information on the Profile Manager, refer to Chapter 6.

The IEAK Profile Manager, shown in Figure 4.5, is accessed via Start|Programs|Microsoft IEAK.

As you'll see in Chapter 6, the files created by the Profile Manager are used to automatically configure a browser's settings. The options available in the Subscriptions area of System Policies And Restrictions are as follows:

- **Maximum KB Of Site Subscription** Defines the maximum kilobytes that can be downloaded per site update.
- **Maximum Number Of Site Subscriptions That Can Be Installed** Limits the number of subscriptions a user can have on the computer.
- **Minimum Number Of Minutes Between Schedule Subscription Updates** Restricts the frequency of updates by requiring a certain amount of time to pass between scheduled updates.
- **Beginning Of Range In Which To Exclude Scheduled Subscription Updates. Measured In Minutes From Midnight** The starting time, in

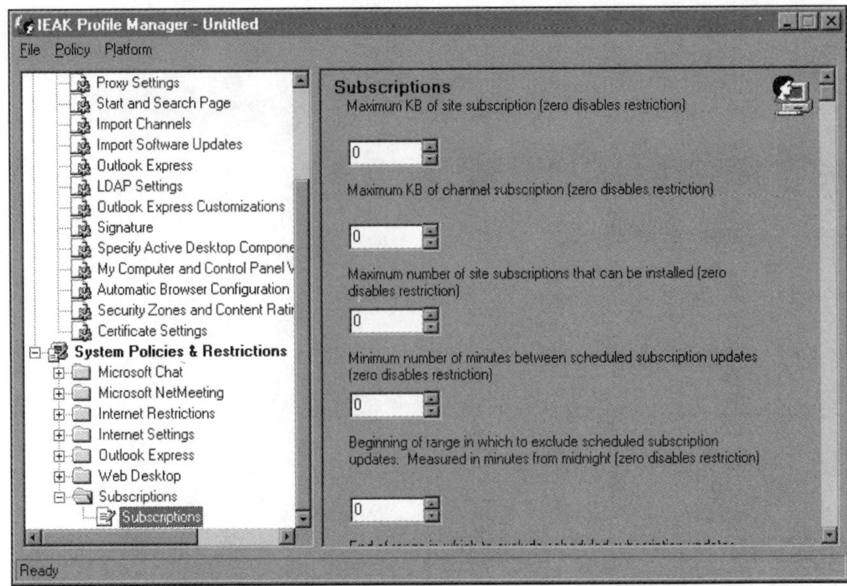

Figure 4.5 The IEAK Profile Manager is used to control client subscription configurations.

minutes from midnight, to exclude updates. For example, a setting of 420 begins the exclusion at 7:00 a.m.

- **End Of Range In Which To Exclude Scheduled Subscription Updates. Measured In Minutes From Midnight** Defines the end of the range of the exclusion.
- **Maximum Site Subscription Crawl Depth** Defines the maximum depth level allowed for Web crawls. If this is set to zero, the user can only update the top-level page.

Note: Except for the Maximum Site Subscription Crawl Depth option, a setting of zero disables the restriction.

There are also a number of settings in the Channel Settings area of the Internet Restrictions folder of the Profile Manager, which pertain to subscriptions. Each of the checkboxes disables the ability to perform a particular subscription task. These settings are:

- **Disables Adding Site Subscriptions** Prevents users from adding site subscriptions.
- **Disables Editing Site Subscriptions** Prevents users from editing site subscriptions.

- **Disables Removing Setting Subscriptions** Prevents users from removing subscriptions or unsubscribing to sites.
- **Disables Update Now And Update All For Channels And Subscriptions** Prevents users from manually updating subscriptions by using Update Now and Update All.
- **Disables All Scheduled Channel And Site Subscriptions** Prevents all automated Web crawls and updates.
- **Disables Unattended Dialing By Subscriptions** Prevents automated dial-up connections initiated by the browser.
- **Disables Password Caching For Channel And Site Subscriptions** Prevents users' authenticated passwords from being automatically transmitted to sites that require authentication. With this option selected, the user is prompted to provide a name and password when connecting to secure sites.
- **Disable Downloading Of Site Subscription Content—Change Notification Will Still Work** Prevents the download of site content to a client computer's cache.
- **Disables Editing And Creating Of Schedule Groups** Prevents users from creating custom schedules for updates.

Managed Webcasting With Active Channels

As mentioned previously, managed Webcasting provides a greater level of control for Web publishers and allows a user to choose the exact information downloaded, rather than downloading a large amount of information and combing through it to find specific information. Managed Webcasting accomplishes this by using the Channel Definition Format (CDF)—an implementation of the Extensible Markup Language (XML)—to create Active Channels, Active Desktop items, and channel-based screen savers. Lastly, unlike basic Webcasting, managed Webcasting can be completely controlled using the IEAK.

In a managed Webcasting environment, you are able to more strictly control the information retrieved. For example, you can define a subset of a particular Web site to be searched, rather than the entire site. This can reduce the amount of traffic generated by an update. In addition, you can more accurately schedule the updates to coincide with content updates on the site, because the information is defined in the CDF file. It is fairly easy to convert an existing Web site into an Active Channel. All that is required is the addition of a CDF file to the site.

Although Active Channels can be used to automatically deliver Web content to browser windows, they can also be configured to deliver information in two other ways: as Active Desktop items and as channel screen savers. Active Desktop items are Web pages that reside directly on the user's desktop. These items usually contain summary information and links that will open a full Web browser with the detailed information. Channel screen savers perform almost the same function, but they are activated as screen savers on the user's computer.

Using Active Channels

Active Channels are normal Web sites that include configuration files in CDF. Because Active Channels are a function of IE4, they can include any Web content supported by IE4. Some of the more advanced Internet items supported by IE4 include Dynamic HTML, ActiveX controls, VBScript, Java applets, ECMA Script, and Active Server Pages.

A typical Active Channel CDF file contains a channel hierarchy or a table of contents for the Web pages that comprise the channel. After a user subscribes to a channel, it appears in both the Internet Explorer channel bar (which is invoked by clicking on the satellite disk icon on the taskbar) and on the desktop channel bar (shown in Figure 4.6), which lists the channels that the user subscribes to on the desktop.

Along with normal channel items, Active Channels can include subchannels, which appear under the top-level channel and operate in the same manner as channels. Subchannels provide an easy way to organize channels that serve large Web sites.

The channel's CDF file is downloaded to the user's computer when the user subscribes to the channel. Channels provide many of the same configuration options as site subscriptions, such as whether to automatically download updated content and how much content to download. However, with Active Channels, users cannot specify the number of levels for site crawls. As with site subscriptions, the downloaded content is cached, and the user can browse the channel offline. Users can use the publisher's update schedule, which is specified in the CDF, or customize the update schedule. Updated Active Channel content is identified the same way as updated site subscriptions—a red gleam appears on the top-level channel's icon when updated information is available. Users can also be notified by email, and, unlike subscriptions, the publisher can include instructions in the CDF file to email the updated Web pages to the users, which are displayed in HTML-enabled email packages or as attachments for non-HTML-enabled programs.

Figure 4.6 The default desktop channel bar.

Active Desktop Items

The Active Desktop is part of the Windows Desktop Update and is discussed in more detail later in this chapter. Active Desktop supports positioning Active Channels directly on the desktop. These items appear in borderless frames on users' desktops and can contain any standard Web content. They are often designed to provide summary information in a small amount of screen space. For this reason, Active Desktop items are often created as scrolling lists to supply information, such as realtime stock or weather information. They also generally include hyperlinks or hotspots that users can click on to open a browser with the more detailed information. The biggest difference between Active Desktop items and Active Channel subscriptions is that users are not notified with a gleam when new Active Desktop information is available, because new information appears on the desktop immediately.

Channel Screen Savers

Web publishers can specify in their CDF that information should be available to the IE4 screen saver. This screen saver displays HTML pages (including Dynamic HTML, ActiveX controls, VBScript, Java applets, and ECMA Script) to provide updated information from the channel. Each of the HTML pages is displayed on the full screen when the computer is idle. The IE4 screen saver automatically cycles through all enabled channel screen savers and provides each channel the same amount of display time (the default is 30 seconds). One difference between the IE4 screen saver and other screen savers is that you can move your mouse and interact with the screen saver without returning to normal operation. This allows you to click on a hyperlink displayed on a screen saver page to invoke the browser and display the detail. If you click on an area of the page that is not an image, link, or object, the screen saver closes.

CDF Files

In their most basic implementations, CDF files are regular text files that contain nothing more than a list of URLs that point to content. This makes basic CDF files easy to create and implement because changes to existing HTML pages aren't required. CDF files can also include more advanced information, such as content-update schedules, hierarchical organizations of the URLs that make up the site, and information that describes individual content items.

Because CDF files deal with the URLs on a site rather than the actual content, they provide structured content indexing, regardless of the content format. A CDF file provides an index or Web site map that accurately describes the type of information on the site. CDF uses logical groupings of information, such as the site's hierarchical structure, to create the site map. Because the CDF file contains information about the site and not actual site content, the CDF file can remain static, even if the content changes often.

CDF's Link-Crawl System

The link-crawl system used by CDF is slightly different than that used by IE for site subscriptions, because the content provider has more control over the content download. By creating a separate CDF file for each category of information on the site, the content provider allows the user to easily monitor specific types of information. For example, a sports statistics site administrator can create separate CDFs for baseball information and hockey information. Users can then configure their browsers to crawl whichever areas of the site interest them the most.

Subscribing To Active Channels And Active Desktop Items

Subscribing to both Active Channels and Active Desktop items requires the content provider to provide a link to initiate the subscription process. For example, in the Active Channel area of the MSNBC site (**www.msnbc.com/tools/channel/guide/intro.asp**), there is a link to add the information to your Active Channels. When you click on this link, you are prompted with a message—similar to the one you receive when subscribing to a site—that asks you whether you would like to download updated information or if you want to be notified when there is new information. The Customize button performs the same tasks with site subscriptions, as well.

> *Note: Microsoft maintains a library of Active Channels called the Microsoft Active Channel Guide. This Web site is automatically accessed when you click on the Channel icon (the satellite dish) on the taskbar. This channel library includes numerous corporate channels, such as MSN, MSNBC, Disney, PointCast, and many, many more.*

Because Active Channels and desktop items are, in essence, variations of Favorites, they provide the same configuration options in the Subscription, Receiving, and Scheduling tabs of the Properties dialog box as subscriptions—with one exception. In the Scheduling tab, there is an added option called Publisher's Recommended Schedule that initiates the update process according to the schedule defined in the CDF. To access the Properties dialog box, right-click on the Favorite in the Favorites menu, and select Properties from the shortcut menu.

Including Predefined Channels In Custom Builds

Using the IEAK 4 Configuration Wizard, you can include preconfigured Active Channels and Active Desktop items in your builds. This is done by configuring the Active Channels on the computer by running the Configuration Wizard and selecting Import Current Channel Configuration on the Customize The Active Channel Bar page. The same steps apply for Active Desktop items (you create Active Desktop items on the computer by running the Configuration Wizard and selecting Import Current Active Desktop Components on the Specify Active Desktop Components page).

Controlling Active Channels And Active Desktop Items

As with site subscriptions, you can use the IEAK Configuration Wizard and the IEAK Profile Manager to control how users use Active Channels and Active Desktop items. Many of the settings are similar to those used to control site subscriptions. The options available in the Subscriptions area of System Policies And Restrictions are as follows:

- **Maximum KB Of Channel Subscription** Defines the maximum kilobytes that can be downloaded per update for each user.
- **Maximum Number Of Channel Subscriptions That Can Be Installed** Defines the maximum number of channels to which a user can subscribe.

Note: A zero value for either of these settings disables the restriction.

As with site subscriptions, a number of settings in the Channel Settings area of the Internet Restrictions folder of the Profile Manager pertain to Active Channels and Active Desktop items. Each of the checkboxes disables the ability to perform a particular channel task. These settings are:

- **Disable Channel UI** Prevents users from accessing the Active Channel user interface. If this option is selected, users cannot manage (add, delete, subscribe, unsubscribe, manually update, or change settings) the channels to which they subscribe.
- **Disables Adding And Subscribing To Channels** Prevents users from adding and subscribing to new channels.
- **Disables Editing Channel Properties And Channel Subscriptions** Prevents users from editing channel settings through the channel's Properties dialog box.
- **Disables Removing Channels And Subscriptions To Channels** Prevents users from removing or unsubscribing from Active Channels on their computer.
- **Disables Channel Logging** Prevents channel logging on the user's computer. Web publishers are able to create channel log files through settings in the CDF for a site. These log files are stored on the user's hard disk and track information about how the channel is used.
- **Disables Update Now And Update All For Channels And Subscriptions** Prevents users from updating their channels or site subscriptions manually.
- **Disables All Scheduled Channel And Site Subscriptions** Prevents automated Web crawls and updates from being initiated from a user's computer.
- **Disables Unattended Dialing By Subscriptions** Prevents automated dial-up connections for channel and site subscription updates.

- **Disables Password Caching For Channel And Site Subscriptions** Prevents users' authentication passwords from being automatically transmitted to sites that require authentication. With this option selected, a user is prompted to provide a name and password when connecting to secure sites.
- **Disable Downloading Of Channel Subscription Content—Change Notification Will Still Work** Prevents channel content updates from downloading to the cache on users' computers. This disables offline browsing of channels.
- **Disables Editing And Creating Of Schedule Groups** Prevents users from creating custom automated update schedules for channels and sites.

True Webcasting Using NetShow

As mentioned earlier, true Webcasting actually pushes content to the client, rather than the client checking for new content periodically. Applications such as Microsoft NetShow use streaming technology to push information to the user's desktop in an efficient and timely fashion. Unlike basic and managed Webcasting, true Webcasting with NetShow requires a special server and requires Web sites to be configured specially.

NetShow takes advantage of the extensible structure of IE to support IP multicasts. However, whereas the hardware on the Internet supports multicasts, not all networking hardware used on intranets can support them. If your network infrastructure is such that IP multicasting is supported, you will be able to use NetShow servers to disseminate information on your network quickly and easily.

The Windows Desktop Update And Active Desktop

The Windows Desktop Update (including Active Desktop) works in conjunction with Webcasting to provide users up-to-date content on their desktop. The Desktop Update includes more than just Active Desktop. It is intended to ease the learning curve by using the same interface as IE to view all information, whether on the Internet, the local hard drive, or a network drive. This consolidation is called *True Web Integration*. The Windows Desktop Update is installed optionally when IE is installed, but it is required for Active Desktop items to operate. The components of the Windows Desktop Update are discussed in the following sections.

The Integrated Start Menu And Taskbar

The first of the Windows components to receive Web-type implementations are the Start menu and Taskbar. Unlike the standard Windows NT Start menu, the Start menu on a system with the Desktop Update installed (shown in Figure 4.7) includes a Favorites menu, removes the Log Off option from the Shut Down dialog box, and adds a Log Off option to the Start menu, just above Shut Down.

Another feature of the new Start menu is the ability to drag items from one area of the Start menu to another. For example, if a user installs a program that creates its own program group, the user can easily move the shortcut for that application by opening the Start menu and dragging the icon to a new location in the Start menu.

Chapter 2's review of Outlook Express describes the Lightweight Directory Access Protocol (LDAP) and its services. LDAP is used to access the Internet's virtual white pages, which are used to locate users listed on LDAP servers. Microsoft has expanded the Find feature of the Start menu to include LDAP

Figure 4.7 The Start menu for a Windows NT system with the Desktop Update installed.

functionality through the People option. Selecting the People option opens the Find People dialog box (shown in Figure 4.8), which can be used to locate people on any LDAP server on the Internet. Microsoft has included settings for six major listings: Four11, Bigfoot, Infospace, Infospace Business, SwitchBoard, and VeriSign.

The Settings option from the Start menu has also been expanded to include Folder Options and Active Desktop settings. The Folder Options dialog box (shown in Figure 4.9) is invoked by selecting the Folder Options Start menu option. The Folder Options dialog box includes settings for how folders are displayed in Explorer, which files are viewed (through the View tab), and the assorted file associations (through the File Types tab). The Active Desktop option allows users to toggle viewing the desktop as a Web Page, customize desktop settings (as discussed later in this chapter), and update the contents of the desktop.

The Taskbar has also been greatly expanded with the Desktop Update. The Taskbar has been integrated closely with IE and the desktop, so it is no longer just a place to locate a user's open applications and check the time. Four toolbars can be added to the Taskbar. Toolbars are added to the Taskbar by right-clicking on the Taskbar and selecting Toolbars from the shortcut menu. Each toolbar can then be selected or deselected as desired. The four toolbars are:

- **The Quick Launch toolbar** This toolbar, which is enabled by default when the Desktop Update is installed, allows one-click launching of applications and, by default, includes Internet Explorer, Outlook Express, Show Desktop, and View Channels. The Quick Launch toolbar is easy to manage. To add an icon to the toolbar, drag it from the desktop, Explorer, or Network Neighborhood. To remove an icon, right-click on

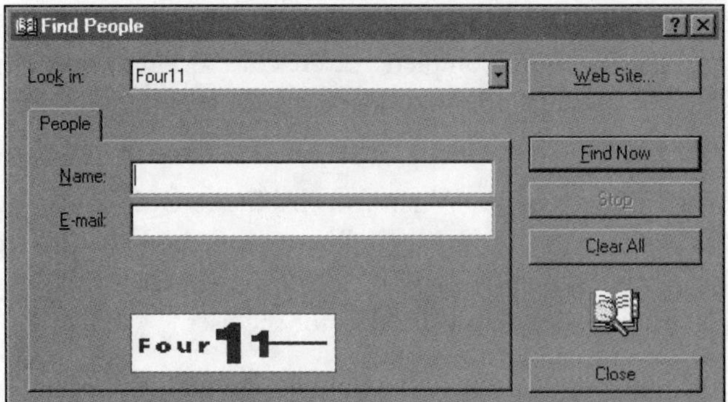

Figure 4.8 The Desktop Update includes the ability to search for people on the Internet.

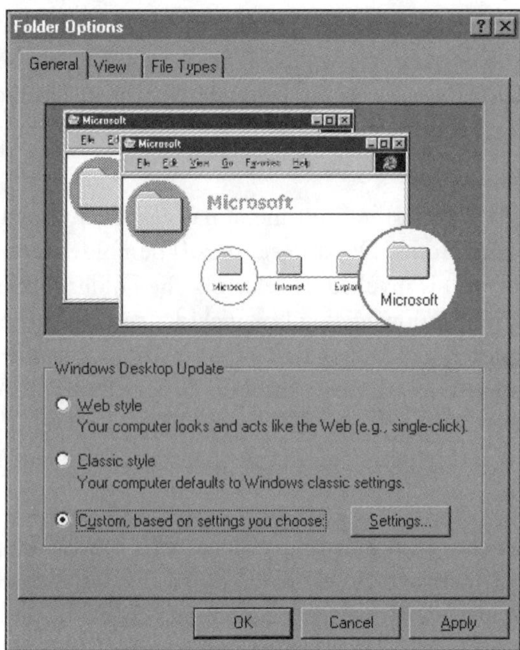

Figure 4.9 Select Folder Options from the Settings menu to invoke the Folder Options dialog box.

the icon, and select Delete from the shortcut menu. The shortcut file is removed and placed in the Recycle Bin.

➤ **The Address bar** This toolbar makes it easy to launch Explorer to the exact location the user wants, whether it is a local drive or the Internet. To use the Address bar, type in the destination and press Enter. Explorer is then launched directly to the address listed in the Address bar. If the user doesn't remember the URL for a site, the drop-down (drop-up, in this case) list and AutoComplete features of Explorer ease this process considerably. Figure 4.10 shows a user's Taskbar with the Address bar enabled.

➤ **The QuickLinks toolbar** When you enable the QuickLinks toolbar, listed as Links in the Taskbar's Toolbars menu, the Internet Explorer QuickLinks bar is displayed. This eases Internet navigation by placing the QuickLinks sites on the Taskbar for the user.

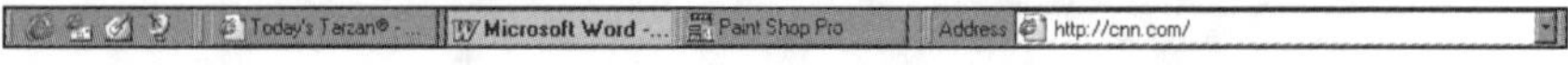

Figure 4.10 A user's Taskbar with the Address bar enabled.

- **The Desktop bar** This toolbar displays the icons that are present on the user's desktop. This enables quicker access to the applications a user displays on the desktop.

It is possible for a user to create a new toolbar by selecting the New Toolbar option from the Toolbars menu of the Taskbar shortcut menu. The user has the option of typing in a URL or a folder address. If a URL is entered, the contents of the Web page are displayed on the toolbar. If a folder is chosen, each file in the folder is displayed on the toolbar. All the toolbars, both custom and default, can be dragged to the desktop to be displayed as floating toolbars. This removes the clutter from the Taskbar and still provides easy access to their features.

The Web View

The Windows Desktop Update allows folders and the desktop to be viewed in Web format (HTML). Figure 4.11 shows the standard Web view for a folder, including a description of the file and, in some cases, a preview image of the file. It is also possible to configure an HTML file that acts as a Web view. Like Active Desktop items, these files can include standard HTML, Dynamic HTML, graphics, ActiveX objects, JavaScript, and VBScript.

Customized Web views of specific directories, particularly those on an intranet, are used to simplify the navigation process for users. For example, particular files can be displayed more prominently in the directory, so users know which files they need. An explanation of the files in the directory can be shown, which ensures that the users select the correct file, rather than display every file in the

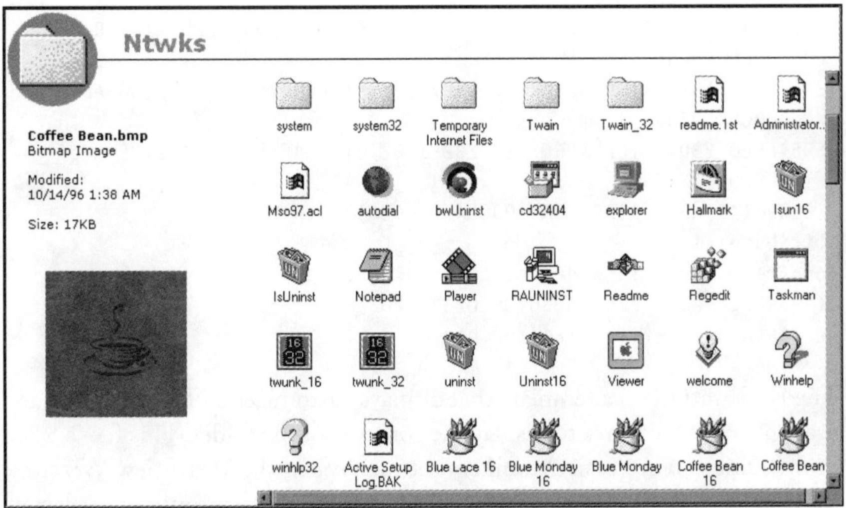

Figure 4.11 The standard Web view for the NTWKS folder.

directory. Links to files can be created that launch installation programs or download specific files to the users' local drives.

> *Note: The Internet Explorer Resource Kit includes a number of sample Web views that can be modified to fit a particular user's needs.*

Customizing Your Web View

The Web view for a particular folder is managed through two files: the Desktop.ini file and the Folder.htt file. These hidden files are created through the Web View Wizard. It is launched by right-clicking on the folder and selecting the Customize This Folder option.

The Desktop.ini file is a standard INI file that is used to inform IE that a particular folder has a custom Web view. This INI file tells IE how to display the contents of the folder (including a background file to be displayed in the icon area), whether thumbnail views have been configured for the folder, and the location of the customized HTML file (if one is used). Following is a sample Desktop.ini file:

```
[.ShellClassInfo]
ConfirmFileOp=0
[{8BEBB290-52D0-11d0-B7F4-00C04FD706EC}]
MenuName=T&humbnails
ToolTipText=T&humbnails
HelpText=Displays items using thumbnail view.
Attributes=0x60000000
[ExtShellFolderViews]
{8BEBB290-52D0-11d0-B7F4-00C04FD706EC}={8BEBB290-52D0-11d0-B7F4-
    00C04FD706EC}
{BE098140-A513-11D0-A3A4-00C04FD706EC}={BE098140-A513-11D0-A3A4-
    00C04FD706EC}
{5984FFE0-28D4-11CF-AE66-08002B2E1262}={5984FFE0-28D4-11CF-AE66-
    08002B2E1262}
[{BE098140-A513-11D0-A3A4-00C04FD706EC}]
Attributes=1
IconArea_Image=D:\folder settings\bkgrnd.jpg
[{5984FFE0-28D4-11CF-AE66-08002B2E1262}]
PersistMoniker=file://Folder.htt
```

The Folder.htt file is a template that displays customized HTML content and uses an ActiveX control to display the contents of the folder. This file is listed in the Desktop.ini **PersistMoniker=** setting. When the Web View Wizard is launched and the Create Or Edit An HTML Document option is selected, it reads the default Folder.htt file from the <*systemroot*>\Web directory. A customized Folder.htt file is saved in the folder you are customizing, and IE will display the new template when the folder is viewed.

It is also possible to supply a new customized HTML page, rather than use Folder.htt. The custom HTML page that is used for the Web view contains many types of Internet information, including ActiveX and scripts. However, unlike standard Web content, the page that is used as a custom Web view can incorporate functionality that is not used in the Internet environment, such as variables (%THISDIRPATH% or %TEMPLATEDIR%), because the custom Web view file is saved in HTT format. The .htt extension means that the MIME filter is activated, rather than the HTML filter. For more information on customizing a Web view, refer to the Internet Explorer Resource Kit.

> *Note: Microsoft recommends that you do not use a custom HTML page to customize the Web view for My Documents because of the way it interacts with Windows. On the other hand, you can modify the Folder.htt file, because it contains the information Windows requires.*

Customizing My Computer And Control Panel

It is also possible to modify how My Computer and the Control Panel appear, but the Desktop.ini and Folder.htt files are not used. The files that are modified for these folders (Mycomp.htt and Controlp.htt) are modified through Registry settings. The PersistMoniker settings for these folders are located in the following Registry keys:

- **My Computer** HKEY_LOCAL_MACHINE\Software\Classes\Clsid\{20D04FE0-3AEA-1069-A2D8-08002B30309D}\shellex\ExtShellFolderViews\{5984FFE0-28D4-11CF-AE66-08002B2E1262}
- **Control Panel** HKEY_LOCAL_MACHINE\Software\Classes\Clsid\{21EC2020-3AEA-1069-A2DD-08002B30309D}\shellex\ExtShellFolderViews\{5984FFE0-28D4-11CF-AE66-08002B2E1262}

Active Desktop

The Active Desktop feature of Internet Explorer is used to customize users' working environments by allowing them to place Internet content—such as Web pages, Java applets, ActiveX controls, and floating frames—directly on their desktops. When combined with the Webcasting features of IE, the user is assured of automatically receiving the most up-to-date information available.

The Active Desktop is actually made up of two separate layers: a layer that handles the desktop icons and a background HTML layer that hosts the actual Active Desktop items. The HTML layer consists of a single HTML file called

Desktop.htm that resides in the Profiles directory for the user. This is a very basic HTML file that includes frame and ActiveX information that tells Active Desktop where to place each item. A user can also manually add static HTML code, such as the computer's name.

Active Desktop items are added by selecting Display Properties|Web. The following lists three ways you can access the Display Properties dialog box:

- Right-click on the desktop, select Properties, and choose the Web tab or double-click on Display in the Control Panel.
- Right-click on the desktop, select Active Desktop, and select Customize My Desktop.
- From the Start menu, select Settings, select Active Desktop, and then select Customize My Desktop.

Using any of the previous steps will take you to the Web tab in the Display Properties dialog box, as shown in Figure 4.12.

To add a new Active Desktop item, follow these steps:

1. After accessing the Web tab of the Display Properties dialog box, click on New.

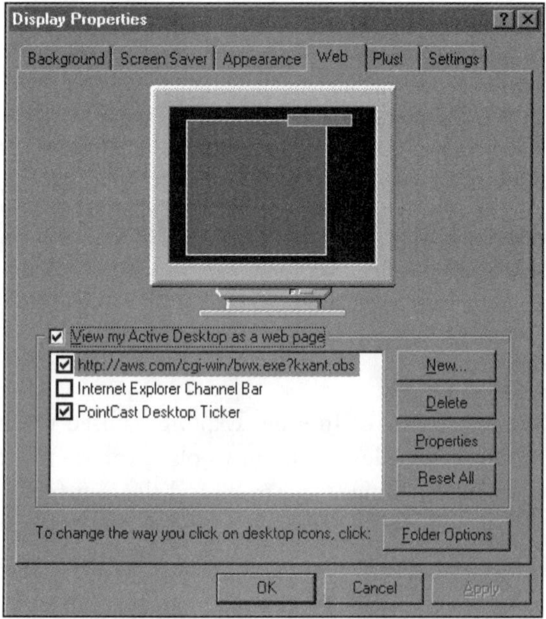

Figure 4.12 Active Desktop items are added through the Web tab in the Display Properties dialog box.

2. Depending on your computer's settings, you might be asked whether you would like to visit the Microsoft Active Desktop Gallery. Click on No.
3. The New Active Desktop Item dialog box, shown in Figure 4.13, will appear. If you know the URL for the site that you would like added to the desktop, enter it and click on OK.
4. If you are not sure of the URL for the site you wish to make an Active Desktop item, click on Browse.
5. Clicking on Browse opens the Favorites folder for Internet Explorer. Select the appropriate site and click on Open. You will be returned to the New Active Desktop Item dialog box.
6. Click on OK. The Add Item To Active Desktop dialog box will open. From here, you are able to customize the subscription, using the same parameters as Active Channels or site subscriptions.
7. To accept the publisher's schedule, click on OK.
8. The updated item is downloaded from the Internet automatically. Click on OK to close the Display Properties dialog box.

The Web tab of Display Properties is also used to disable and delete Active Desktop items. To disable an item, uncheck the box next to its name. To delete an item, click on Delete.

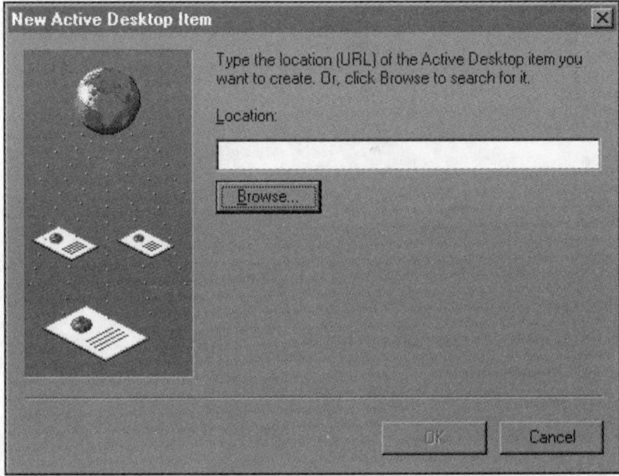

Figure 4.13 Desktop items are added through the New Active Desktop Item dialog box.

Controlling Active Desktop Items

As with site subscriptions and Active Channels, you can use the IEAK Configuration Wizard or Profile Manager to control Active Desktop items. The pertinent options available in the Web Desktop folder of the System Policies And Restrictions area are rather self-explanatory and are as follows:

- Disable all desktop items
- Disable adding any new desktop items
- Disable deleting any desktop items
- Disable editing any desktop items
- Disable closing any desktop items

Exam Prep Questions

Question 1

Which of the following applications are used by administrators to manage access to Active Channels?

- ❑ a. IEAK Configuration Wizard
- ❑ b. Internet Explorer Management System
- ❑ c. IEAK Channel Administrator
- ❑ d. IEAK Profile Manager

The correct answers to this question are a and d. The IEAK Configuration Wizard and IEAK Profile Manager are used to control access to Active Channels. Answers b and c are fictitious; therefore, they are incorrect.

Question 2

By default, how many layers past the initial page will a Web crawl search a site?

- ❍ a. 0
- ❍ b. 1
- ❍ c. 2
- ❍ d. 3

The correct answer to this question is a. By default, the Web crawl will only search the initial page of a subscribed site, although the user can modify this option to search up to three layers deep.

Question 3

Which file is added to a standard Web site to create an Active Channel?

- ❍ a. JavaScript
- ❍ b. HTML
- ❍ c. XML
- ❍ d. CDF

The correct answer to this question is d. A CDF file is added to an existing site to create an Active Channel. Whereas Active Channels can contain both JavaScript and HTML documents, they have no role in creating the channel. Therefore, answers a and b are incorrect. Whereas CDF is a subset of XML, XML itself does not have the ability to create an Active Channel. Therefore, answer c is incorrect.

Question 4

Which of the following are possible ways to create an Active Desktop item?

- ❑ a. Right-click on any Web page in IE and select Add To Desktop.
- ❑ b. Click on a link supplied by a Web publisher.
- ❑ c. Define it in the Registry.
- ❑ d. Use the Web tab of the Display Properties dialog box.

The correct answers to this question are b and d. An Active Desktop item is created by clicking on a link supplied by the Web publisher or using the Web tab of the Display Properties dialog box. There is no Add To Desktop option in the shortcut menu that is invoked when you right-click on a Web page. Therefore, answer a is incorrect. It is not possible to create an Active Desktop item through the Registry. Therefore, answer c is incorrect.

Question 5

Which of the following accurately pairs the type of Webcasting with the IE component?

- ❍ a. Basic Webcasting—Active Desktop items
- ❍ b. Managed Webcasting—Active Channels
- ❍ c. True Webcasting—site subscriptions
- ❍ d. True Webcasting—Active Channels

The correct answer to this question is b. Managed Webcasting uses Active Channels to regularly update a computer's cache of information. Basic Webcasting uses site subscriptions to check for new content on a Web site. Therefore, answer a is incorrect. True Webcasting uses push technology, such as NetShow, to disseminate information. Therefore, answers c and d are incorrect.

Question 6

Which of the following file locations are managed through the Registry?

- ❑ a. Desktop.ini
- ❑ b. Controlp.htt
- ❑ c. Mycomp.htt
- ❑ d. Desktop.htt

The correct answers to this question are b and c. The Controlp.htt and Mycomp.htt file locations are managed through Registry settings under the HKEY_LOCAL_MACHINE\Software subkey. The Desktop.ini file is located in the directory being viewed. Therefore, answer a is incorrect. The Desktop.htt file doesn't exist. Therefore, answer d is incorrect.

Question 7

Which of the following protocols is used to locate users on the Internet?

- ❍ a. LDAP
- ❍ b. HTTP
- ❍ c. SSL
- ❍ d. HTML

The correct answer to this question is a. The Lightweight Directory Access Protocol is used to search specific servers for user information. HTTP is the transport protocol for HTML, which is the markup language used for Web pages. Therefore, answers b and d are incorrect. SSL is a protocol that is used to securely transfer data over the Internet. Therefore, answer c is incorrect.

Question 8

A site subscription is actually a Favorite that is checked regularly by Internet Explorer.

- ❍ a. True
- ❍ b. False

The correct answer to this question is True. The site subscription process is initiated through the Favorites function of IE.

Question 9

Which of the following components are defined using a CDF file?

- ❑ a. Active Channel
- ❑ b. Active Desktop item
- ❑ c. Site subscription
- ❑ d. Channel screen saver

Answers a, b, and d are correct. As part of the Active Channel structure, a CDF file can define Active Channels, Active Desktop items, and channel screen savers. A site subscription is a manual process controlled by the user, rather than a CDF file. Therefore, answer c is incorrect.

Question 10

Which of the following type of Webcasting provides the lowest level of interaction between the Web publisher and the user?

- ❍ a. True Webcasting
- ❍ b. Managed Webcasting
- ❍ c. Basic Webcasting
- ❍ d. Advanced Webcasting

The correct answer to this question is c. Basic Webcasting provides the lowest level of interaction between the Web publisher and the user because the user dictates when searches are initiated. The Web publisher plays no role in this decision. In a true Webcasting environment, the Web publisher is in nearly complete control over how information is disseminated. Therefore, answer a is incorrect. In a managed Webcasting environment, the user can elect to accept the schedule created by the publisher, which is a fairly high level of interaction. Therefore, answer b is incorrect. Advanced Webcasting does not exist in the Microsoft model. Therefore, answer d is incorrect.

Need To Know More?

Microsoft Press: *Microsoft Internet Explorer Resource Kit.* Redmond, WA, 1998. ISBN 1-57231-842-2. Part 4 (Chapters 15 through 17) is dedicated to Webcasting, whereas Part 3 (Chapters 12 through 14) is dedicated to the Windows Desktop Update. Each of these sections contains valuable information regarding all aspects of this chapter. They also include sample CDF files and more detailed information on these subjects.

Search TechNet using keywords within the Internet Explorer and Internet Explorer Administration Kit areas. Both areas provide detailed information on Webcasting and the Windows Desktop Update.

The Microsoft Knowledge Base provides detailed information on all products, including Internet Explorer and Internet Explorer Administration Kit. It also provides detailed information on both Webcasting and the Windows Desktop Update. Searches on Webcasting, desktop update, and CDF all provide detailed information. The Microsoft Knowledge Base is located at **http://support.microsoft.com/support/a.asp?M=S**.

For more detailed information on NetShow and its use in true Webcasting, refer to the Microsoft NetShow sites at **www.microsoft.com/netshow**.

Microsoft NetMeeting

Terms you'll need to understand:

- √ DirectX 5
- √ H.323
- √ ILS (Internet Locator Service)
- √ ITU (International Telecommunications Union)
- √ LDAP (Lightweight Directory Access Protocol)
- √ T.120
- √ TCP/IP (Transmission Control Protocol/Internet Protocol)
- √ USB (Universal Serial Bus)

Techniques you'll need to master:

- √ Sharing applications over a TCP/IP connection
- √ Communicating with other users with a text-based interface in realtime
- √ Understanding voice "phone calls" with or without video over the Internet
- √ Understanding whiteboard shared collaboration

In this chapter, you'll explore Microsoft's NetMeeting application. You'll also learn how to exploit NetMeeting's conferencing capabilities, including audio and video. You'll learn how to use a regular modem with this program and how to find users with the Internet Locator Service (ILS). In addition, you'll look at each of the NetMeeting extensions, including whiteboard and file transfer, and you'll examine NetMeeting System Policies.

NetMeeting Overview

When *InfoWorld* gave NetMeeting the 1997 Product Of The Year Award, it referred to NetMeeting as the most overlooked product from Microsoft. The beta release of NetMeeting V.1.0 could have easily turned the world upside down, but even today, NetMeeting is still mostly ignored by computer professionals. Perhaps it is because NetMeeting is so revolutionary that it is overlooked—the classic fear of the unknown. It doesn't matter if you work in a large organization or if you're a sole proprietor, NetMeeting has the capability to completely change the way you do your job. In this chapter, you'll examine the power of NetMeeting, which will not only help you do well on the exam but should be considered a testimonial to NetMeeting's capabilities.

Microsoft NetMeeting is software used to enable conferencing in realtime via the Internet or an intranet. You find and connect to other users using an Internet Locator Service (ILS), such as Four11. An ILS allows users to find each other, then communicate in realtime using both audio and video. It also allows users to work together on almost any Windows application, even if only one computer has the application loaded. Furthermore, users can exchange or mark up graphics on an electronic whiteboard, transfer files, and use a text-based chat program. NetMeeting can do this with as little as a standard modem and dial-up Internet account.

NetMeeting uses international collaboration and conferencing standards, so it can easily be used with similar software from other vendors, such as Intel's ProShare. Microsoft considers the following features key points of NetMeeting:

- T.120 standard
- Multipoint conferencing capabilities defined by the International Telecommunications Union (ITU)
- H.323 standards-based video conferencing
- Lightweight Directory Access Protocol (LDAP) standard support
- Support for NT 4 and system policies
- NetMeeting Mail Extension

Services Offered

NetMeeting 2.1 incorporates several new features that are supported by new operating systems, such as Windows 98. Some of the technologies that complement NetMeeting's new features include DirectX 5, which allows communication with video cameras with Universal Serial Bus (USB), and the new video device driver model. Windows 95 and NT 4 with Service Pack 3 also support NetMeeting. NetMeeting 2.1 has enhanced H.323 support, to allow both gateway support and Multipoint Conferencing Units (MCUs), in addition to the previous support of T.120. It also has an Outlook-type bar, which gives it the same look and feel as the Outlook family of programs. This bar contains icons for frequently used functions, such as Directory, SpeedDial, Current Call, and History. Let's look at a few of these services—T.120, H.323, and ILS—now.

T.120

The T.120 standard was designed with several goals in mind. The first of these goals is its ability to allow participants to send and receive data in realtime with error correction by using a number of connection types, including TCP/IP. These standards support common topologies, including cascaded, daisy chain, and star configurations. Regardless of which configuration you select, one computer in the chain must be a top provider. When using NetMeeting, the person that begins a conference is the top provider. Figure 5.1 illustrates a cascade

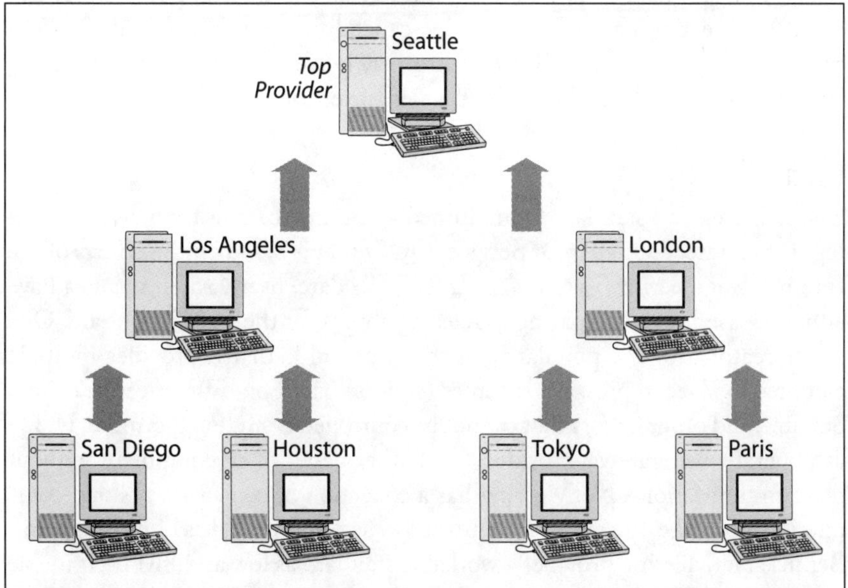

Figure 5.1 A cascade topology that shows the provider hierarchy.

topology in which the top provider is labeled "Seattle". Although this figure denotes a cascade topology, it could just as easily be a star or daisy chain topology.

If NetMeeting starts and finds no conferences running, it will create one locally. However, if a conference is already in session, NetMeeting notifies the caller, who is then given the option to join the remote conference. The Host Meeting feature, which is accessed through the Call menu, automatically determines the top provider based on the conference selected, as opposed to the calling order.

Data is moved according to the topology of the conference, which is actually determined by who calls whom. In the example, the following order is established:

- Seattle calls Los Angeles and London
- Los Angeles calls San Diego and Houston
- London calls Tokyo and Paris

The critical point here is that two conferences cannot be joined together—that is, if London calls Tokyo and Paris first, they cannot join the conference with Seattle, Los Angeles, San Diego, and Houston. Rather, Paris needs to call Los Angeles and San Diego, while Tokyo calls Houston and Seattle.

During the conference, if Los Angeles shares an application with other conference callers, the data displays in realtime to Seattle, San Diego, and Houston. If Los Angeles hangs up, San Diego and Houston are dropped as well. Because NetMeeting has audio and video capabilities, San Diego and Houston can continue to see and talk to each other; however, the data conferencing capabilities will be lost when Los Angeles leaves the conference.

H.323

The ITU created a standard for multimedia communications for networks lacking in guaranteed Quality Of Service (QOS) that is based on the efforts of the Internet Engineering Task Force (IETF). To date, over 125 companies have either released or are preparing to release support for the H.323 standard. One of the reasons for the popularity of this protocol is that it provides multiple compression/decompression schemes (codecs) based on differences in delays, bit rates, and other factors that cannot be controlled easily. Furthermore, H.323 can operate over gateways, bridges, and other networking equipment without platform limitations. NetMeeting has a collection of codecs that allows communications to be optimized for rates as low as 4.8Kbps and as high as 64Kbps. Because NetMeeting provides a workable standard as low as 4.8Kbps, it is able to use a 28.8Kbps dial-up modem for realtime audio and video.

ILS (Internet Locator Service)

NetMeeting and other programs in the Internet Explorer 4 suite support the Lightweight Directory Access Protocol (LDAP), covered in Chapter 6. By using LDAP, many applications have one common method for information exchange that has been designed for the Internet's slower speed. NetMeeting's functionality is heavily dependent on LDAP V3, because it includes provisions for a dynamic directory service. This type of service was first seen publicly with the Microsoft Internet Locator Service (ILS), which is an option of the Internet Information Server (IIS). The ILS publishes a list of connected users that includes information such as user name, online/offline status, audio/video capability, city, state/province, country, and other comments. In addition, it indicates whether the person listed is currently on another call. The phrase *dynamic directory* is well-suited to this environment, because you can watch users sign in and drop off from the ILS. Within a few minutes of a person arriving or leaving, the directory is updated. There are a number of ILS servers available on the Internet today. By strict definition, there are actually two server types—ILS and User Locator Service (ULS). The differences between these types of servers are discussed later in the chapter. This book uses the acronym ILS to refer to servers other than Microsoft servers.

NetMeeting Features

Now, let's take a tour of the features of NetMeeting to see it in action. Alternatives include conferencing, sharing applications, transferring files, and using whiteboard and chat. And you can add NetMeeting extensions, which are explained later.

Conferencing

Click on the Directory icon in the left-hand bar to view potential conferencing partners (see Figure 5.2). After you find the person you want to communicate with, select the name on the list, as shown in Figure 5.3. Because you are initiating this call, you are automatically the top provider.

Depending on a number of factors, such as available bandwidth and line congestion, it might take several minutes for your connection with the other person to become available. After the connection is made and the call is accepted, you will see a call window, similar to Figure 5.4. Notice that the title bar indicates that one connection has been made—you have entered a collaboration meeting.

Depending on a number of local conditions, such as whether both parties have a video camera, it is possible to have a virtual meeting with both audio and

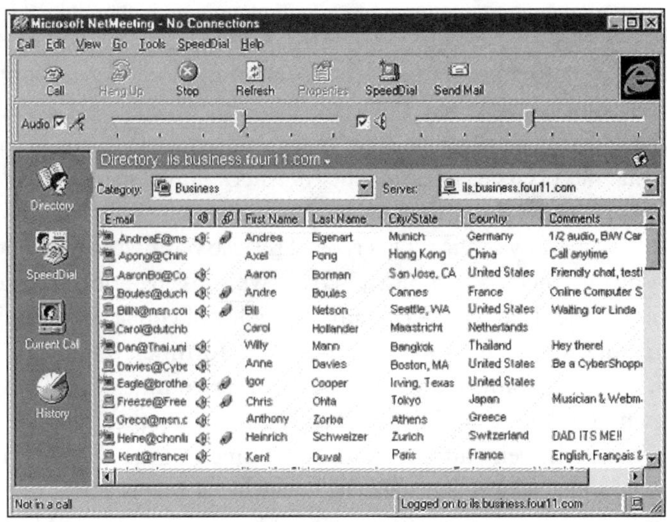

Figure 5.2 The NetMeeting Directory.

video. To use audio, each party must have a sound card and a microphone and speakers. In addition, both parties must have video cameras before you can use the video feature. Video quality is adjustable by resolution and refresh speed, and it is measured in frames per second for any given bandwidth available. The next section describes NetMeeting's video capabilities in more detail.

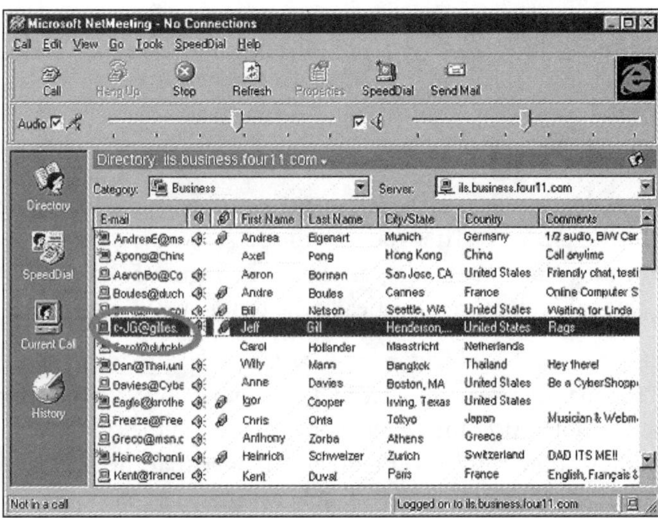

Figure 5.3 NetMeeting Directory selection.

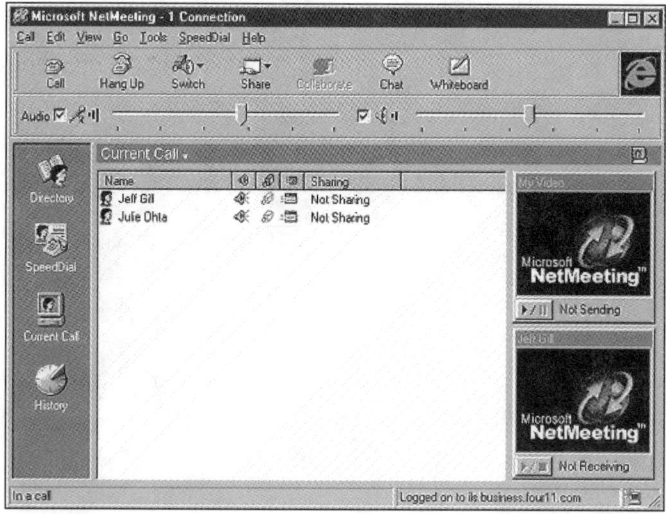

Figure 5.4 NetMeeting Current Call window.

Video Conferencing

It is possible for more than two people to join a single meeting. However, NetMeeting's audio and video capabilities limit the number of users communicating over audio/video to two. If a user with the appropriate audio/video (A/V) hardware wishes to join an existing conference, that user cannot utilize the A/V components until one of the existing A/V users drops out of the conference. You can quickly see if someone has audio and/or video capabilities by looking at the icons on the directory screen (see Figure 5.5). If the icon for a speaker is shown, the user is configured for audio. If the camera icon is shown, the user is configured for video.

The parties involved in the video conference shown in Figure 5.6 each have a color video camera connected to their system. NetMeeting supports video at connection speeds as low as 28.8Kbps. However, the video refresh rate is very slow at low bandwidth speeds.

While the first two people in the virtual meeting are discussing a topic with an audio and video feed, the rest of the group can be involved in a realtime text-based chat. While this might not be as fun as the virtual meeting with audio and video, it is a realtime meeting of workers collaborating on a project.

For example, let's say that there is a third user who would like to have a "face-to-face" meeting with one of the existing collaborators who is using video. The third user indicates this desire using the text-based chat option. One of the existing A/V users can easily switch to this new user by clicking on the Switch

Figure 5.5 The NetMeeting audio and video icons.

pull-down menu and selecting the new user. In Figure 5.7, the user has been switched to Vic Leone.

Again, the amount of time it takes to connect to the new user depends on the available bandwidth and the amount of traffic that is occurring on the Internet. Notice in Figure 5.7 that Jeff's audio and video icons have been grayed out because the audio and video options are no longer available to him.

Figure 5.6 NetMeeting video images.

Figure 5.7 You are now video conferencing with Vic in NetMeeting.

Multipoint Application Sharing

Notice that, until this point, each of the figures has shown the words *Not Sharing* next to a user's name. NetMeeting allows any person who has an application on their computer to start the application and share it for collaboration with another. For example, suppose Craig's company has written a custom application in which you have expressed an interest. By using NetMeeting, you can arrange to meet with Craig at Four11. He can show you the program over the Internet, without having it installed on your system.

This section steps you through program collaboration using NetMeeting. In Figure 5.8, the person who has the application to be shared selects Share and then selects the program to share.

The application being shared is now visible to the other person in the collaboration (again, the speed in which this action takes place depends on network factors, such as bandwidth). By using this option, it is possible for the other person to run the program without actually having a copy of it installed on their computer. Without a copy of the program, the person using the program remotely can only use what is available on the screen. As an example, consider Microsoft Word for Windows. If the user that is sharing the application does not have Bookshelf installed, the remote user cannot use Bookshelf. If they do have Bookshelf installed, and the remote user makes a request for it, the program requests a CD to be installed, and the person sharing Word must install the CD for the remote user. Figure 5.9 shows Word being shared in collaboration with a remote user.

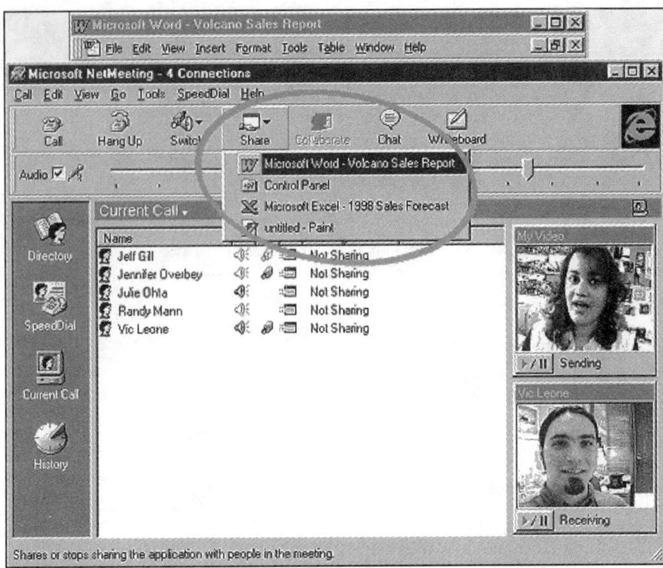

Figure 5.8 The NetMeeting Share pull-down menu.

Suppose the remote user has changes they would like to make to the document. The person sharing the application simply has to select Collaborate from the toolbar, which is shown in Figure 5.10. Notice that the directory now states

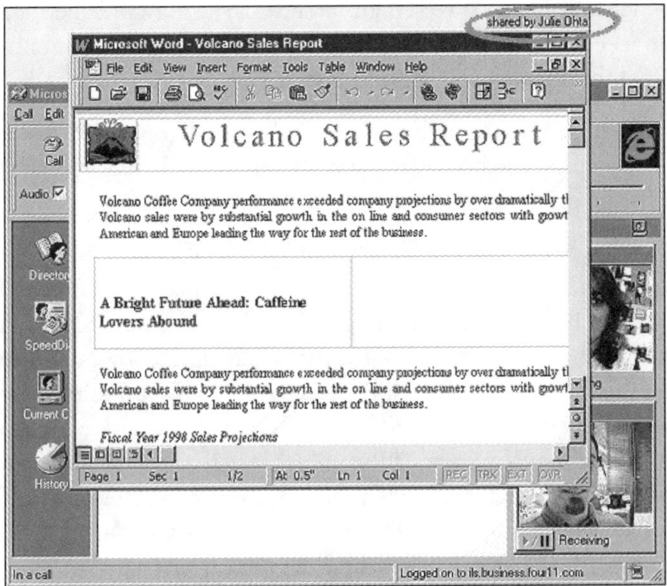

Figure 5.9 Word for Windows is shared in collaboration.

Figure 5.10 The NetMeeting Collaborate icon.

that the users are Not Collaborating, rather than Not Sharing. This indicates that the users are ready to collaborate and can do so when ready.

After a user allows collaboration to take place with a document, the remote viewer can begin to make changes, while viewing and speaking with the document creator (see Figure 5.11).

Whiteboard

Another way NetMeeting participants can share information is with the electronic whiteboard. This feature has the capability to increase productivity and efficiency. This section presents the features of NetMeeting's whiteboard.

If you've been in a conference room or classroom in recent years, you've seen a grease board, also called a *whiteboard*. The whiteboard included with NetMeeting takes the grease board idea into the virtual world. Click on Whiteboard in the toolbar to use this feature (see Figure 5.12).

If you have ever used MS Paint, then you are familiar with both the pluses and minuses of using the whiteboard in NetMeeting. If you find whiteboard useful enough to warrant frequent use, it might be a good idea to invest in a digitizing tablet. A digitizing tablet, which converts pen strokes to digital images on the screen, is as necessary to NetMeeting's whiteboard as a mouse is for Windows. You can operate the whiteboard without one, but it's extremely difficult. Without a tablet, you must use your mouse to create the image on the screen, a difficult

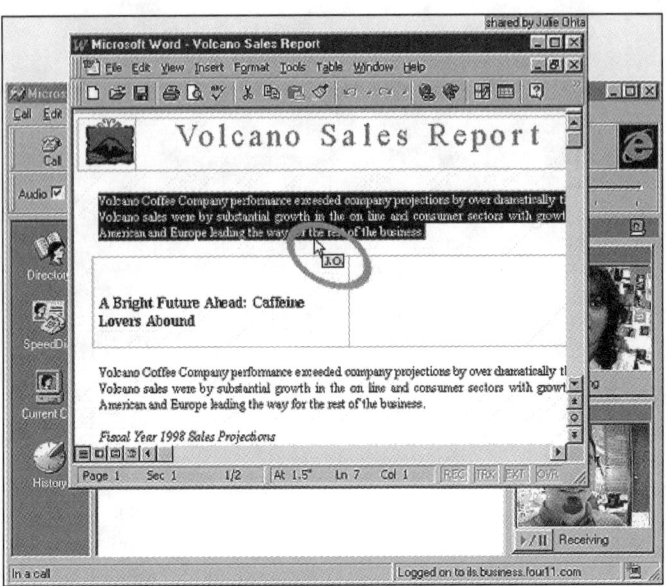

Figure 5.11 The document can be edited by either party.

task, even for the best artists. With a tablet, it's much easier to get your point across because it's just like drawing on a chalkboard or a physical whiteboard.

Figure 5.13 shows a conference that uses whiteboard to illustrate the structure of NetMeeting. Unlike A/V connections, the whiteboard is limited to six users, not two, which greatly enhances its appeal for large virtual conferences.

Figure 5.12 The NetMeeting Whiteboard icon.

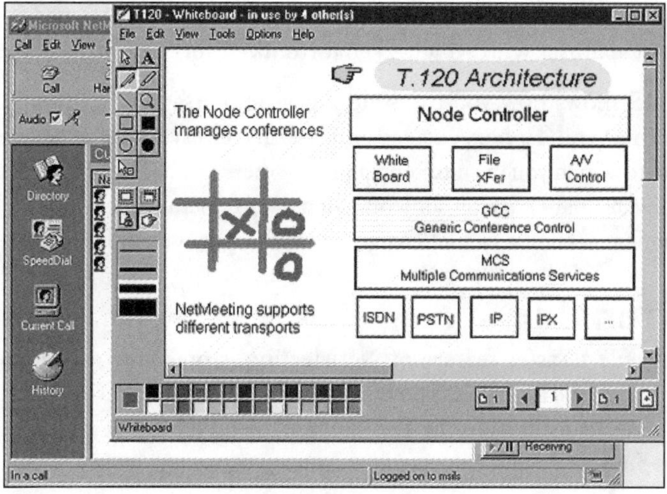

Figure 5.13 A NetMeeting whiteboard in action.

Chat

Earlier in this chapter, it was mentioned that users unable to use the audio and video functions of NetMeeting (due to hardware limitations or other people using A/V) were still able to communicate using text-based chat. As you might have noticed in previous figures, Chat is another icon available through the main NetMeeting application. Figure 5.14 highlights the Chat icon. In comparison to live audio and video over the Internet, text-based chat seems a bit mundane;

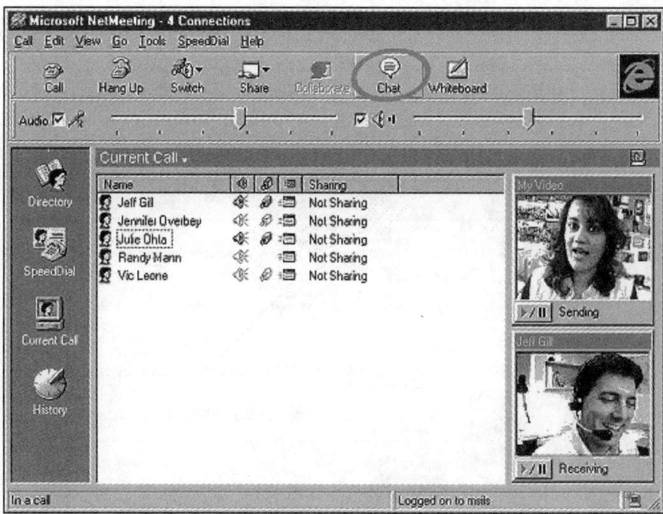

Figure 5.14 The NetMeeting Chat icon.

however, notice that many collaborators can interface, and it is possible to select a particular user with which to chat (think of this as a whisper mode).

Figure 5.15 shows how you can send a private message using the pull-down menu in the Send To box. Instead of selecting Everyone In Chat, select the individual to which you wish to send a private message. Before you start thinking about a private chat or asking someone for a date, remember each person can save his or her chat session to a file! Don't say anything you wouldn't want repeated.

File Transfer

While the file transfer feature of NetMeeting is not quite as evident as the other components, it is no less powerful or valuable. File transfer is initiated by selecting File Transfer from the Tools menu, then selecting Send File, as shown in Figure 5.16.

This process requires no intervention on the part of the receiver. NetMeeting automatically opens for file receipt after the sender sends a file. Notice that a window similar to a Save As dialog box opens for file selection. Once you select a file, click on Send to start the transfer (see Figure 5.17). Figure 5.18 shows a successfully transferred file.

To locate the sent file, select File Transfer from the Tools menu on the receiving computer and select Open Received Files.

Extending NetMeeting

NetMeeting can be extended for intranet use, enabling you to add your own products and/or services. To do this, download the NetMeeting 2.1 Software

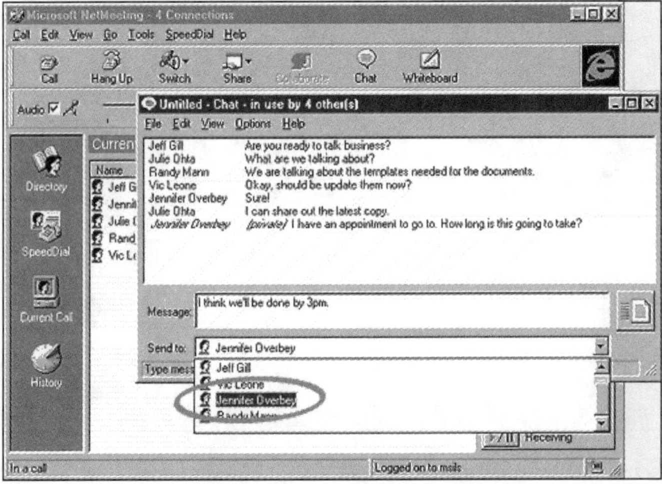

Figure 5.15 Send private messages using chat's Send To pull-down menu.

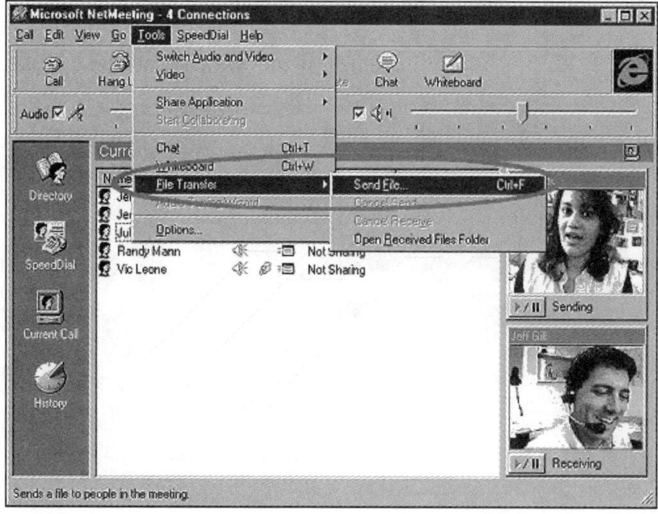

Figure 5.16 File transfer is available on the Tools menu.

Developers Kit (SDK) from the NetMeeting site at **www.microsoft.com/netmeeting**. This SDK provides extensions for ActiveX, JavaScript, or Object Linking and Embedding (OLE) Component Object Model (COM). Another extension of NetMeeting is the addition of the Mail Extension. This extension works very closely with Outlook and Exchange clients and allows a user to place a call through NetMeeting directly from their Address book. This means that a user can open their Address book and immediately decide whether to

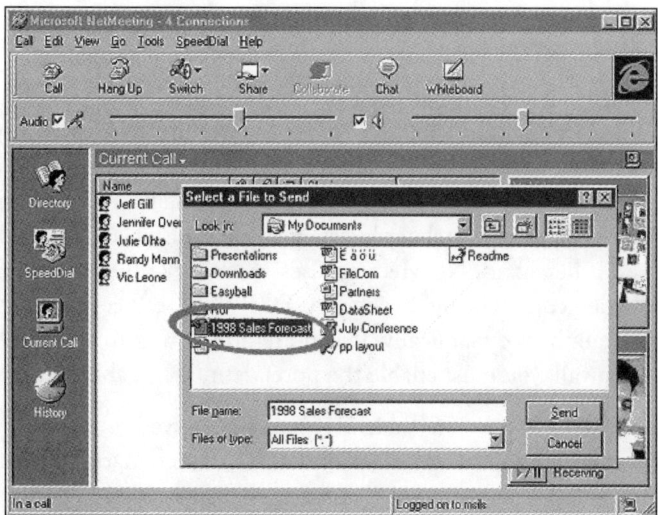

Figure 5.17 The NetMeeting Select A File To Send dialog box.

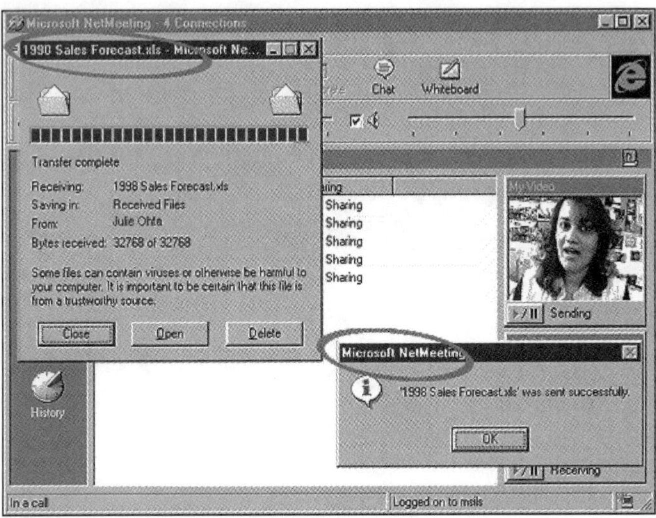

Figure 5.18 The file has been successfully transferred.

send a text message or attempt a NetMeeting call. If the NetMeeting call fails, the user can easily revert to sending a text message.

Proxy Settings

Many corporate networks today are configured to access the Internet through proxy servers and firewalls. Because NetMeeting uses many specialized protocols, you cannot use the most interesting parts of NetMeeting unless you configure the proxy settings. The following sections examine firewall requirements and proxy server settings for NetMeeting.

Many firewalls can support both primary and secondary TCP and UDP connections. In many environments, a firewall is configured to allow only primary TCP connections, because TCP is a connection-oriented protocol and it's considered more reliable and secure than UDP. NetMeeting uses a TCP connection for application sharing, whiteboard, text chat, file transfer, and directory lookups. On the other hand, NetMeeting uses secondary UDP connections for audio and video conferencing. Secondary TCP and UDP connections are assigned port numbers dynamically. If you are attempting to use NetMeeting through a firewall, you must enable the ports defined in Table 5.1.

The numbered TCP ports in Table 5.1 must be allowed to pass through the firewall for NetMeeting to operate completely. All secondary TCP and UDP connections are selected dynamically on any port from 1024 to 65535.

Table 5.1 Required NetMeeting TCP and UDP ports.

Port	Used For
389	ILS (TCP)
522	User Location Service (ULS) TCP
1503	T.120 (TCP)
1720	H.323 call setup (TCP)
1731	Audio call control (TCP)
Dynamic	H.323 call control (TCP)
Dynamic	H.323 streaming (RTP over UDP)

You might run into the same challenges with a proxy server, if it doesn't have a generic method of connection handling. For more information on firewalls, how they operate, and how to set them up, see the book *Internet Firewalls and Network Security* (see the "Need To Know More?" section at the end of this chapter).

Gatekeepers are part of the H.323 standard and are not included as part of the implementation of NetMeeting. Instead, Microsoft chose to use the NT domain model and system policies. The Internet Explorer Administration Kit (IEAK) is used to configure many of the system policies that designate how clients use NetMeeting, as you'll see in later chapters.

Client Configuration

Out of the box, the NetMeeting client is able to use all the available options. In many cases, however, especially in corporate environments, this is not desirable. After you determine what features users should have to be productive, you can quickly establish policies through the System Policies And Restrictions section of IEAK. There are many cases in which ILSs or ULSs available on the Internet do not promote the most business-like behavior. Although this might be entertaining, it is not really conducive to a productive business environment.

Before creating system policies, it is wise to consider what your users need to do their work in a productive manner with as few distractions as possible. Areas to look at include:

- File transfer
- Application sharing
- Audio and video feeds

When considering the appropriate configuration for NetMeeting on a network, it is important to incorporate the function of the company and the departmental roles. Engineering might need whiteboard capabilities, but it is doubtful that customer service will require this feature. However, customer service might benefit greatly from audio, and possibly file transfer, capabilities. You will serve your firm well by designing and locking down services based on group needs. The following section covers the NetMeeting Administration configuration options that can be used to limit NetMeeting's functionality for particular users or groups.

Administrative Configuration Options

This section lists the administration configurations available for various sections of the System Policies And Restrictions area of the IEAK Wizard or Profile Manager. For Applications Sharing, the options available are:

- **Disable All Application Sharing** Disables the Share Application button on the Tools menu.
- **Prevent User From Sharing Clipboard** Indicates that the clipboard is available to the user only, and that it cannot be shared.
- **Prevent User From Sharing Windows** Prevents the Windows application from being shared by users.
- **Prevent User From Sharing Explorer** Prevents the Explorer window from being shared. Note: Preventing users from sharing Explorer does not prevent them from sharing Windows, and vice versa. If this is required, disable both options.
- **Prevent User From Collaborating** Prevents user input from a specified person on a collaboration.

For the Restrict File Transfer dialog box, the options available are:

- **Prevent User From Sending Files** The user can receive files but cannot send them.
- **Prevent User From Receiving Files** The user can send files but cannot receive them.

For the Restricting Use Of Options dialog box, the options available are:

- **Disable The General Options page** Prevents changes in network settings (Tools|Options|General Tab), file transfer, accepting calls, and auto start of NetMeeting.
- **Disable My Information page** Prevents changes to addresses and categories.

- **Disable Calling options** Prevents changes to directory and speed-dial options.
- **Disable Audio options** Prevents changes to the microphone and H.323 gateway.
- **Disable Video options** Prevents changes to video quality, video camera properties, and image size.
- **Disable Protocol options** Prevents changing TCP/IP to null modem.
- **Prevent User From Answering Calls** Prevents notification of incoming calls.
- **Prevent User From Audio features** Prevents audio communication.

For the Restrict Video dialog box, the options available are:

- **Prevent User From Sending Video** Disables all video options.
- **Prevent User From Receiving Video** Prevents the user from seeing video.
- **Prevent User From Using Directory** Prevents all users from changing servers and server options, such as logging on/off, resolving addresses, and viewing directories. Does not affect Web browser directory services.

The only option available in the Set Default Directory Server section is Directory Server. This option sets the default ILS/ULS when starting NetMeeting.

In the Set Exchange Server For NetMeeting Address section, you can modify the Exchange Server Property option. This option selects the Exchange attribute that the Exchange extension will use to determine the NetMeeting address. If you cannot use one of the extensions listed, it must be added to the Registry manually. Refer to an Exchange reference book for more information.

The Preset User Information Category option is configured during the installation of NetMeeting. To change the category, you must uninstall and reinstall NetMeeting. A few of the categories available are Personal, Business, and Adult.

To enable T.120 for TCP/IP, select Enable TCP/IP T.120 protocol.

The Set NetMeeting home page option allows you to set the URL for Help|Microsoft On The Web|Product News.

The Set Limit For Audio/Video Throughput option allows you to set the average audio/video throughput limit in bps. This does not affect file transfer speed.

Exam Prep Questions

Question 1

ILS stands for which of the following?

- ❍ a. Internet Logic System
- ❍ b. International Language Service
- ❍ c. Internet Locator Service
- ❍ d. Internet Local System

The correct answer is c. ILS stands for Internet Locator Service. This is the name of the directory service that is used as an online version of a phone book for finding others on the Internet. Although all the other answers sound reasonable, no such terms exist. Therefore, answers a, b, and d are incorrect.

Question 2

Which operating systems support NetMeeting version 2.1?

- ❑ a. Windows 9x
- ❑ b. Windows NT 3.51 Service Pack 5 or higher
- ❑ c. Windows 3.x
- ❑ d. Windows NT 4 Service Pack 3 or higher

The correct answers are a and d. Windows 9x and Windows NT4 SP3 or higher are supported with NetMeeting version 2.1. Because changes have been made since the earlier version of NetMeeting, and system requirements have kept pace with operating systems, answers b and c are incorrect.

Question 3

Which of the following are valid ILS servers?

- ❑ a. Build your own
- ❑ b. Four11
- ❑ c. Microsoft
- ❑ d. None of the above

The correct answers are a, b, and c. Build your own, Four11, and Microsoft are valid ILS servers.

Question 4

When setting up NetMeeting behind a firewall, which well-known port(s) must be open?

- ❍ a. 389, 522, 1720, 1731
- ❍ b. 80, 820, 525, 1800
- ❍ c. 486, 900, 1335, 1730
- ❍ d. 322, 520, 1530, 1721

The correct answer is a. The port numbers listed are used for TCP, ULS, H.323, and Audio connections for NetMeeting. The other ports listed, although valid ports, are used for a number of different applications, none of them NetMeeting. Therefore, answers b, c, and d are incorrect.

Question 5

Besides the well-known ports, which of the following ports must be opened dynamically for NetMeeting to securely cross a firewall?

- ❍ a. 125
- ❍ b. 110
- ❍ c. 1024—65535
- ❍ d. None of the above

The correct answer is c. The 1024 through 65535 should be opened dynamically for NetMeeting and closed after use to produce an effective firewall. 125 and 110 are incorrect because the question specifically excludes the well-known port range, and all ports up to 1024 are classified as well-known ports. Therefore, answers a and b are incorrect.

Question 6

Which are the protocols used in ports besides the well-known ports?

❑ a. IP

❑ b. IPX

❑ c. RTP

❑ d. TCP

The correct answers are c and d. RTP and TCP are the protocols used in ports besides the well-known ports. RTP is from H.323 for streaming, whereas TCP is used dynamically for H.323 call control. IP is the Internet Protocol. IPX is the protocol used to connect to NetWare applications. Therefore, answers a and b are incorrect.

Question 7

What is the maximum number of collaborators that can meet over an electronic whiteboard?

❍ a. 2

❍ b. 1

❍ c. 4

❍ d. 6

The correct answer is d. A maximum of six collaborators can meet over an electronic whiteboard. The electronic whiteboard is not audio or video based; if it were, the number of collaborators would be limited to two. Therefore, answer a is incorrect. Answers b and c are invalid options.

Question 8

In NetMeeting, what is the low-end cutoff speed of realtime video?

❍ a. 33.6Kbps

❍ b. 128Kbps

❍ c. 56Kbps

❍ d. 28.8Kbps

The correct answer is d. 28.8Kbps is the low-end cutoff speed of realtime video in NetMeeting. 33.6Kbps, 128Kbps, and 56Kbps are all higher speeds. Therefore, answers a, b, and c are incorrect.

Question 9

A collaborator from NetMeeting can save notes from a chat forum.

❍ a. True

❍ b. False

The correct answer is a, True. You can also save chat notes to a database.

Question 10

The electronic whiteboard has the look and feel of which Microsoft program?

❍ a. Notepad

❍ b. Paint

❍ c. Explorer

❍ d. All of the above

The correct answer is b, Paint. Paint and NetMeeting's whiteboard use the same toolbar, and both text and graphic tools appear on the left side of the electronic whiteboard. The other choices don't mean anything in this context. Therefore, answers a, c, and d are incorrect.

Question 11

Which protocol is the ILS dynamic directory based in?

❍ a. HTTP

❍ b. LDAP

❍ c. POP3

❍ d. None of the above

The correct answer is b. The Lightweight Directory Access Protocol (LDAP) is used to create a dynamic phone book of those who are currently online.

HTTP is the protocol used for Web page transport. Therefore, answer a is incorrect. POP3 is the post office protocol used for email transfer on the Internet. Therefore, answer c is incorrect.

Question 12

NetMeeting has been recently upgraded to support USB-based cameras.

❍ a. True

❍ b. False

The correct answer is a, True. The Universal Serial Bus upgrade allows inexpensive USB-based cameras to be used with NetMeeting.

Question 13

Windows 98 has specific changes incorporated into it to improve the performance of NetMeeting.

❍ a. True

❍ b. False

The correct answer is a, True. Windows 98 contains changes designed to improve NetMeeting's performance. This is seen in the new video driver model, which comes with NT 5, as well.

Question 14

It is possible to collaborate with other NetMeeting users, even if they do not have a copy of the application you wish to share.

❍ a. True

❍ b. False

The correct answer is a, True. NetMeeting allows others to share an application over the Internet.

Need To Know More?

Siyan, Karanjit. *Internet Firewalls and Network Security*. New Riders, Indianapolis, IN, 1995. ISBN 1-56205-437-6. This book is a good starting point for learning about firewalls and how to set them up.

For additional information on video conferencing, visit the International Multimedia Teleconferencing Consortium Web site at **www.imtc.org**. It is a nonprofit organization for the creation and adoption of international standards of multipoint document and video teleconferencing.

The International Telecommunications Union is a United Nations group. It is the keeper of the T.120 and H.323 standards. Go to its Web site at **http://www.itu.ch/home/Search** and search for *T.120* and *H.323*.

Visit the Microsoft Web site at **www.microsoft.com/netmeeting** for an extensive look at NetMeeting and all its features.

6

Working With The IEAK Profile Manager

Terms you'll need to understand:

- √ IEAK Configuration Wizard
- √ IEAK Profile Manager
- √ JScript
- √ Auto-configure URL
- √ Auto-proxy (JS or PAC) file
- √ Configuration (INS) file
- √ Policy template (ADM) file
- √ Policy and restriction information (INF) file
- √ Cabinet (CAB) file

Techniques you'll need to master:

- √ Understanding the options available through the IEAK Configuration Wizard and the IEAK Profile Manager
- √ Using the different modes of the IEAK Configuration Wizard and the unique customizations offered in each
- √ Understanding the role of INS, INF, CAB, and ADM files
- √ Working with the IEAK Profile Manager to modify configuration files
- √ Understanding the steps necessary to implement an Automatic Configuration solution
- √ Creating and using a JScript Auto-proxy solution

The main impetus behind the Internet Explorer Administration Kit (IEAK) is to create customized builds that predefine users' Internet Explorer settings. In this chapter, we'll review the IEAK Configuration Wizard and examine the key aspects of the Profile Manager's features and functions. We'll also discuss the methods of deploying Automatic Configuration to maintain and manage users' Internet and desktop settings, and we'll delve into the specific files associated with Automatic Configuration and Automatic Proxy.

Profile Manager Overview

As mentioned in Chapter 5, the IEAK Configuration Wizard allows administrators to create customized builds of Internet Explorer (IE). The IE package is composed of a set of CAB files corresponding to the components specified during the build process, as well as configuration (INS) files, which contain all the options specified in the wizard. Users can run the Setup program included in the package to install the customized browser and components.

If the configuration files are placed on a central server, IE4's Automatic Browser Configuration feature enables administrators to manage the users' settings remotely. IEAK's Profile Manager provides an interface for the options available in these configuration files.

Note: Automatic Configuration is also a feature in IE3. In IE3, the Profile Manager is referred to as the INS Editor.

Options Available In The Profile Manager

The Profile Manager has a tree-view pane. The left pane displays a list of objects. When you select one of these objects, the right pane lists the configurable options available for the selected option, as shown in Figure 6.1.

Visual familiarity with the Profile Manager is very important. Practice creating and editing configuration files using the Profile Manager.

The left pane's objects are organized into two major areas, Wizard Settings and System Policies And Restrictions, which are discussed in the following sections. Also discussed are INS and ADM files. INS files are produced by the Profile Manager and contain settings for Internet Explorer. ADM files are profile templates that are created the first time IEAK or the Configuration Wizard is run.

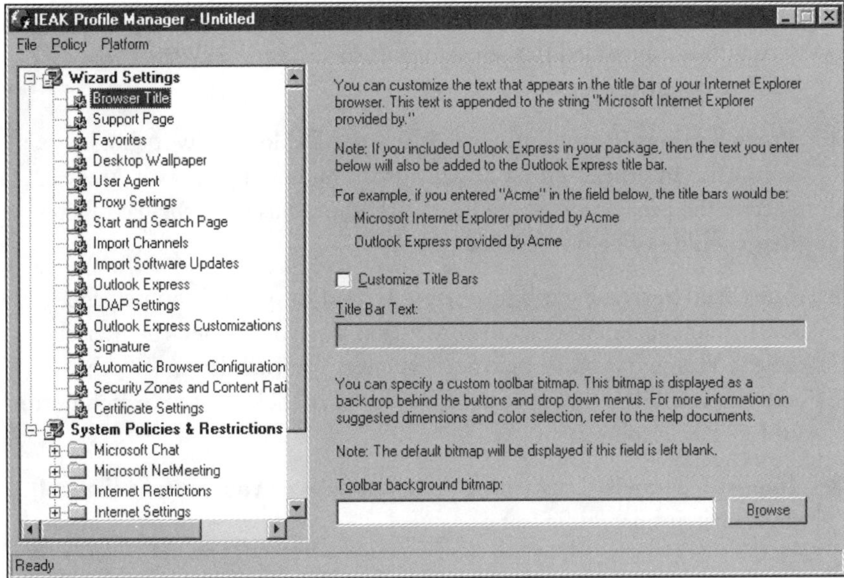

Figure 6.1 The IEAK Profile Manager.

Wizard Settings

The options available in Stages 4 and 5 of the IEAK Configuration Wizard correspond directly to the objects in the Wizard Settings area of the Profile Manager. You can specify the following objects and customizations:

- **Browser Title** The text you enter in this option appears in the title bar of Internet Explorer and Outlook Express after the words "Microsoft Internet Explorer provided by". This object also includes an option to incorporate a custom toolbar background bitmap.
- **Support Page** Internet Explorer retrieves the page specified here when a user chooses Help|Online Support.
- **Favorites** This option is used to customize users' Favorites folders and QuickLinks by specifying URLs to be included or by importing existing Favorites from your computer.
- **Desktop Wallpaper** This option enables you to specify a custom desktop wallpaper file, either an HTML page or an image. This setting takes precedence if you choose to import your desktop settings later.
- **User Agent** A user agent string is a quick description of the browser you are using. Many Web sites like to gather this information to keep statistics on the types of browsers visiting their site or to provide users

with content customized for their type of browser. You can specify a string to be appended to the user agent so you can track the usage of your custom browser.

- **Proxy Settings** Proxy settings tell Internet Explorer how it should access the Internet—either directly or through a proxy server. You can specify the proxy servers, if any, that IE should use and the list of sites that should not be proxied.
- **Start And Search Page** This setting is used to specify a home page URL that is opened when the browser is started or when the user clicks on the Home button in Internet Explorer. You can also specify the search pane URL that is opened when a user clicks on the Search button in Internet Explorer.
- **Import Channels** This setting is used to import your current channel and subscription configuration.
- **Import Software Updates** This option is used to import your current Software Distribution Channel configuration.
- **Outlook Express** This option is used to specify Outlook Express mail and news servers. You can also choose whether to make OE the default mail and news clients and whether to use Secure Password Authentication.
- **LDAP Settings** This setting is used to specify a Lightweight Directory Access Protocol (LDAP) directory service and its settings to provide users with a directory for finding users.
- **Outlook Express Customizations** This setting is used to specify a file or URL to be used as the Outlook Express InfoPane, as well as an HTML file that is included as the first message in users' Inboxes.
- **Signature** This option is used to append a standard line, such as a corporate disclaimer, to all Outlook Express mail messages and news postings.
- **Automatic Browser Configuration** This option is used to specify an Auto-configure URL and/or Auto-proxy URL and the interval, in minutes, at which the Automatic Browser Configuration will refresh itself.
- **Security Zones And Content Ratings** This option is used to import your Security Zone settings and content rating settings.
- **Certificate Settings** This option is used to import your current Certificate Authorities and Authenticode Security information.

System Policies And Restrictions

The Systems Policies And Restrictions area corresponds to all of the options available in the last screen when running the IEAK Configuration Wizard in Corporate Administrator Mode. This area enables you to specify desktop, shell, and security settings for your users.

What is most unique about this area is that you can control, or *lock down*, certain features and functions. When features are locked down, they either don't appear or are grayed out.

Although Microsoft documentation mentions that locked down features will be grayed out, this might not necessarily be the case. For the most part, users are able to view and seemingly modify Internet settings; however, changing the options in the browser does not actually work because of a Microsoft policy.

The following items are listed in the System Polices And Restrictions area of the Profile Manager:

- **Microsoft Chat** This option is used to preset the default server, character, and profile settings for Microsoft Chat users.
- **Microsoft NetMeeting** This item is used to disable NetMeeting features that might cause an extraordinary amount of stress on your network. You can even set a limit for audio/video throughput. The NetMeeting object also allows you to configure server information and protocol settings.
- **Internet Restrictions** This object actually allows you to completely disable the features found in IE4. You can also specify the default URL for downloading ActiveX controls.
- **Internet Settings** This option is used to set defaults for General settings, such as colors, fonts, and languages, and Advanced Settings, which correspond to the Advanced tab under Internet Properties of the View menu in IE. It also allows you to specify modem settings, such as the connection type and other connection options.
- **Outlook Express** This setting is used to place Outlook Express mail and news in the Restricted Sites Zone to disable almost all active content, and you can change the default format (HTML versus text) of email messages and news posts. You also have the opportunity to turn on or off certain folder and message navigational elements.

- **Web Desktop** This item is used to disable certain shell operating system features dealing with the desktop, Start menu, shell, printers, and system.
- **Subscriptions** This option enables you to control network utilization. You can set subscription and channel restrictions. For example, you can set the maximum number of levels a subscription can crawl, and you can specify the maximum amount of data that can be downloaded.

In contrast, the IEAK Configuration Wizard includes the following stages:

- **Stage 1: Gathering Information** Identifies your company information, your role in the organization (Corporate Administrator, Internet Service Provider, or Content Provider/Developer), and what types of builds you want to make. Only Internet Service Providers (ISPs) receive a Single Floppy option.
- **Stage 2: Specifying Active Setup Information** Defines where you download the components using Automatic Version Synchronization (AVS) and defines the components to be included in your package.
- **Stage 3: Customizing Active Setup** Defines the way Setup appears and works. You can specify whether to download sites on the Internet or intranet, and Setup will automatically balance the use of each of the URLs for optimum download performance. If you have chosen the Corporate Administrator role, you can choose to use a silent installation and define where the custom package is installed on the client.
- **Stage 4: Customizing The Browser** Identifies customizations to Internet Explorer general settings.
- **Stage 5: Component Customization (If Necessary)** Identifies customizations to email, news, and LDAP settings. It also includes a screen where certain system polices and settings can be set, depending on the role you defined for yourself in Stage 1.

The role you choose in Stage 1 defines the types of customizations you can make. The following are the types of modes available for the Configuration Wizard and the unique browser customization screens available for each role in Stage 4 of the wizard:

- Corporate Administrator Mode:
  - Import the predefined channel bar from your computer.
  - Import the desktop toolbar settings from your computer.
  - Add software distribution channels.
  - Define Auto-configure settings.

    - Import settings for Security Zones.
    - Import settings for content ratings.
    - Import Certificate Authorities.
    - Import Authenticode Security information.
- Internet Service Provider (ISP) Mode:
    - Add one channel.
    - Delete channels.
    - Add a custom desktop component.
    - Define an Internet Sign-up Server method.
    - Add custom sign-up files.
    - Define Dial-Up Networking parameters.
- Internet Content Provider/Developer Mode:
    - Add one channel.
    - Delete channels.
    - Add a custom desktop component.

Also, in the final screen—Systems Policies And Restrictions—ISPs can only specify settings for the following objects:

- Microsoft Chat
- Microsoft NetMeeting
- Internet Settings
- Outlook Express

Internet Content Providers/Developers can only specify settings for:

- Microsoft Chat
- Internet Settings

INS Files

INS (Internet setup) files are text-based files that contain cross-platform Internet Explorer configuration information. When you create an IE package using the IEAK Configuration Wizard, a configuration file called INSTALL.INS is created.

The following sections can be found in the INSTALL.INS file:

- **[Branding]** Defines the basic information needed while building an Internet Explorer package.
- **[Batch]** Defines the type of IE builds the IEAK should make.
- **[ActiveSetup]** Specifies the Setup Wizard's title and background bitmap.
- **[ActiveSetupSites]** Identifies the IE download sites.
- **[Internet_Mail]** Defines mail and news servers and other mail and news options defined in the wizard settings.
- **[URL]** Specifies IE's welcome page, Home page, Search page, Help page, QuickLinks, and Auto-configure URLs.
- **[Favorites]** Specifies URLs to be added to IE's list of Favorites.
- **[Desktop Objects]** Defines channel bar settings and the desktop wallpaper path.
- **[Custom Wallpaper]** Identifies whether to import custom wallpaper.
- **[Subscriptions]** Specifies subscriptions to be included with IE.
- **[Proxy]** Defines IE proxy settings.
- **[Security Imports]** Specifies whether site certificates, Authenticode certificates, ratings settings, and security settings should be imported.
- **[ExtRegInf]** Identifies the INF files to be used to configure or lock down users' settings.
- **[Internet_News]** Specifies an NNTP server and other news settings defined in the IEAK Wizard.
- **[LDAP]** Defines an LDAP server name and other LDAP settings defined in the IEAK Wizard.
- **[Signature]** Identifies signature information for news postings.
- **[Mail_Signature]** Identifies signature information for mail messages.
- **[SWUpdates]** Defines software description information as defined in the IEAK Wizard.

For organizations in which various user groups require unique settings, administrators can create multiple *USERGROUP*.INS files. For example, suppose you have a new Internet server that only the user group Developers should be able to access without using a proxy. You could use the IEAK Profile Manager to change its INS file, which would typically be called DEVELOPERS.INS. The new settings are used on the next update interval specified in the IEAK or when users open their browser.

The following is an example of code you might see in this example's *USERGROUP*.INS file:

```
[Internet_Mail]
Window_Title=Welcome to Acme Mail
Use_IMAP=No
SMTP_Server=mail.acmecompany.com
POP_Server=mail.acmecompany.com
Default_Client=No
Infopane=http://www.acmecompany.com/infopane/developers.htm

[URL]
Home_Page=http://www.acmecompany.com/developers/index.asp
Search_Page=http://www.acmecompany.com/developers/search.asp
AutoConfigURL=http://www.acmecompany.com/ieconfig/developers.ins

[Proxy]
HTTP_Proxy_Server=acmeproxy:80
FTP_Proxy_Server=acmeproxy:80
Gopher_Proxy_Server=acmeproxy:80
Secure_Proxy_Server=acmeproxy:80
Socks_Proxy_Server=acmeproxy:80
Use_Same_Proxy=1
Proxy_Override=<local>;new-server.acmecompany.com
Proxy_Enable=1

[ExtRegInf]
CHAT=*,CHAT.INF,DefaultInstall
CONF=*,CONF.INF,DefaultInstall
INETRES=*,INETRES.INF,DefaultInstall
INETSET=*,INETSET.INF,DefaultInstall
OE=*,OE.INF,DefaultInstall
SHELL=*,SHELL.INF,DefaultInstall
SUBS=*,SUBS.INF,DefaultInstall
```

To create a *USERGROUP*.INS file, perform the following steps:

1. From within the IEAK Profile Manager, choose File|Open.
2. Choose the INSTALL.INS file located in the language subfolder of the Ie4site folder for your package. INSTALL.INS is used as a template.
3. Make the changes you want to set for the user group.

4. Choose File|Save As.
5. The Save As dialog box will appear (see Figure 6.2). Save the configuration as *USERGROUP*.INS, where *USERGROUP* is the name of the user group that is to receive these settings. Also, specify the Auto-configure URL to the location in which this INS file should reside, and name the associated CAB files appropriately.

The Profile Manager makes the maintenance of these configuration files practically effortless. When changes need to be made, simply open the *USERGROUP*.INS file in the Profile Manager, make the changes, then save it. The associated CAB files are updated automatically.

ADM Files

You might be familiar with Windows NT ADM files, which are used as templates for user and system policy (POL) files. A POL file is a collection of elements that define a user's desktop and computing environment.

The IEAK uses the Windows policies technology and creates nine default policy templates of its own the first time either the IEAK Profile Manager or the IEAK Configuration Wizard is run. The policies reside in the \Program Files\IEAK\Policies directory. Table 6.1 describes each of these ADM files.

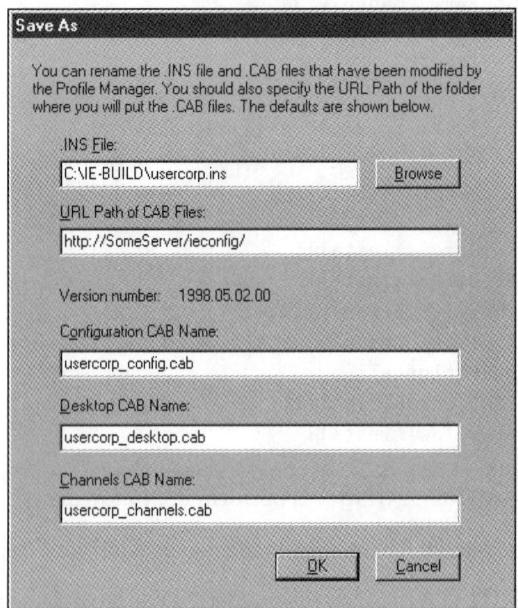

Figure 6.2 The Save As dialog box in Profile Manager.

Table 6.1 Vital statistics about default policy files for the IEAK.

Policy Template	Subject	Customizable Settings
CHAT.ADM	Microsoft Chat	Microsoft Chat settings
CONF.ADM	NetMeeting	NetMeeting user and computer access privileges
INETRES.ADM	Internet Restrictions	Various Internet settings; specified Internet code download settings
INETSET.ADM	Internet Settings	IE general and advanced settings and modem settings
OE.ADM	Outlook Express	Outlook Express settings
SHELL.ADM	Web Desktop	Use of certain shell operating system functions
SUBS.ADM	Subscriptions	Channel and subscription settings

Each of these policy templates appears automatically as an object within the System Policies And Restrictions area of the Profile Manager. To modify additional settings, administrators can create custom policy files and add them to the Profile Manager. To add a new policy object, perform the following steps:

1. Open or create an INS file.
2. Choose Policy|Import from the File menu. Browse to where your custom ADM file resides.
3. Choose Policy|Check Duplicate Keys to check for duplicate Registry keys in the templates and delete any duplicates from your templates.

When you save changes to system policies and restrictions, the IEAK Policy Manager creates corresponding INF files and packages them in cabinet (CAB) files. For example, if you create a NetMeeting policy file, a file called *CONF.INF* is generated, or if you import a custom policy template called *KEYS.ADM* and create a policy file with it, a file called *KEYS.INF* is created. The INS files refer to the INF files to create the appropriate Registry keys. The cabinet files are unpacked automatically when users download them.

Deploying Automatic Browser Configuration

Internet Explorer's Automatic Browser Configuration feature enables administrators to control users' Internet and desktop settings remotely. Typically, a custom package is created for each user group that needs unique settings. The packages are deployed with Automatic Configuration enabled and set with the appropriate Auto-configure URL.

Corporate administrators can use the IEAK Resource Kit to create one single "intelligent" build. Corporate administrators can use an Auto-configure URL that points to a custom Active Server Page to figure out what type of INS to return to a user based on the user's NT domain. A sample set of files is included in the \Program Files\IEAK\reskit\corp directory. This process requires IIS 3 or above.

The first time the customized Internet Explorer is run after installation, it connects to the specified Auto-configure URL and configures the browser settings. The settings can be refreshed based on any one of the following events:

- When the time interval specified in the IEAK is met.
- Each time IE is started. This is the case if no time interval has been configured.
- When the Automatic Configuration is refreshed manually by the user.

To set up Automatic Browser Configuration after IE has been deployed, the IE custom package must be recompiled with the new Automatic Configuration information, then redistributed.

However, existing users do not necessarily have to reinstall their browsers to utilize the Auto-configure URL functionality. Users can set this functionality manually by following these steps:

1. From within Internet Explorer, choose View|Internet Options.
2. Select the Connections tab.
3. Click on the Configure button.
4. Type the URL of the Auto-configuration file in the URL box (see Figure 6.3).
5. Select Refresh to refresh the Auto-configuration information.

To set up Automatic Configuration, perform the following steps:

1. Set up Custom Packages with Auto-configuration settings.
2. Create user configuration files.
3. Digitally sign Auto-configuration cabinet files.

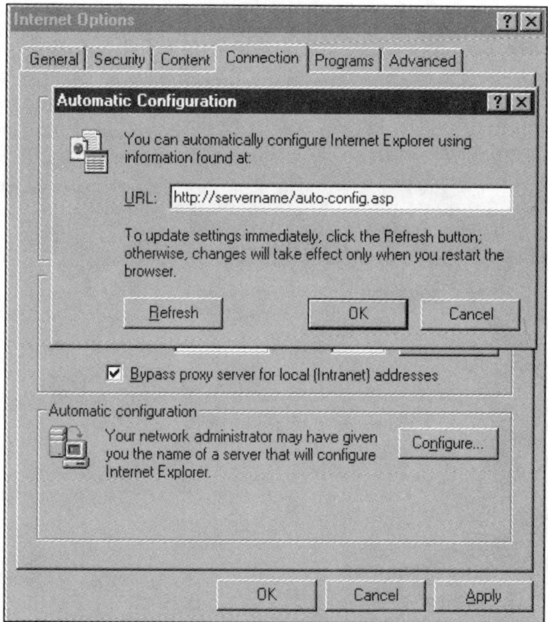

Figure 6.3 Internet Explorer Automatic Configuration dialog box.

4. Configure Automatic Configuration servers.

These steps are detailed in the following sections.

Set Up Custom Packages With Auto-configuration Settings

To build a custom package, start the IEAK Configuration Wizard and specify the settings you want to include.

Set aside at least one hour to build your first Internet Explorer Kit. Building subsequent packages requires much less time because the Administration Kit remembers most of the options you specified previously.

Stage 4 of the IEAK Configuration Wizard enables users to set Automatic Browser Configuration information, as shown in Figure 6.4.

If you specify either an Auto-proxy URL or an Auto-configure URL, IE includes this setting in the Auto-configure URL section of its Connection Properties. If you specify both types of URLs, the Auto-proxy URL is incorporated into the INS file.

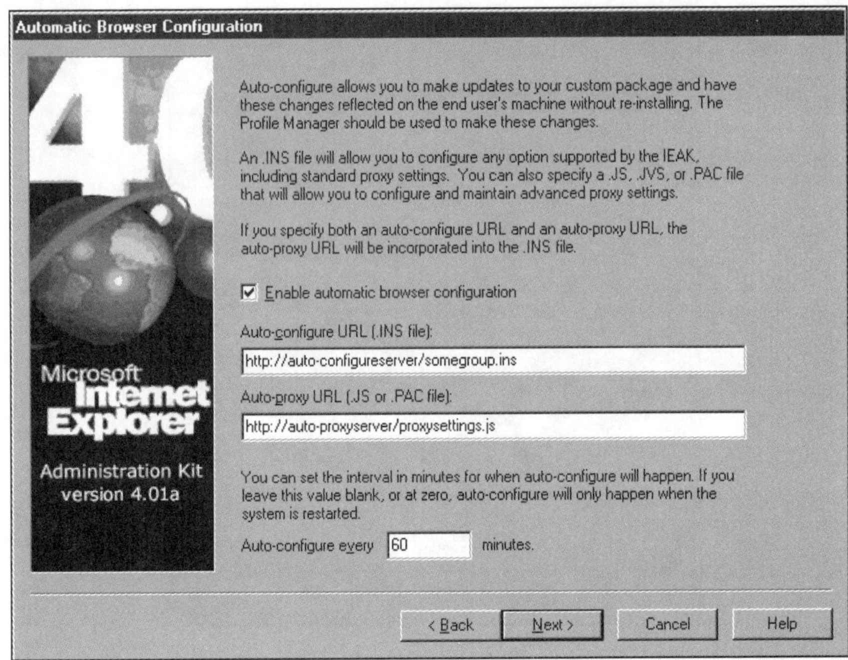

Figure 6.4 The IEAK Automatic Browser Configuration dialog box.

To enable Automatic Configuration, select the Enable Automatic Browser Configuration checkbox. Then, complete the following fields as appropriate:

- **Auto-configure URL** This URL points to the Auto-configuration (INS) file for this custom package. For example, if the INS or ASP Auto-configuration file resided in the ieconfig directory on the server named AcmeServer, the Auto-configure URL would be **http://AcmeServer/ieconfig/filename**. It does not support the **file://** protocol.
- **Auto-proxy URL** This URL points to an Auto-proxy (JS, JVS, or PAC) file to configure proxy settings dynamically.
- **Auto-configure every xx minutes** This is the time interval that Internet Explorer should check for updates to the Auto-configuration information. If this field is left blank or has a value of 0, IE will only refresh the Auto-configuration information when IE is restarted or when the user refreshes it manually.

After configuring the previous fields, the IEAK Configuration Wizard places the following entries in the [URL] section of the INSTALL.INS file:

```
AutoConfig=1
AutoConfigURL=http://URL/user-configuration file name
```

```
AutoConfigJSURL=http://URL/auto-proxy file name
AutoConfigTime=auto-configuration interval
```

Create User Configuration Files

As discussed previously, USERGROUP.INS files can be created to specify settings for each user group in your organization. When IE refreshes its Auto-configure URL, it processes the contents of the USERGROUP.INS file and makes changes as necessary.

Internet Explorer also downloads and unpacks the CAB files for Windows to process. The unpacked INF files are used by Windows to change system policies and restrictions corresponding to the System Policies And Restrictions section of the Profile Manager. When the Auto-configuration CAB files are downloaded to a user's system and unpacked, Windows checks to see if any of the INF files have changed. If they have, the settings in the new INF files take effect.

Digitally Sign Auto-configuration Cabinet Files

You must sign the Auto-configuration cabinet (CAB) files digitally before they can be deployed for use.

Digital certificates are a part of Authenticode technology, which identifies the source of a signed program and verifies that the program has not changed. You can obtain a digital certificate from a Certificate Authority (CA), such as VeriSign.

After you have installed the key, a digital certificate is generated. At this point, you can sign your CAB files using code signing tools, such as the Code Signing Wizard (SIGNCODE.EXE), which can be found in the IEAK Resource Kit in the \Program Files\IEAK\reskit\addons\tools folder.

Configure Automatic Configuration Servers

By now, you have probably identified an appropriate server that will act as a central repository for the Auto-configuration files. To configure the server to act as an Automatic Configuration server, you must install Web server software, such as Microsoft Internet Information Server (IIS).

You should then copy the configuration and cabinet files into the directory specified by the Auto-configure URL. For example, if the Auto-configure URL is **http://www.acmeserver.com/ieconfig/ie.ins**, copy the INS and CAB files to the ieconfig subdirectory in the root of the Web server.

After completing the previous steps, you can deploy Internet Explorer to your users, and their settings will be configured automatically from the Auto-configuration server.

Auto-proxy Files

As an alternative to setting users' proxy settings with an INS file, IE can be configured to use an Auto-proxy (JS or PAC) file to set the address of the proxy to use for each of the following protocols:

- HTTP
- Secure
- FTP
- Gopher
- Socks

Auto-proxy files can also define the hosts that should be exceptions to using the proxy server dynamically.

Auto-proxy files are written in JScript (Microsoft's implementation of JavaScript) and are created using a text editor. When an Auto-proxy file is specified in the user's Connection settings, the script simply determines whether IE should use a proxy or connect to a host directly.

The following code is a sample JScript function that you might see in an Auto-proxy file:

```
function FindProxyForURL(url, host)
 {
   if (isPlainHostName(host))
     return "DIRECT";
   else
     return "PROXY acmeproxy:80";
 }
```

The **isPlainHostName()** function checks to see if there are any dots in the host name. If there are, then IE is told to use the proxy server named *acmeproxy* on port **80**. If the host does not have dots, the host is assumed to be local, and IE does not use the proxy to retrieve the page.

Exam Prep Questions

Question 1

Which of the following items can an ISP configure using the IEAK Configuration Wizard?

- ❍ a. Add multiple channels to users' channel bars
- ❍ b. Add a custom desktop component
- ❍ c. Add software distribution channels
- ❍ d. Define proxy settings
- ❍ e. Define security settings

The correct answer to this question is b. ISPs can add a custom desktop component. ISPs can add only one channel and can delete all other channels. Therefore, answer a is incorrect. Only Corporate Administrators have the ability to add software distribution channels, define proxy settings, and define security settings. Therefore, answers c, d, and e are incorrect.

Question 2

Which of the following administrator roles does the IEAK Configuration Wizard support?

- ❑ a. Internet Service Provider
- ❑ b. Webmaster
- ❑ c. Internet Service Manager
- ❑ d. Internet Content Provider
- ❑ e. Corporate Administrator

Answers a, d, and e are correct. The IEAK Configuration Wizard contains different screens for Internet Service Providers, Internet Content Providers, and Corporate Administrators.

Question 3

What is the most efficient method of modifying users' Internet settings after Internet Explorer has been deployed?

- ❍ a. Create and include a batch file in users' login scripts that changes users' Registry settings as needed.
- ❍ b. If the customized IE package has the Auto-configuration feature enabled, simply place the modified configuration file(s) on the specified central Auto-configuration server.
- ❍ c. Require users to enable Automatic Configuration manually using the Connection tab of their Internet Explorer Properties dialog box.
- ❍ d. Create a new customized Internet Explorer package that includes the changes. Redistribute the new browser to your users.

The correct answer is b. If users are directed to an Auto-configure URL, simply modifying the configuration files at that URL will update users' Internet settings at the specified interval or when the user reopens the browser. Although the remaining options are possible methods of updating users' Internet settings, they are not the most efficient methods. Therefore, answers a, c, and d are incorrect.

Question 4

You need a customization code to run the IEAK Profile Manager.

- ❍ a. True
- ❍ b. False

The correct answer to this question is b. A customization code is only required to build an IE package, which is accomplished with the IEAK Configuration Wizard.

Question 5

Which of the following browser settings can be pre-set using the IEAK?

- ❑ a. Favorites
- ❑ b. QuickLinks
- ❑ c. Proxy server names
- ❑ d. Default cache size
- ❑ e. Default font size
- ❑ f. Default history size

The correct answers to this question are a, b, c, and e. Favorites, QuickLinks, proxy server names, and the default font size can all be specified using the IEAK. Internet Explorer's default cache size and default history size cannot be set using the IEAK. Therefore, answers d and f are incorrect.

Question 6

If an IE advanced setting is modified in the IEAK, which of the following would be true?

- ❍ a. The specified setting is locked, but the remaining advanced settings can be modified by the user.
- ❍ b. All advanced settings are locked and cannot be modified by the user.
- ❍ c. The user can override all changes to the advanced settings.
- ❍ d. The setting is configured but not locked down.

The correct answer is b. If an IE advanced setting is modified in the IEAK, all advanced settings are locked and cannot be modified by the user. Answers a, c, and d are incorrect.

Question 7

Which of the following objects are available for modification in the IEAK Profile?

- ❑ a. Email signature
- ❑ b. LDAP settings
- ❑ c. Automatic Browser Configuration
- ❑ d. Certificate settings
- ❑ e. Proxy settings
- ❑ f. Favorites

Answers a, b, c, d, e, and f are correct. All the objects mentioned can be modified using the IEAK Profile Manager.

Question 8

Which of the following types of files can be updated using the IEAK Profile Manager?

- ❑ a. TXT
- ❑ b. INS
- ❑ c. ADM
- ❑ d. CAB
- ❑ e. INF

The correct answers to this question are b, d, and e. The Profile Manager updates INS files and its accompanying INF files, which are then packaged into updated CAB files. TXT files are not used with the Profile Manager, and ADM files are only used as templates—they are not updated with the Profile Manager. Therefore, answers a and c are incorrect.

Question 9

How many custom components can be added to an IE package with the Configuration Wizard?

❍ a. 4

❍ b. 12

❍ c. Depends on the user role you choose in Stage 1

❍ d. 10

The correct answer to this question is d. No matter which role you choose in the IEAK, you can include up to 10 custom components in your package. Therefore, answers a, b, and c incorrect.

Question 10

Which of the following configurations are available to a Corporate Administrator only?

❑ a. Choose to create a silent installation (with no user prompts)

❑ b. Specify the install path on the client

❑ c. Choose whether to implement the Windows desktop

❑ d. Import Security Zone settings

❑ e. Import Authenticode certificate information

❑ f. Append a default signature to users' email messages and news postings

Answers a, b, c, d, e, and f are correct. All the configurations mentioned are only available to Corporate Administrators.

Question 11

Which of the System Profiles And Policies objects are available for configuration by an ISP in the Configuration Wizard?

- ❑ a. Microsoft NetMeeting
- ❑ b. Internet Settings
- ❑ c. Internet Restrictions
- ❑ d. Microsoft Chat
- ❑ e. Outlook Express

The correct answers to this question are a, b, d, and e. ISPs can control settings for NetMeeting, Internet settings, Microsoft Chat, and Outlook Express. ISPs cannot change options in the Internet Restrictions object. Therefore, answer c is incorrect.

Need To Know More?

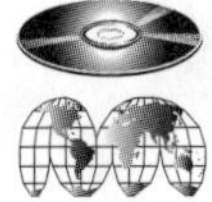

Search the TechNet CD (or its online version at **www.microsoft.com**) using the keywords *Profile Manager* and *Automatic Configuration*. The TechNet CD also includes a copy of the *IEAK Corporate Deployment Guide*. This is excellent reading to learn more about using the Profile Manager to create an Auto-configuration solution.

For more detailed information on the IEAK Profile Manager, refer to the Microsoft IEAK Web site at **http://ieak.microsoft.com**.

7

Corporate Administrator Mode

Terms you'll need to understand:

- ✓ AVS (Automatic Version Synchronization)
- ✓ GUID (globally unique identifer)
- ✓ InfoPane
- ✓ INS
- ✓ JS
- ✓ LDAP (Lightweight Directory Access Protocol)
- ✓ PAC
- ✓ Permissions
- ✓ System Policies And Restrictions
- ✓ Silent install

Techniques you'll need to master:

- ✓ Customizing signatures
- ✓ Configuring proxy server settings
- ✓ Creating restrictions

In this chapter, you'll explore Internet Explorer 4 Administration Kit in the Corporate Administrator mode. You'll also read about what you need to know to make the IEAK useful. You'll explore a unique type of IE4 download—silent mode. Finally, you will learn many IEAK productivity tips and tricks.

Installing Internet Explorer (Corporate Administrator)

Unfortunately, for many users, setting up IEAK can be a challenging experience. This section takes a look at the more salient points of the IEAK Corporate Administrator mode and discusses how to make IEAK work for you. The most important points to remember about Corporate Administrator mode are:

- When creating a download for silent mode, which is discussed later in this chapter, only one download site is available.
- When creating a download for silent mode, all options are preset.
- When creating a Corporate Administrator mode download, preset the proxy settings.
- Signature files can hold legal disclaimers.

It's important to remember each of these when preparing for the exam, as well as when using IEAK in Corporate Administrator mode. The following sections explore some of the more practical aspects of installing IEAK.

Automatic Version Synchronization

The IEAK can be your friend; however, unless you learn how to properly set up the IEAK, it can be your worst enemy. You can install the IEAK by downloading it from the Internet or ordering a CD-ROM from Microsoft. The following looks at the pros and cons of the installation options.

Downloading The IEAK From The Internet

If you plan on downloading the IEAK from the Internet, your first setup task concerns selecting a download site. If you live near Microsoft, it's a natural assumption that the best place to download the latest and greatest files is from the Redmond site. Theoretically, this should result in faster transmissions, and you will feel like a good Netizan by not bogging down the entire Internet with your download. Microsoft has about 50 servers available to support requests. Although that is a great deal of servers, it is actually not enough to support the amount of traffic Microsoft has most of the time. Because of this, you will most likely get a slower transfer rate going through Redmond.

After selecting a download server, you must next consider Internet traffic. Speaking from experience, you should never attempt to perform an Automatic Version Synchronization (AVS) when the Internet is busy. Unlike the Internet Explorer 4 Setup program, the AVS doesn't simply pick up where it left off in the event of a download failure. You must start over from scratch. This is no small matter, because the download time is measured in hours.

Automatic Version Synchronization (AVS) ensures that you have the latest versions of all Internet Explorer components before proceeding with the build. It does this by connecting to the download site you selected and comparing file dates and times.

After you select a download site and an optimum download time, you are ready to download the IEAK. The first time you download the IEAK, you need to download the latest files. This is called *synchronizing*. If you elect to not synchronize the applications for your first build, the Next button will be grayed out and unusable. So, although you don't have to synchronize, you won't be able to complete a build without it. You *must* use AVS to create your first build. On subsequent builds, you can decide whether or not to synchronize your files, but it's usually a good idea.

Internet Explorer 4's Service Pack 1 (SP1) is one of many programs that need to be updated by AVS before beginning your build. NetMeeting, MS Wallet, and so forth, also must be part of your first AVS. After completing SP1's long download, the AVS continues to attempt to synchronize the rest of the package. As an example, though most companies are using much faster connections, a full AVS synchronization over a 28.8Kbps connection takes about 12 hours.

Please keep in mind that if your synchronization attempt fails anywhere along the way, you must begin your AVS all over again, starting with SP1. Whether the failure is a disconnect by your ISP, a burst of Internet traffic that causes a time out, or simply bad luck, it can lead to a very frustrating series of attempts. Keep this in mind before you promise a custom Internet Explorer 4.01 build to your supervisor. Hopefully, Microsoft will update the AVS so that it will synchronize a single program (as opposed to the entire package at once) or perhaps pick up at the point of failure. Of course, the faster your Internet connection, the more likely you'll complete the synchronization.

Installing IEAK From A CD-ROM

Instead of downloading the IEAK from the Internet, you might find that it is more convenient to install the IEAK from a CD-ROM. After encountering the frustration of attempting to download version 4, many administrators have chosen to order the CD, rather than attempt a download again. A CD installation provides more stability and can be considerably faster. Of course, you will still have to go through the synchronization process, but it won't take as long as downloading. On the downside, updates to Internet Explorer are simply coming too fast to keep CDs up-to-date. So, when you install the IEAK from a CD, you risk installing outdated versions of some of the applications.

When you load the IEAK CD, you should see the screen shown in Figure 7.1. To install the IEAK, simply select the Install Internet Explorer Administration Kit icon.

After the installation has been completed, you are ready to run a setup for your first build. To start the IEAK Wizard, select it from the Microsoft IEAK group in the Programs area of the Start menu. The first setup dialog box outlines the steps involved in creating a custom build of IE4. Clicking on Next opens a dialog box that outlines Stage 1 of the build process.

Stage 1: Entering IE4 Build Information

Review the details regarding Stage 1 of the installation process, then begin the process:

1. Click on Next. You should see the Enter Company Name And Customization Code dialog box, as shown in Figure 7.2.
2. Enter your company name and customization code (Microsoft provides you with a customization code).

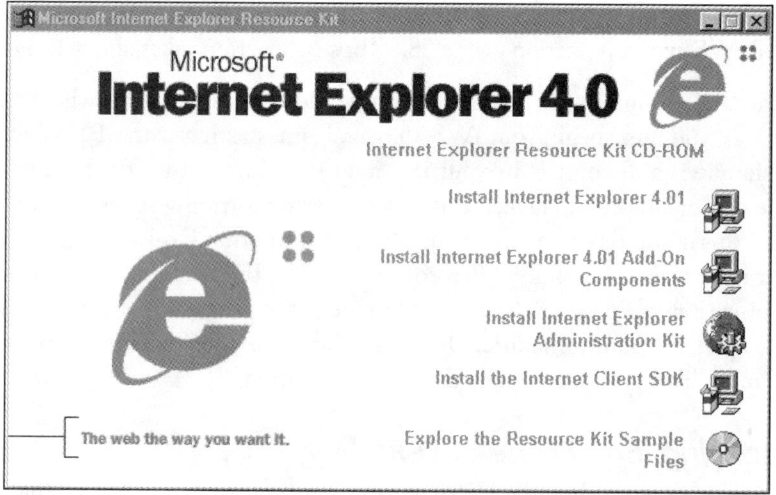

Figure 7.1 The IEAK CD contains everything you need to prepare an installation and set up the Automatic Version Synchronization.

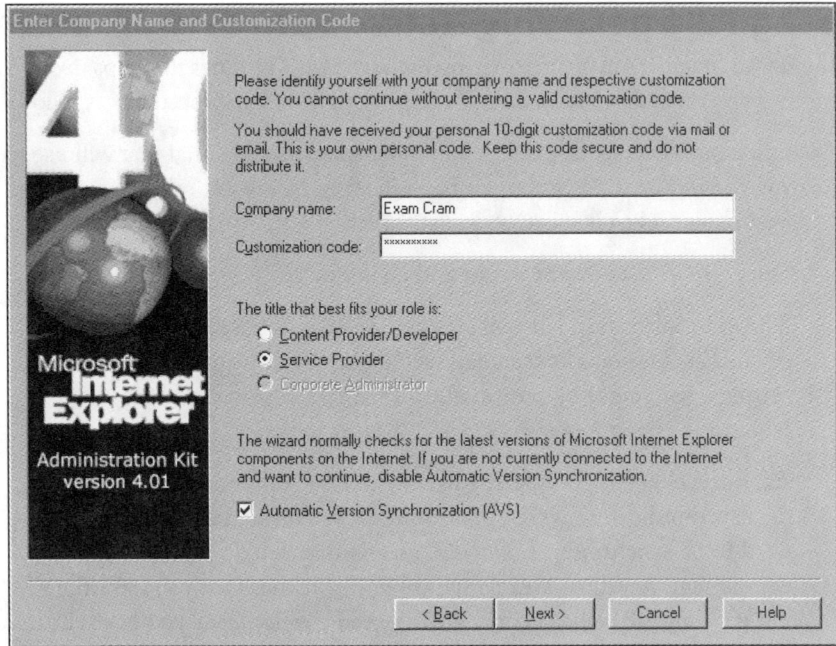

Figure 7.2 The Enter Company Name And Customization Code dialog box is used to begin the installation process.

The available options are directly related to the customization key type that you received from Microsoft. You must get a key version for each type of installation.

3. Click on Next and specify the platform for which you are creating an IE4 build. The available options are:

   - Windows 95/NT 4
   - Windows 3.11/WFW/NT 3.51
   - Unix

4. Click on Next, then choose the language for the build you are creating.

5. Click on Next, then specify the type of distribution for the build:

   - Server-based directory
   - CD-ROM
   - Floppy disks

6. Click on Next to proceed to Stage 2.

Stage 2: Specifying Active Setup Parameters

Similar to Stage 1, the opening dialog box in Stage 2 outlines the steps involved in the stage. Read the details, then continue with the setup procedures as follows:

1. Click on Next. At this point, you must select the site that you will use to run the required AVS. Remember, selecting Microsoft might not be the best choice, even if it is the closest server.

2. Select the site you want to use and click on Next.

   The Administration Kit will check to see if you have the latest versions of all IE4 components installed (see Figure 7.3). Depending on your IE settings, you might be prompted to trust the information being sent by Microsoft. Select Yes to proceed.

   After the check is complete, a list of the IE4 components will be displayed indicating which files are the most up to date and which files need to be synchronized. A red X means that you do not have that component. A yellow ! (exclamation point) means that you have the file, but it is not the latest version, and a green check means you have the latest version available (see Figure 7.4).

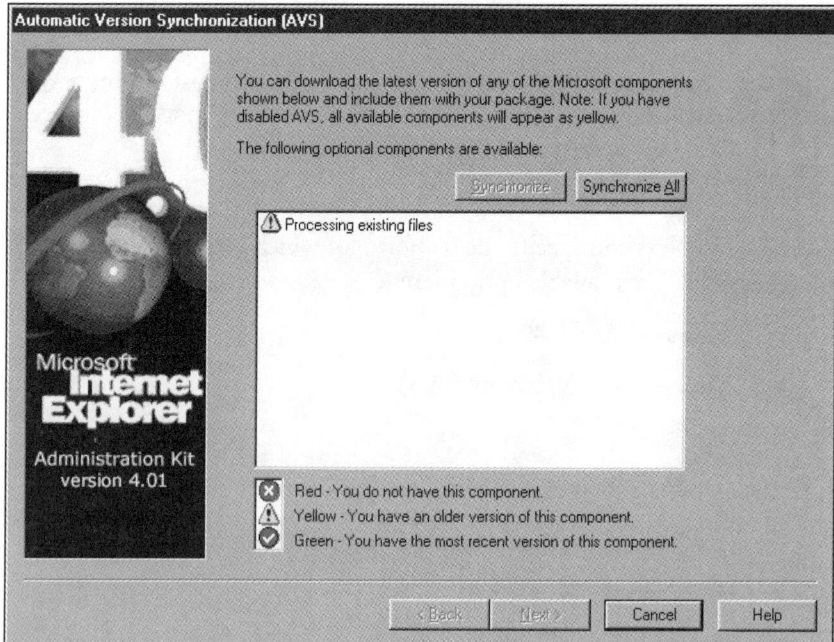

Figure 7.3 The Automatic Version Synchronization process checks your files to verify whether you have the latest versions of IE4 components.

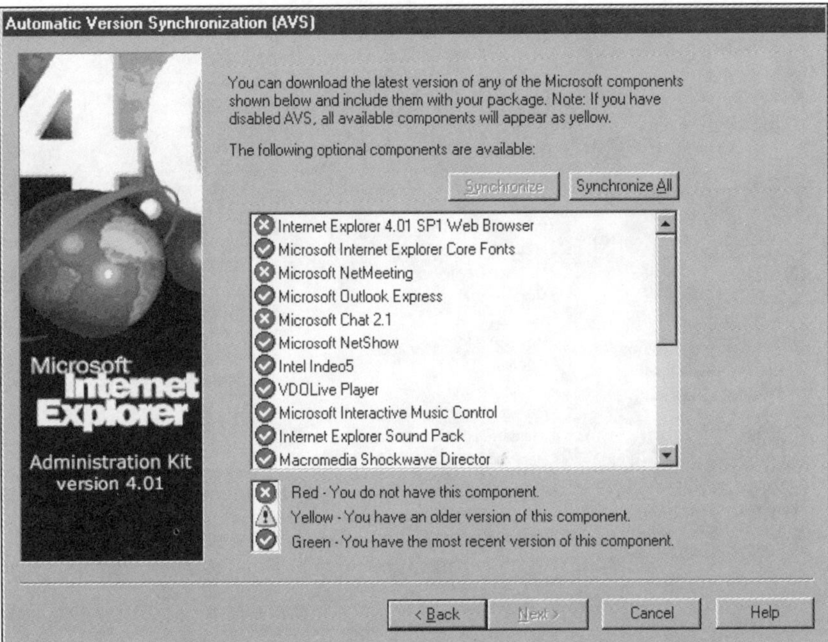

Figure 7.4 After Automatic Version Synchronization, the Internet Explorer Administration Kit will inform you as to which applications are current and which need to be updated.

3. Notice in Figure 7.4 that Internet Explorer, NetMeeting, and Chat have not been installed. In this case, the components marked with the red X indicate that a previous install was not completed successfully and, therefore, they must be re-downloaded. If you run into this situation, your best bet is to choose Synchronize All and wait as the latest versions of the programs are installed. Remember, if you're downloading from the Internet, this might take the better part of a day, depending on your connection speed and the number of applications to synchronize. Throughout the update, you might be prompted to trust the information received from Microsoft. Click on Yes to proceed.

4. Eventually, you will get a fully synchronized image set, as shown in Figure 7.5. It is in your best interest to have the latest versions of all IE components. Notice that you cannot choose Next until all files are synchronized. Once you're ready to go, click on Next to proceed.

   The next screen gives you the opportunity to add custom components to the build.

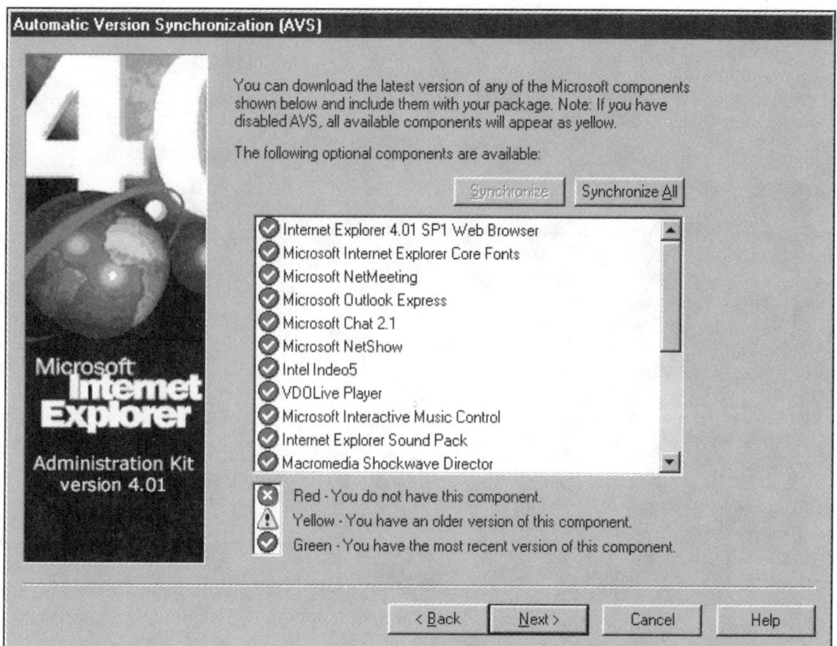

Figure 7.5 Eventually, you will get a fully synchronized image set for your custom builds.

If you are converting from Netscape installations that have helper files, the helper files are not brought over during the conversion. This is the time to install any custom helper files that you might need in Internet Explorer.

Figure 7.6 shows the Specify Custom Active Setup Components dialog box. Through this dialog box, you can specify up to 10 custom components that your users can install at the same time they install the browser. Custom components can be either self-extracting EXE or CAB files. The entries in the dialog box are as follows:

- **Component** Designates the name of the component to be added. This is the name that will appear in the setup screen when users install the component.
- **Location** Defines the location of the EXE or CAB files.
- **Command** Defines the command to be run to extract the CAB files. This option is used only with CAB files.
- **GUID** Specifies the globally unique identifier for the application. Many applications might already have a GUID. If so, enter the

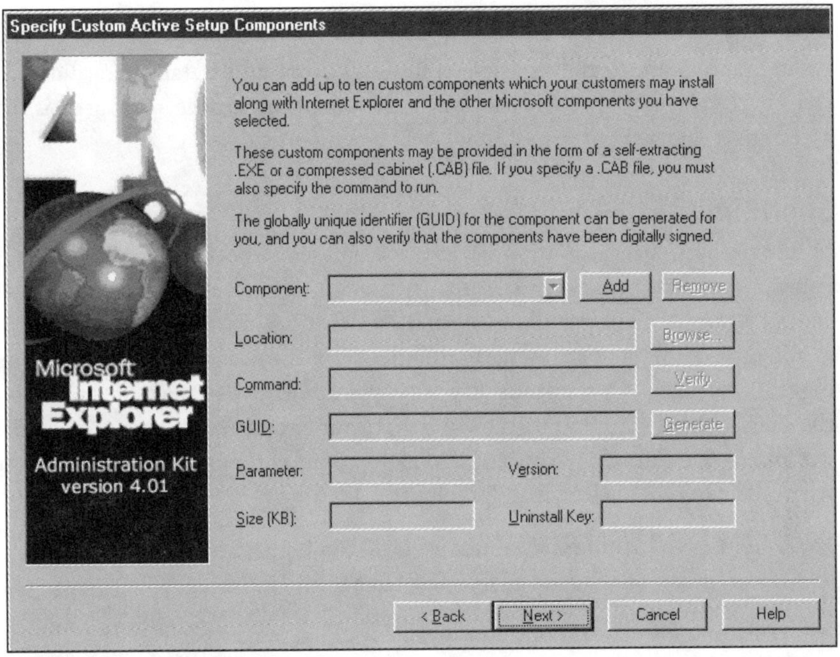

Figure 7.6 Custom components are added through the Specify Custom Active Setup Components dialog box.

information here. If not, use the Generate option to create a GUID for the application.

- **Parameter** Lists the parameters of a self-extracting EXE file, if you are using a self-extracting EXE file.
- **Size (KB)** Enters the size of the program in kilobytes.
- **Version** Enters the version number of the application.
- **Uninstall Key** Enters the Registry information for use by the uninstall program.

5. After you've completed the required information, click on Next to proceed. The Configuration Wizard will display any trusted publishers installed on your machine. Remember that any active setup will only acknowledge custom packages as trusted. Therefore, you must choose a publisher to sign your files. This completes Stage 2.
6. Click on Next to move on to Stage 3: Customizing Active Setup. The good news is that the potentially most challenging aspects are now behind you.

Stage 3: Customizing Active Setup

As in Stages 1 and 2, the first screen in Stage 3 presents details regarding the steps in the stage. As you will see, one of the important aspects of Stage 3 is the ability to create a silent install.

Silent Install

While running the installation wizard, you will see a checkbox that asks you if you want to "Install package silently." Although this screen might seem innocent, it is not. A silent install of Internet Explorer 4.01 installs all components, as you have configured them, without input from the user. This means that the biggest challenge of a silent install is that you are forced to make decisions on the users' behalf, which in turn means that your choices must be well thought out and tested before deployment. Considerations you must take into account when deciding on a silent install include:

- Whether to include the Windows Desktop Update or Active Desktop. If not, it can be made available at a later time.
- Only one installation option is available. This makes perfect sense, if you think about it. Because users will not be able to make installation choices, there's no reason to make multiple choices available.
- Only one site is available for downloads. If you're using a regular install, your users can have up to 10 install options and up to 10 download sites.

As you can see, choosing a silent install limits the options available to you in regard to installation choices (CD and multiple floppies are not available) and the number of download sites. After deciding to use a silent install and choosing the options to be used, thoroughly test the custom build before deployment on your network. Now, let's back up a little and work through the process of completing Stage 3.

Completing Stage 3

1. After reading the opening screen, click on Next. You will see either the Customize The AutoRun Screen For CD-ROM Installations dialog box or the Customize The Active Setup Wizard dialog box, depending on the type of installation you're performing (download or CD-ROM).

   The information in the dialog boxes is similar in that you can specify the text that will appear in the title bar and the bitmap that will be displayed during installation. Note that the CD splash screen bitmap must be a 256-color bitmap image, 540×357 pixels. After completing the CD-ROM

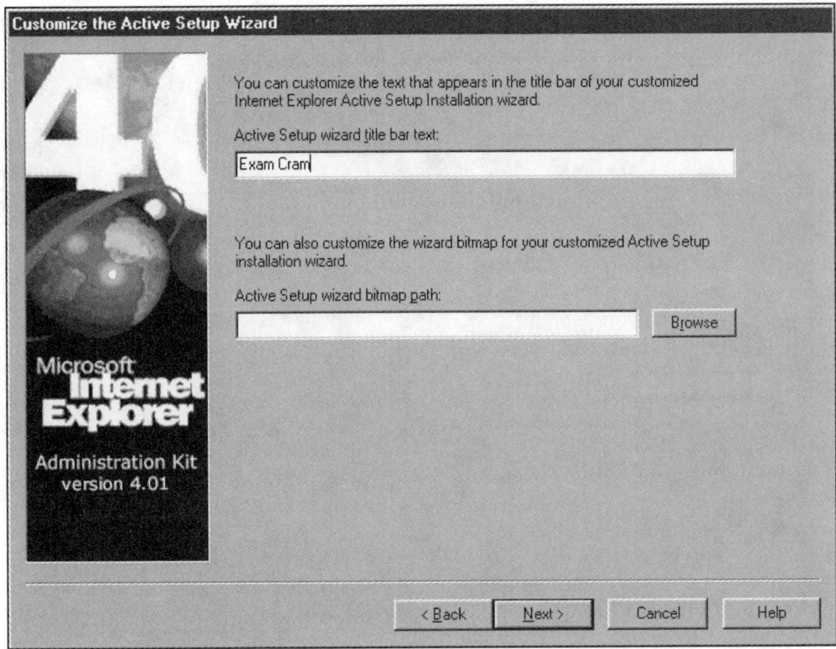

Figure 7.7 Through the Customize The Active Setup Wizard dialog box, you can define the title bar text and background image to be displayed.

options dialog box, the Customize The Active Setup Wizard dialog box, shown in Figure 7.7, appears.

2. Click on Next to invoke the custom components install section. This section allows you to specify the text that will appear in the title bar during this portion of the installation.

3. Click on Next to move to the Select Silent Install dialog box.

4. Select whether to use a silent install, then click on Next to bring up the Select Installation Options dialog box, as shown in Figure 7.8.

   Among the options available is whether to provide a minimal, standard, or full installation of IE. In addition, you have the option of creating up to 10 different packages containing different variations of the available applications.

5. Create a new option by clicking on New and entering the requested information. The Description text box provides information about which options are available for a particular build. If the component you want is not in the Components Available list, click on the Back button

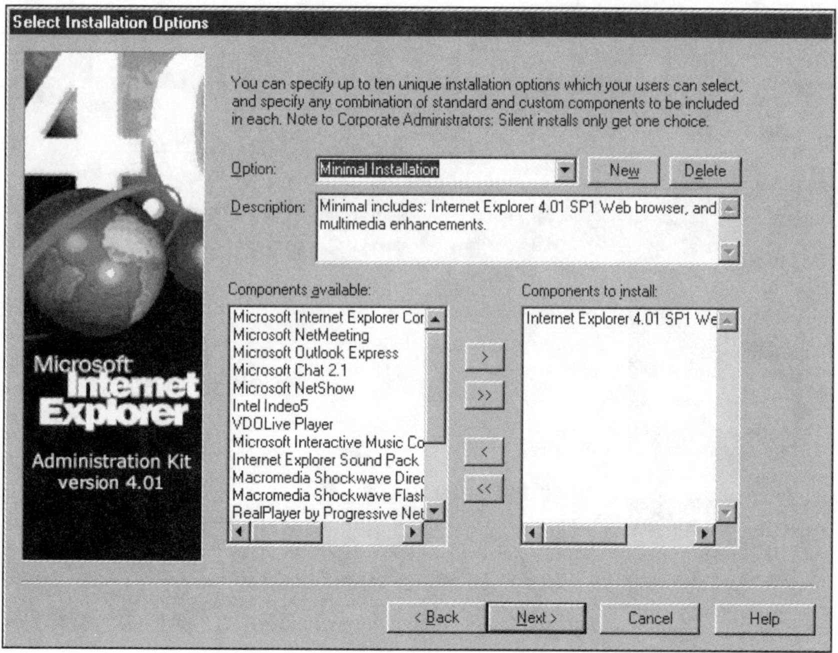

Figure 7.8 A minimal custom build that will distribute just the Service Pack 1 for Internet Explorer 4.01.

until you reach the Automatic Version Synchronization page, then add the desired component.

6. After completing the installation options, click on Next to open the Specify Download URLs dialog box, as shown in Figure 7.9.

   This dialog box is used to configure up to 10 download sites for your custom build of IE4. You must specify the name of each site, its URL, and its region. Use the Add and Remove buttons to modify the listings.

7. After you've added all download sites to your list, click on Next to proceed to the Select Version Information And Add-on Component URL dialog box, as shown in Figure 7.10.

   A version number is very important in creating your builds, because it ensures that the most recent versions of the files are used each time a new custom build is created. The wizard automatically populates this section, but you can override the version number if you wish. For these settings, the first digit is the most significant (that is, version number 3 0 0 0 is newer than 2 6 7 8). As the screen states, a configuration identifier can be up to eight digits long. The caveat here is to ensure that the version numbers match by using the same company name in Stage 1

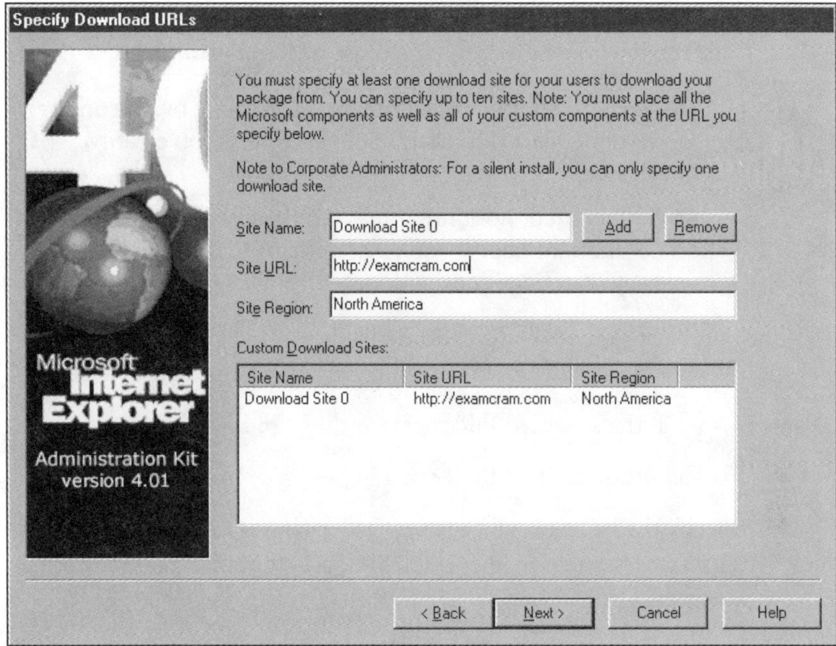

Figure 7.9 Unless you're using a silent install, you can define up to 10 download sites.

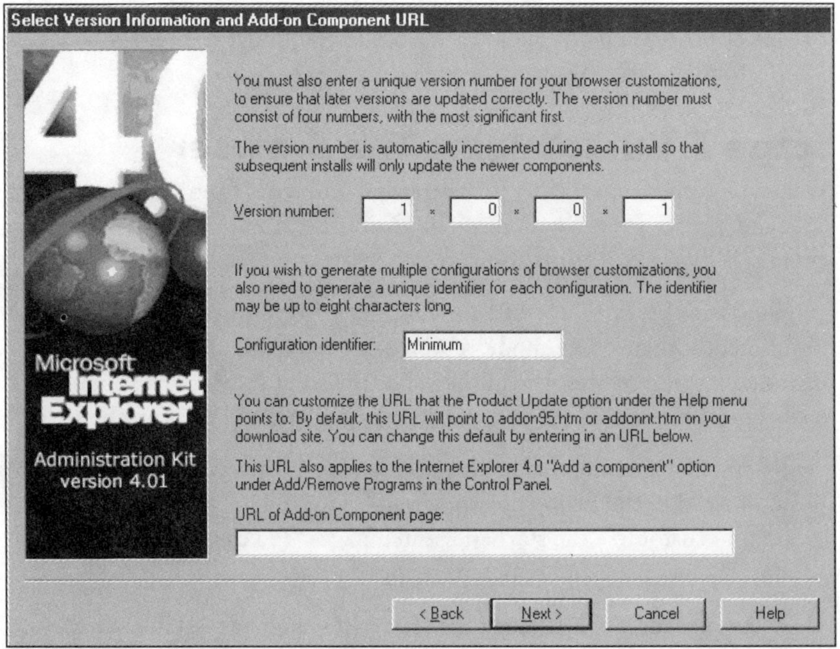

Figure 7.10 Specify a version number for the build you are creating.

each time the wizard is run. You are also given the option at the bottom of the screen to enter a URL for an Add-on Component page.

The version number will automatically increase by one on the fourth digit (least significant digit) each time you create a new build.

Addon95.htm or Addonnt.htm is required in the URL of the Add-on Component page if you want updates to be available to the users by selecting Product Updates from IE's Help menu.

8. Click on Next to move to the next dialog box, which allows you to specify where to install IE. There are three available options:

   - Install in the specified folder within the Windows folder.
   - Install in the specified folder within the Program Files folder.
   - Specify the full path of a custom folder. (If the folder does not exist on a user's hard drive, the installation program will create the folder automatically.)

9. Click on Next to proceed to the final wizard dialog box in Stage 3. This dialog box is used to determine whether the Desktop Update should be loaded. You have the option of allowing users to determine if they want Desktop Update installed.

10. Select the desired option and click on Next to move to Stage 4: Customizing The Browser.

Stage 4: Customizing The Browser

At this stage, the Corporate Administrator mode varies from the Content Provider and Service Provider modes. The Corporate Administrator mode allows you to specify proxy settings for all users.

Installing Internet Explorer 4.01 for Corporate Administrator mode starts out no differently than other modes covered in this book. The first dialog box presented in Stage 4 after the initial list of the steps provides the opportunity to customize the text in the title bar and the background used on the toolbar:

1. Review the opening dialog box, click on Next, then click on Next again to proceed to the dialog box shown in Figure 7.11. This dialog box is used to customize the start and search pages. You can define the same start (home) page and search page for all users.

2. After entering the URLs for the start and search pages, click on Next to proceed to the next dialog box, which allows you to specify an online support page.

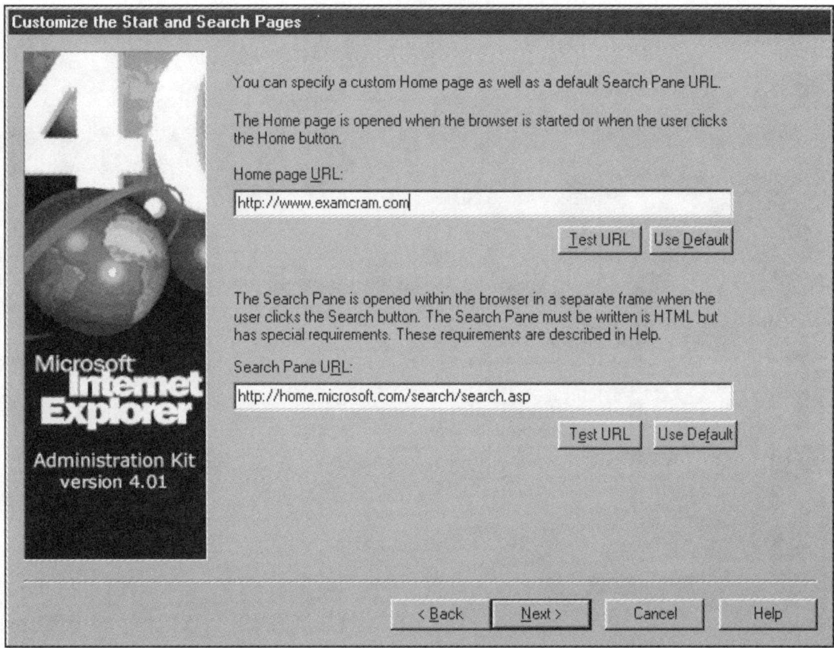
Customize the Start and Search Pages
Microsoft Internet Explorer
Administration Kit version 4.01
You can specify a custom Home page as well as a default Search Pane URL.
The Home page is opened when the browser is started or when the user clicks the Home button.
Home page URL:
http://www.examcram.com
Test URL
Use Default
The Search Pane is opened within the browser in a separate frame when the user clicks the Search button. The Search Pane must be written is HTML but has special requirements. These requirements are described in Help.
Search Pane URL:
http://home.microsoft.com/search/search.asp
Test URL
Use Default
< Back
Next >
Cancel
Help

Figure 7.11 Defining standard start and search pages.

3. Click on Next to continue.

   The next dialog box enables you to define the Favorites folder and links that are installed on each user's computer. If you look closely at the fine print of the license agreement, you'll find that you can delete any links that are directly competitive to your business.

   For example, let's say a company publishes an online, high-technology magazine. Because *Wired* is in the same business, the company can delete any links to *Wired* (see Figure 7.12) without violating the license agreement.

4. After removing any link references to competitors, you can add links pointing to your own Web site. Keep in mind that you can have sites that update via channel definition format, as well (see Chapter 4 on Webcasting). To be sure that no channels conflict with your business, choose the Delete Existing Internet Explorer Channels option in the Customize The Active Channel Bar dialog box.

Throughout the remainder of Stage 4, you are prompted for various input, such as automatic configuration scripts and whether to display the Internet Explorer Welcome page. The most important of the remaining configuration settings are the proxy settings.

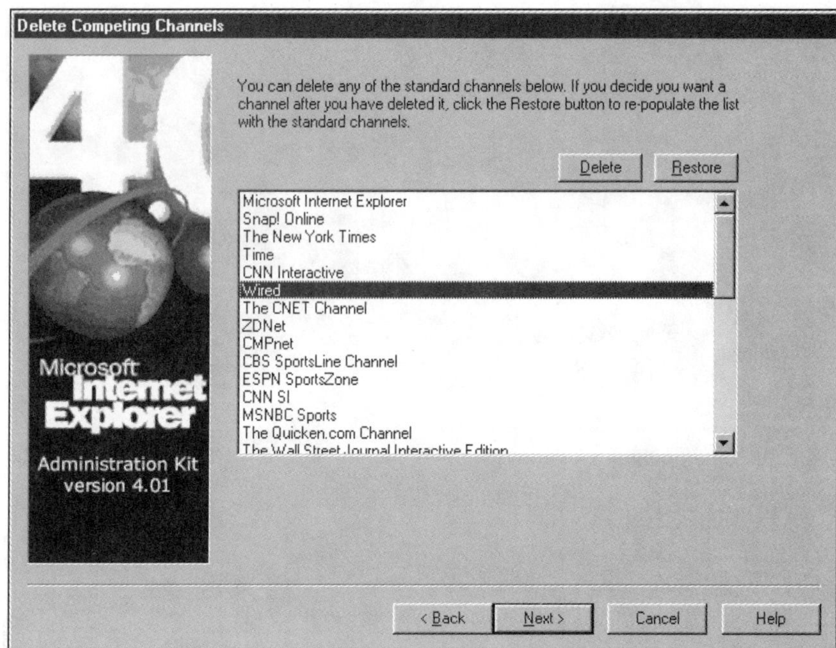

Figure 7.12 Links to competing companies can be deleted.

You can configure proxy servers in a couple ways. You can use Auto-proxy files to automatically set these configuration options. These files have extensions of either .JS or .PAC.

Auto-proxy setting files can be created with a configuration file for a user group. The .JS or .PAC file extension is the identifier for these file types.

The other option is available through the Specify Proxy Settings dialog box, shown in Figure 7.13.

That covers the dialog boxes in Stage 4 that apply to Corporate Administrator mode. The last stage, Stage 5, focuses on customizing the components of your build.

Stage 5: Customizing Components

Several items are of interest in this stage when in Corporate Administrator mode. It's important to note that although these items are not exclusive to running the Internet Explorer Administration Kit in Corporate Administrator mode, the programs involved could easily be tested in a corporate setting.

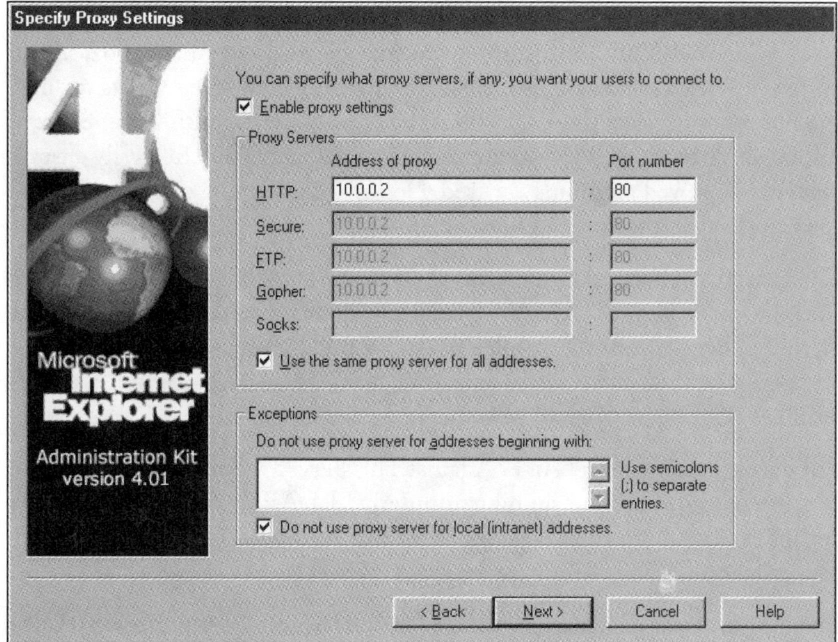

Figure 7.13 Set proxy configurations using the Specify Proxy Settings dialog box.

Because the number and type of dialog boxes varies greatly depending on the type of build you are creating, the following sections cover the most often-used and important configuration options. For this reason, there might be screens displayed during your build that are not discussed here. For more information, refer to the IE Resource Kit.

Some of the most important options in Stage 5 include:

- Specifying users' Outlook Express news and mail settings
- Specifying Lightweight Directory Access Protocol (LDAP) server settings
- Specifying default signatures to provide a corporate disclaimer or signature in Internet newsgroups or email messages
- Specifying system policies and restrictions as well as locking down a variety of application, browser, and system settings

Default corporate disclaimers that are locked in place can be used to meet legal notification requirements.

The first of the Stage 5 dialog boxes that should be examined carefully is the Specify Internet Mail Servers, Domain, And News Server dialog box, shown in Figure 7.14. This dialog box is used to not only enter the settings for mail and news, but to make these selections the default selections. Later in Stage 5, you can ensure that the user cannot make any changes. This effectively ensures that only approved programs are used. Notice at the bottom of the screen that you can also use a secured method of authentication.

The next area of particular interest is the Specify LDAP Server Settings dialog box, shown in Figure 7.15. A few entries on this screen deserve attention. Friendly Name is simply a display name for the user. Home Page means the home page of the LDAP server (not your firm's home page). Search Base determines where in the hierarchy to begin a search.

The checkbox for Check Names Against This Server When Sending Mail can be a useful tool if you are running an internal LDAP server. If your network depends on a public LDAP server, as shown in Figure 7.15, your users will have a long wait while this huge database is checked.

The next important dialog box is the Outlook Express Customizations dialog box, as shown in Figure 7.16. Pay particular attention to the InfoPane section.

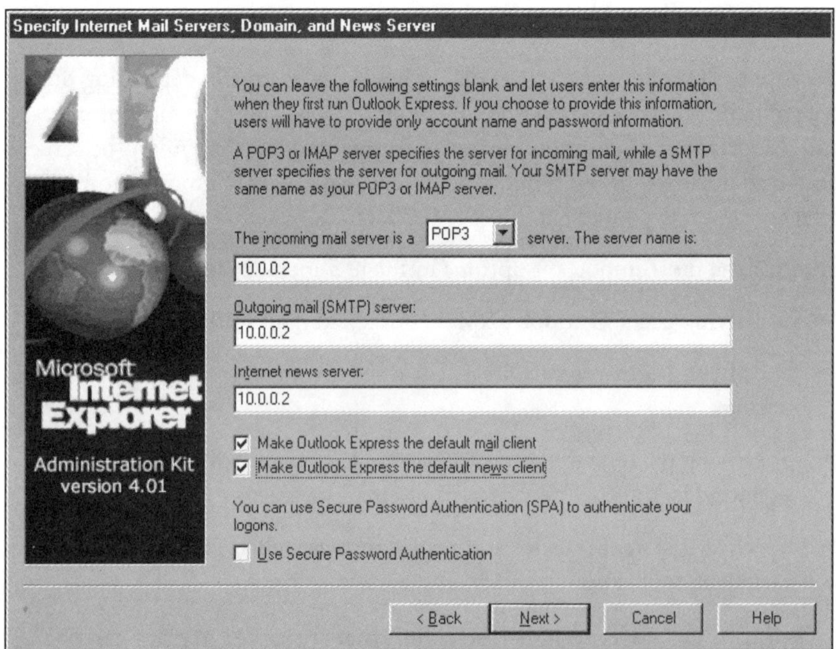

Figure 7.14 Default mail server, domain, and news server settings.

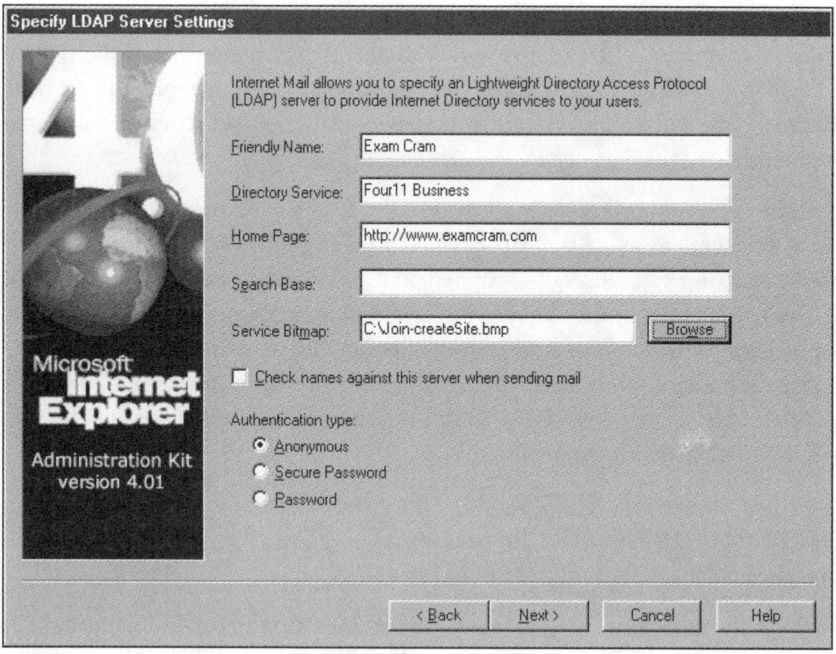

Figure 7.15 Defining LDAP server settings.

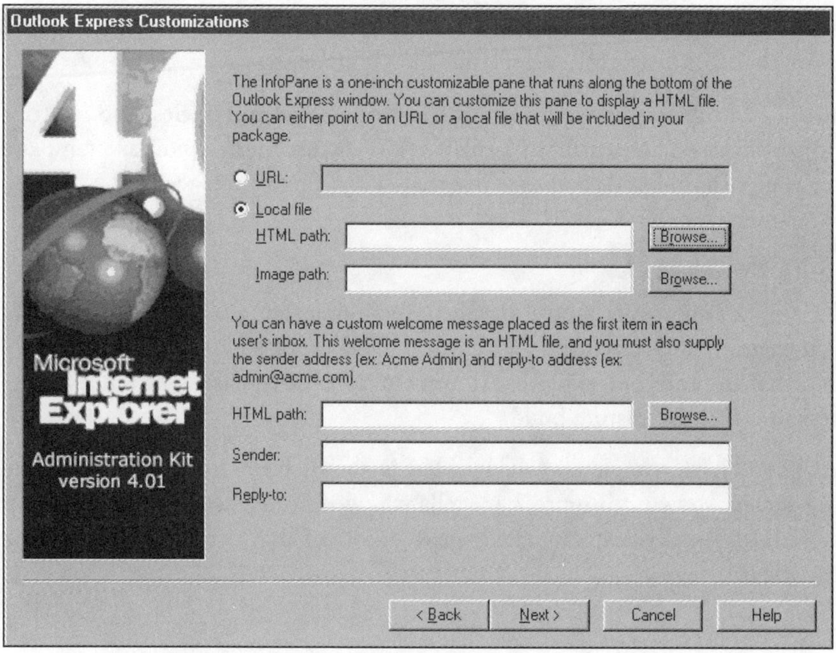

Figure 7.16 The InfoPane is a one-inch pane that displays at the bottom of an Outlook Express window.

The InfoPane can display either a local file or a URL. The display does not expand, so data must be kept to less than one inch. An example of the type of information included in the InfoPane might be local support phone numbers. Because you can enter a URL in this window, this data could be updated frequently.

Another very important dialog box deals with the signature files that are attached to every message sent from the client computer. There is nothing tricky about entering signatures, and many users are already familiar with them. In Corporate Administrator mode, a disclaimer is frequently used to separate employees' views from official company policy. The maximum size is 1K and text only. Entries can be made for email and/or newsgroups, with the same or separate text. From a technical standpoint, there is no magic here. Just be sure you remember that it can be done.

Now it is time to take a look at one of the most interesting parts of the custom build: System Policies And Restrictions. The good news is, this isn't tough, and the custom build is almost complete.

Perhaps the most confusing areas of the Internet Explorer Administration Kit are those that deal with System Policies And Restrictions. The confusion arises not from the creation of policies and restrictions, but from the fact that the Internet Explorer Configuration Wizard looks and operates the same as System Policies And Restrictions in the Profile Manager. This fact has caused more than a little confusion for some IEAK students.

Included in the appendix is a list of the various System Policies And Restrictions options that are currently available. You can use the appendix as a template for your custom builds and to verify that everything is in place.

The Build

Figure 7.17 shows an interesting phenomenon in the IEAK build process. As you examine the screen, notice that the build process happens automatically and that the Internet Explorer Administration Kit actually uses a DOS process to create the custom build.

After you have completed your build, it is almost ready for distribution. The last screen, shown in Figure 7.18, tells you where the custom build has been stored. It's usually best to make a written note of this location before exiting the wizard.

This completes your tour of installing the Internet Explorer Administration Kit in the Corporate Administrator mode. The goal of this chapter is to provide you with a strong foundation based on the Corporate Administrator build that you can expand on when creating other types of builds, which are discussed in other chapters.

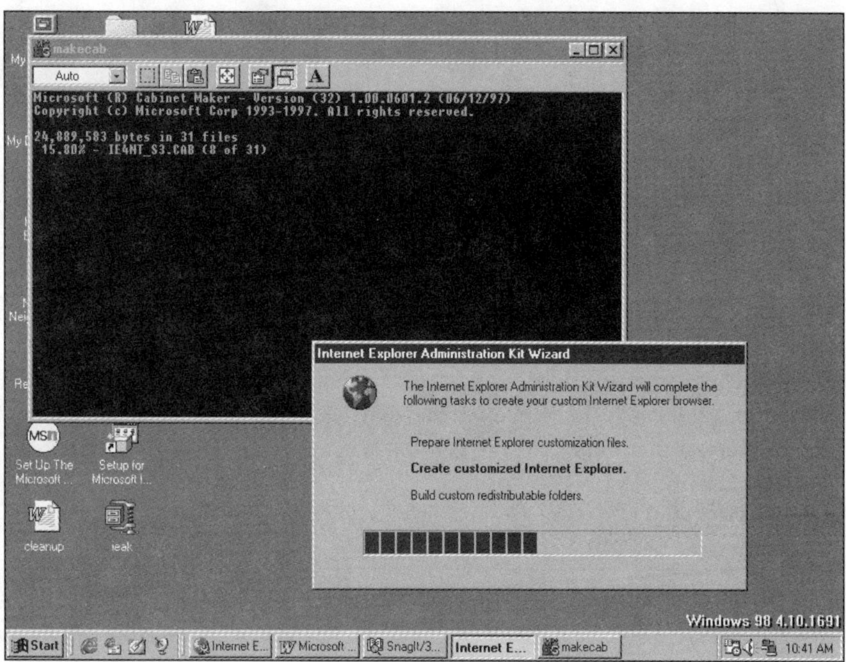

Figure 7.17 Notice that the custom build process opens a DOS window and calls the program Cabinet Maker to create the build.

Figure 7.18 The Internet Explorer Administration Kit displays a window listing the location of the custom build.

Exam Prep Questions

Question 1

When customizing the Internet Explorer Administration Kit using Corporate Administrator mode, which setting(s) can be modified? [Choose all correct answers]

- ❑ a. Security zones
- ❑ b. Proxy settings
- ❑ c. Connection Manager
- ❑ d. Default desktop

The correct answers to this question are a, b, and d. The Corporate Administrator mode is unique in allowing the configuration of proxy server settings. Using policies and restrictions, an administrator can configure user desktops as well as security settings. The Connection Manager is a separate program. Therefore, answer c is incorrect.

Question 2

Your company requires you to restrict user access to several Internet sites by using a proxy server. What settings in the Exceptions window can accomplish your task?

- ❑ a. Server host names (NetBIOS names)
- ❑ b. Local domain names in your intranet
- ❑ c. IP addresses
- ❑ d. Fully Qualified Domain Names

The correct answers to this question are c and d. The Exceptions window can contain Fully Qualified Domain Names, IP addresses, and computer host names. Neither NetBIOS names nor intranet domain names can be added to the Exceptions window to provide this functionality. Therefore, answers a and b are incorrect.

Question 3

You are creating a custom browser package using the Corporate Administrator mode. Company policy declares that some Web sites based on the site's domain are forbidden. Which of the following will allow you to implement these restrictions? [Choose all correct answers]

- ❑ a. Configuration file with a .JS extension
- ❑ b. Configuration file with a .PCA extension
- ❑ c. Configuration file with a .PAC extension
- ❑ d. Configuration file with an .INS extension

The correct answers to this question are a and c. Either JS or PAC files can be used to configure proxy settings. The .PCA extension does not represent a real file type. Therefore, answer b is incorrect. INS files are Auto-configuration files, but not for proxy settings. Therefore, answer d is incorrect.

Question 4

When creating a build of Internet Explorer 4.01 using Corporate Administrator mode, your choices for distribution include downloading, CD-ROM, multiple floppies, and single floppy.

- ❍ a. True
- ❍ b. False

The correct answer to this question is b, False. This answer would have been true if single floppy was omitted from the question. The single floppy option is only available in the ISP mode.

Question 5

Workers in different departments must download components from the Internet. The employees gain access to the Internet from a central Web page that contains hyperlinks to the download sites. Previous experience has shown that some Web sites have been known to contain outdated information, while others have been known to contain adult material.

Required Result:

Prompt the users before downloading ActiveX controls from trusted sites.

Optional Desired Results:

Block user access to sites containing adult material.

Prevent access to sites that have outdated information.

Prevent access to ActiveX controls from untrusted sites.

Proposed Solution:

Place the trusted sites in the Restricted Sites Zone, and place the untrusted sites in the Internet Zone. Set the security level to High for both zones.

Which result does the proposed solution provide?

- ❍ a. The proposed solution provides the required result and all optional desired results.
- ❍ b. The proposed solution provides the required result and only one optional desired result.
- ❍ c. The proposed solution provides only the required result.
- ❍ d. The proposed solution does not produce the required result.

The correct answer to this question is d. This question requires careful reading. Notice the proposed solution called for blocking a trusted site, not an *untrusted* site. Consider this a hint to read your test questions carefully! Furthermore, high security prevents Internet Explorer from downloading ActiveX controls from all sites. Security settings cannot block user access to specific sites. The content advisor will not help you with outdated content. It will only block access based on the language, nudity, sex, and violence ratings of its content. Currently, ratings are set on a voluntary basis by each page's Webmaster.

Question 6

> Your company has decided to standardize the corporate Internet browser and require users to upgrade to Internet Explorer 4.01. Some users have concerns that they will lose their list of favorite Web sites. Which of the following users will need to manually reconstruct their Favorites list in Internet Explorer 4.01?
>
> ❍ a. Netscape users
>
> ❍ b. Internet Explorer 3 users
>
> ❍ c. All users
>
> ❍ d. All users who were not using Netscape or Internet Explorer

The correct answer to this question is d. IE4 automatically imports Favorites from IE3 and Bookmarks from Netscape.

Question 7

> You have an intranet that includes a component download server and an installation server. The component server has been moved to another part of your intranet, but the installation server (which contains the IE4Site\En folder) has remained in its original place. What must you do to provide the installation server with access to the new component download server?
>
> ❍ a. You must update the IE4Sites.dat file.
>
> ❍ b. You must delete the IE4Site\En folder.
>
> ❍ c. You must update the Install.ins file.
>
> ❍ d. You must re-install Internet Explorer 4.01.

The correct answer to this question is a. The local folder holds customizations and settings for your custom browser package. It does not contain the components of the custom browser—it's merely a pointer to a location from which you can download. When the download site specified in the IE4Sites.dat file changes, then the IE4Sites.dat file must be updated to reflect that change.

Question 8

You are creating a custom build of Internet Explorer 4.01 and would like to add a corporate disclaimer to all email messages and news postings. Which of the following will accomplish this?

❍ a. Modifying the INS file in the IEAK Profile Manager.

❍ b. Adding the disclaimer by selecting Include a Signature when creating your custom build.

❍ c. Both a and b.

❍ d. None of the above.

The correct answer to this question is c. Signatures can be added to email messages and news postings using the IEAK Profile Manager or the build wizard.

Need To Know More?

Microsoft Press: *Microsoft Internet Explorer Resource Kit.* Redmond, WA, 1998. ISBN 1-57321-842-2. Part 9 discusses deployment and maintenance and covers much of the material in this chapter.

TechNet. Searches on keywords within the Internet Explorer and Internet Explorer Administration Kit areas provide detailed information on both general build options and the Corporate Administrator mode.

The Microsoft Knowledge Base provides detailed information on all products, including Internet Explorer and Internet Explorer Administration Kit (including Corporate Administrator mode and general build options). The Microsoft Knowledge Base is located at **http://support.microsoft.com/support/a.asp?M=S**.

8

Internet Service Provider Mode

Terms you'll need to understand:

- √ DNS (Domain Name System)
- √ GUID (globally unique identifer)
- √ InfoPane
- √ INS
- √ JS
- √ Lightweight Directory Access Protocol (LDAP)
- √ PAC
- √ Permissions
- √ Security Zones
- √ System Policies And Restrictions

Techniques you'll need to master:

- √ Customizing signatures
- √ Proxy server settings
- √ Restrictions

In this chapter, we explore the Internet Explorer 4 Administration Kit (IEAK) in the Internet Service Provider (ISP) mode. We also show you what you need to know to master Security Zones. Finally, we explore the unique way to install IE with a single floppy, which is available only in ISP mode.

Installing Internet Explorer (ISP Mode)

As you learned in Chapter 7, there is always good news and bad news when dealing with IEAK build modes. The good news is that the exam likely will contain very little about ISP mode. The bad news is that we still have to cover this topic.

When creating a custom build for Internet Explorer 4.01 in ISP mode, you can have a single-floppy build, which points to the URL at your site. This option is unique to ISP mode. An ISP can also distribute with multiple floppies or CD-ROM. An ISP, and only an ISP, can distribute in these three ways; you cannot use a local download site as you can in Corporate Administrator mode.

You will need a solid understanding of Security Zones for the exam, so let's examine Security Zones first and then do a quick custom build of the IEAK in ISP mode so that we can see a few screens we have not seen before. Let's also change how the AVS is set up so that the differences you see between Corporate Administrator mode and ISP mode give you a solid understanding of Automatic Version Synchronization (AVS).

Security Zones

Security Zones, when properly set up, are an invaluable asset. Conversely, haphazardly created Security Zones invite disaster. Just as in learning how to correctly build custom versions of IE, you must learn how to set up Security Zones, or they will be the source of untold grief. The first trick centers on understanding the types of Security Zones and what they are designed to do. Let's examine these now.

Overview Of Security Zones

The idea behind Security Zones is to allow the system administrator to create different groups of Web sites that a user can visit safely. Microsoft calls each of these groups a *zone*. Each zone has different levels of what is allowed and, in some cases, what is not allowed. Internet Explorer includes four predefined zones, as follows:

- **Local Intranet Zone** This is the default for all sites within a local area network (LAN). The Local Intranet Zone is the home to Web applications that require access to a user's hard disk. Because sites in this zone have access to a user's hard disk, this zone grants a high degree of trust.
- **Trusted Sites Zone** This zone is used to specify Internet sites that you know you can trust. Examples of such sites are vendors you do business with regularly and other servers for your company located off-site.
- **Internet Zone** This zone includes all sites that are neither trusted nor restricted. By default, the Internet Zone is set to medium security, meaning that you are prompted to allow many actions that could damage your system. In addition, you are not able to download unsigned ActiveX controls. See Table 8.1 for more information on the configuration of this, and all, default zones.
- **Restricted Sites Zone** This zone is reserved for sites that you know for sure are bad places to go. The security level for this zone is set to high, meaning that most ActiveX options are completely disabled.

There is also a fifth, implied zone—the Local Machine Zone. Most administrators are not aware of this zone because it is not configurable. However, this lack of configuration within the Local Machine Zone does not preclude it from being a zone. A Local Machine Zone can be configured only in the Registry.

The Local Machine Zone is not a major focus of the test, but be sure to know that there are five Security Zones, not four.

By default, the Local Machine Zone has almost zero security, meaning that everything is trusted. As an administrator, you can extend the Local Machine Zone security to restrict network or other drives if you need to.

The goal of Security Zones is to provide an easy way to set an appropriate level of security for most common environments. Although each zone is configurable, each does come with a default feature set. Experience shows that unless there is a driving need to modify these zones, it is best to leave them set as the defaults. The defaults are described in Table 8.1.

You can customize the default settings for your particular needs. Now that the idea of Security Zones has been laid out, it is time to set up some Security Zones.

Table 8.1 The default Security Zone settings.

Security Option	Low Level	Medium Level	High Level
ActiveX controls safe for scripting	Enable	Enable	Enable
Run ActiveX controls	Enable	Enable	Disable
Download signed ActiveX controls	Enable	Prompt	Disable
Download unsigned ActiveX controls	Prompt	Disable	Disable
Start and script ActiveX not marked as safe	Prompt	Prompt	Disable
Java permissions	Low safety	High safety	High safety
Active scripts	Enable	Enable	Enable
Java applets scripts	Enable	Enable	Enable
File downloads	Enable	Enable	Disable
Font downloads	Enable	Enable	Prompt
User Logins	Automatic	Automatic in intranet with current user name/password	Prompt for user name/password
Send nonencrypted form data	Enable	Prompt	Prompt
Open applications from an IFrame	Enable	Prompt	Disable
Install desktop components	Enable	Prompt	Disable
Drag-and-drop support	Enable	Enable	Disable
Channel permissions	Low safety	Medium safety	High safety

Setting Up Security Zones

It is easy to see what a machine's current Security Zone configuration is by using the IEAK Configuration Wizard or the IEAK Profile Manager. You can also check this by selecting Internet Options from the View menu in IE and selecting the Security tab, as shown in Figure 8.1.

If you have a site that is referenced by both its IP address and its domain name (e.g., 200.200.200.200 and **www.examcram.com**, respectively), it is imperative to configure both references to the same zone. Failing to include both methods in a zone could lead to security problems. For example, if 200.200.200.200 were set as a Trusted Sites Zone, **www.examcram.com** could still belong in the Internet Zone, which offers fewer privileges.

At times, you might need to customize a particular setting to fit a particular environment. This is where the Custom setting option comes into play. Figure 8.2 shows the Security Settings dialog box, which is accessed by selecting Custom and clicking on Settings.

Note: Security settings in IE4 are not the same as those in IE3. This means that any upgrade from IE3 will not preserve security settings.

Internet Zone

By default, unless another option is selected, a site is assumed to be in the Internet Zone. What that means for a particular site is shown in Table 8.1.

Local Intranet Zone

Because the Local Intranet Zone has a security rating that can otherwise be labeled nil, it is important to be sure that sites within this zone are secured behind a firewall that has been properly configured. Both parts of that last sentence are important: a real firewall *and* a properly configured one. A firewall that is installed wide open is the same as not installing a firewall at all.

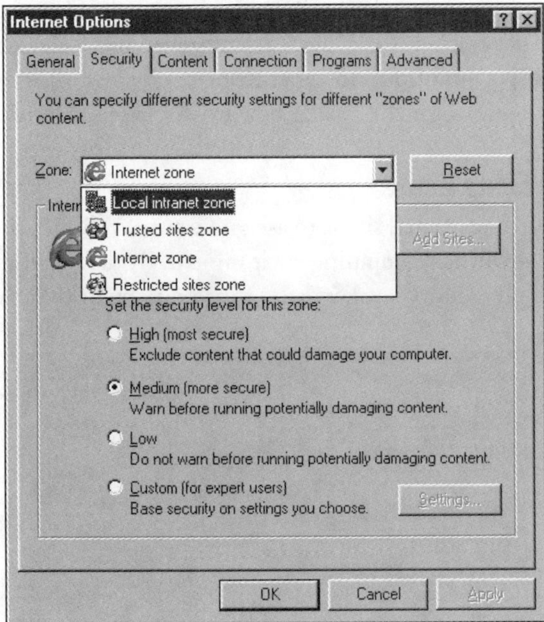

Figure 8.1 Viewing the default current Security Zone configuration.

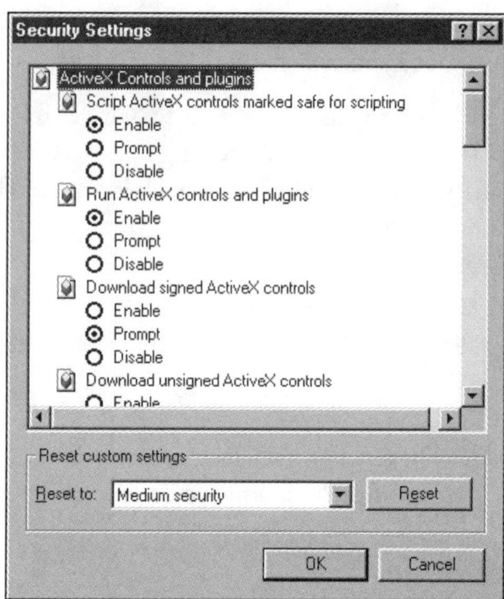

Figure 8.2 The advanced options for the Custom Security Settings.

If you do not make any changes, the default Local Intranet Zone is made up of local domains and any proxy exceptions that are in the Specify Proxy Setting dialog box. Setting up site configuration for the Local Internet Zone is easy. To do so, select View|Internet Options|Security. Then select Local Intranet Zone, and the Add Sites button will convert from grayed out to selectable. Click on Add Sites to display the Local Intranet Zone dialog box, shown in Figure 8.3. The checkbox options for this dialog box are discussed in Table 8.2.

Restricted Sites Zone

The idea behind a restricted site is to assign known Web sites that are harmful to the well-being of your computing environment. By default, restricted sites are placed in the high security level, which offers only the most secure operations.

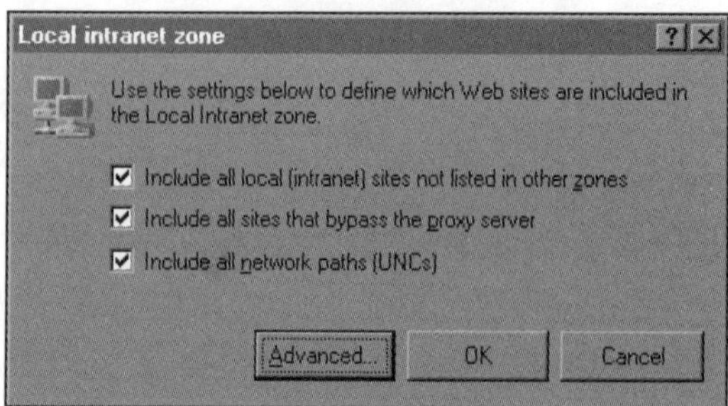

Figure 8.3 The three configuration options for the Local Intranet Zone.

Table 8.2 The configuration options for the Local Intranet Zone.

Option	Description
Include all local (intranet) sites not listed in other zones	These sites have names that do not include periods. For example, **http://home.microsoft.com** has periods and therefore is not local. This rule applies to files as well as to URLs.
Include all sites that bypass the proxy server	Typically, when using TCP/IP as the primary protocol, it is wise to exclude the local machines that have IP addresses. If you have some special reason for including local machines in a proxy configuration, this setting should be cleared. If there is no proxy server, this setting has no effect.
Include all network paths (UNCs)	Network paths are usually used in a LAN environment and should be made part of the Local Intranet Zone. If you have a specific reason not to include them, the checkbox for this option should be unchecked.

Because of performance restrictions, Web pages displayed from a restricted site might not function correctly or at all.

Trusted Sites Zone

By default, a trusted site is granted a low security level. A *trusted site* is one that you do business with regularly. The common term for this type of commerce is *extranet*. Typically, an extranet is used to place orders for goods or services, to check on delivery schedules, and to perform other normal business functions that otherwise would take more effort to coordinate. If none of the above fit your needs, go to a custom zone, described in the next section.

Custom Zone

A custom zone allows you to fine-tune operations to fit any need that simply doesn't fit into the predefined Security Zones. An example of custom controls was shown in Figure 8.2. Many custom controls are available, but listing all the choices here would not help you much in your studies. Instead, we encourage you to look at the custom setting on your browser. Before we look at building with the IEAK in the ISP mode, let's tie up some loose ends.

Other Considerations

By now, you are likely familiar with the different types of user authentication, because you have already seen those used with Windows NT or Internet Information Server. A quick reminder follows:

- **Anonymous login** Sets security to zero.
- **Prompt for user name and password** Checks the user ID and password supplied by the user.
- **Automatic login only in Intranet Zone** Queries users for IDs and passwords in other zones. After a value has been entered, the values are used throughout the session.
- **Automatic logon with current username and password** Uses NT Challenge/Response authentication.
- **IFrames** This is not something you need to be concerned with. However, you should know that forms can submit pages in different ways. SSL layers are not affected and are always allowed. Non-SSL data submission has three options:
    - **Enable** Allows information on pages in this zone to be submitted without user intervention.
    - **Prompt** Asks the user whether sending information is OK.
    - **Disable** Prevents information that uses HTML from being submitted.

This concludes our discussion of the important points of the ISP mode. Now, we'll walk through an actual build, where we'll see how this mode differs from the other modes. Armed with this book and some experience in custom builds, you should not fear IEAK. That having been said, it is time to create a custom build with IEAK in ISP mode.

Custom Builds With IEAK In ISP mode

Stage 1: Entering IE4 Build Information

1. The first step in creating any build with IEAK is to enter your customization key. Which key you enter determines which build mode you are able to use. Figure 8.4 shows that we have selected the Service Provider (ISP) mode.
2. Now comes the fun part: waiting. Even if AVS is disabled, you must select a download site and continue to check your files as if AVS were turned on. If you are on a 28.8K modem, take a coffee break or, even better, get a meal. The computer will wait for you.

   With AVS turned off, the only difference is that all your files have the exclamation point (!) in the yellow triangle. As we saw in Chapter 7, you

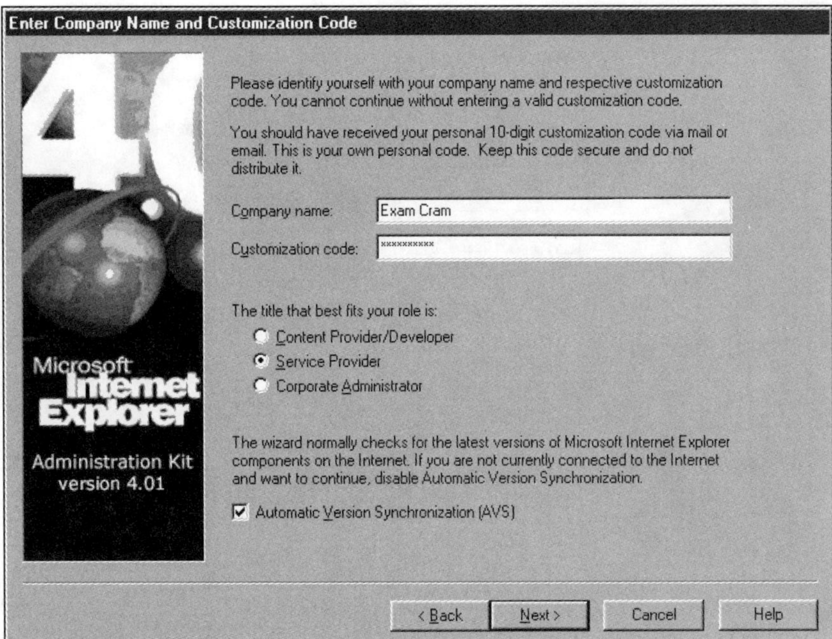

Figure 8.4 Beginning a build in ISP mode with AVS enabled.

must perform an AVS the first time you perform a build. If you have updated your files recently, you need to wait only a few seconds for AVS to verify that your files are up to date. Figure 8.5 shows the beginning of a build with AVS disabled. Because disabling AVS does not really save time, keep the peace of mind that comes from knowing the exact status of the components of your custom build, and leave AVS turned on.

3. The next step, selecting a language, is the same in all custom builds. The next screen, shown in Figure 8.6, is where you specify the setup options and where a new option is revealed: specifying a single floppy for installation.

Stage 2: Specifying Active Setup Parameters

In this stage, you must select a download site for your updates even if AVS is turned off. After clicking on Next, you will see the results of AVS. As shown in Figure 8.5, with AVS turned off, everything is reported out of date. Stage 2 continues the same as all the other builds (see Chapter 7 for details).

Stage 3: Customizing Active Setup

The first part of Stage 3 parallels that of the other two builds. The next critical juncture comes deep into Stage 3, when the chance to specify download URLs

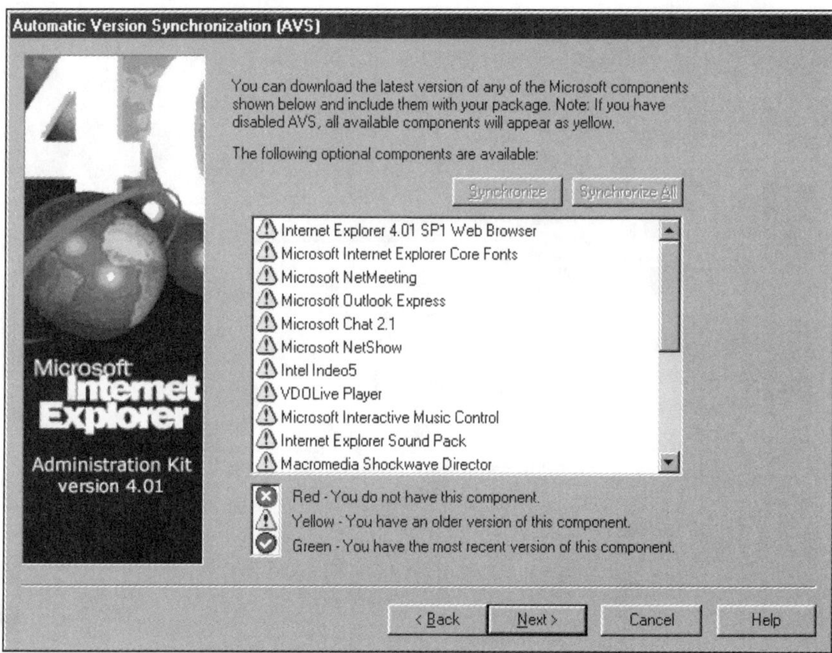

Figure 8.5 The start of a build with AVS disabled.

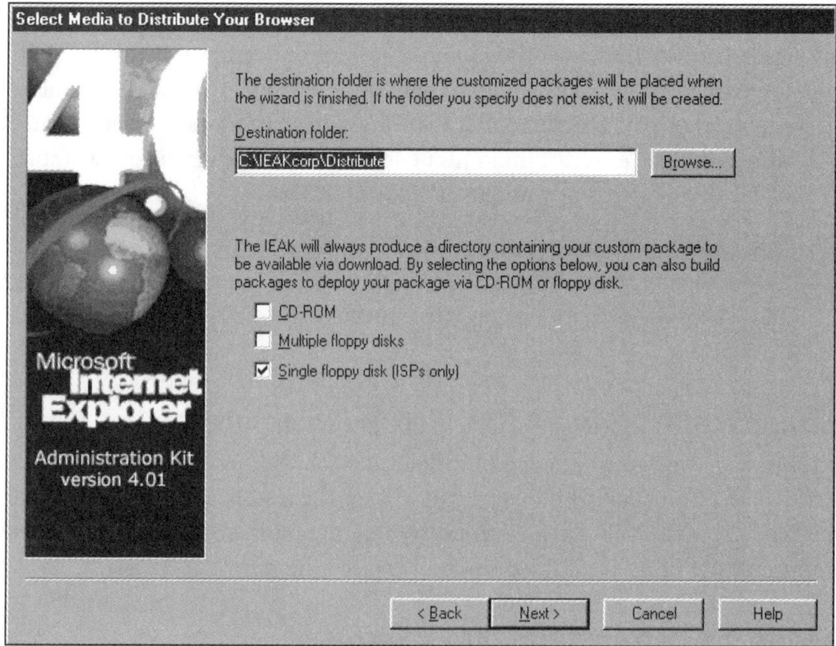

Figure 8.6 Creating a single floppy in ISP mode.

comes into play. This option is vital if you are using a single-floppy mode. Internet Explorer and related programs cannot fit on a single floppy. Therefore, the single-disk mode is not much more than a 400K setup file with a set of pointers indicating where the programs reside. This pointer file is a generic file named *signup.isp*. You will find sample ISP files within the IE Resource Kit with names such as *signup1.isp* and *signup2.isp*. You can select one of these samples, but be sure to rename it *signup.ISP*. When your new client initiates a setup, their system will create a unique INS file.

As you move through Stage 3, remember that you can configure items (e.g., your own channel in the Channel Guide) and create a custom help file that can be used by Internet Explorer 4.01.

Stage 4: Customizing The Browser

Stage 4 is largely identical in all the builds. The last wizard page in Stage 4 reveals the Customize Security Zone Settings radio button and a Modify Setting bar. This is your chance to update the Security Zones as you see fit for this custom build.

Stage 5: Customizing Components

This stage deals with specifying settings of many types: news, mail, server, application, browser, and system. Now is a great time to include customizations such as the InfoPane. If you don't remember the details of this stage, refer to Chapter 7.

The main thing you should remember about ISP mode after walking through this process and reading this chapter is that ISP mode is the only mode that allows you to custom build a package with a single floppy.

Content Provider/ Developer Mode

So far, we've discussed only two of the three modes of the IEAK Wizard: Corporate Administrator and ISP. The remaining mode, Content Provider/ Developer, offers the fewest configuration options for the build and most closely resembles ISP mode. In fact, you can use the customization code for ISP or Corporate Administrator to create a build in Content Provider/Developer mode. Because you've already been through builds in both of the other modes, Table 8.3 lists only the stages, dialog boxes, and options that are available through Content Provider/Developer mode.

Table 8.3 Content Provider/Developer mode options.

Stage	Dialog box	Option
1	Enter Company Name and Customization Keycode	All
	Select a Platform	Windows 95/NT4.0
		Windows 3.11/ WFW/NT 3.51
	Select a Language	All
	Media Type to Distribute the Browser	Destination folder for your Custom Build
		Multiple Floppies
		CD-ROM
2	Select a Download Location	All
	Automatic Version Synchronization	All
	Active Setup Components	All
	Specify Trusted Publishers	All
3	Autorun Screen for CD-ROM installs	All
	Customize Active Setup Wizard	All
	Custom Component Install	All
	Select Install Option	All
	Specify Download URLs	All
	Choose Version Number	All
4	Customize the Window Title and Toolbar Background	All
	Customize the Start & Search Pages	All
	Specify an Online Support Page for the Browser	All
	Favorites Folder and Links Customization	All
	Customize the Welcome Message and Desktop Wallpaper	All
	Customize the Active Channel Bar	All
	Delete Competing Channels	All
	Add a Custom Desktop Component	All
	User Agent String Customization	All
5	None	
6	System Policies And Restrictions	Internet Settings
		Microsoft Chat

Exam Prep Questions

Question 1

You are creating a custom build of Internet Explorer 4.01 using an Internet Service Provider (ISP) customization code. Which of the following best describes how users will access your sign-up server?

- ❍ a. A generic ISP file will be used to arrive at the sign-up server. A unique INS file will be created when the new user begins creating an account.
- ❍ b. A generic INS file will be used to arrive at the sign-up server. A generic ISP file will be created when the new user begins creating an account.
- ❍ c. A unique ISP file will be used to arrive at the sign-up server. A unique INS file will be created when the new user begins creating an account.
- ❍ d. A unique ISP file will be used to arrive at the sign-up server. A generic INS file will be created when the new user begins creating an account.

The correct answer is a. New installs are pointed to the sign-up server by the generic ISP file. You can find a sample file in the Resource Kit to create your own ISP file. Usually, all users sign up using the same ISP file. Unique INS files are created for each user when they begin the sign-up process.

Question 2

When creating a custom build of Internet Explorer 4.01 in the Service Provider (ISP) mode, which choices are available for distributing your custom build?

- ❍ a. Single floppy
- ❍ b. Multiple floppy
- ❍ c. CD-ROM
- ❍ d. All of the above

The correct answer is d. Only ISP mode allows a single floppy as well as multiple floppies or CD-ROM. The other two modes—Corporate Administrator mode and Content Provider/Developer mode—require either multiple floppies or CD-ROM.

Question 3

You want to make signing up with your firm's ISP business as easy as possible for new users. You plan to use the silent download option so that an IE4 install appears automatically on your client's computers. You tell this to the CIO, who tells you to go forward. You find that this works great.

❍ a. True

❍ b. False

The correct answer is False. Only the Corporate Administrator mode allows for a silent install. This mode is not available in either ISP or Content Provider/Developer mode.

Question 4

You are creating a custom build of Internet Explorer 4.01 with an ISP customization code. You have created a custom package for Internet Explorer 4.01. The people you are sending the custom build to are not connected to the Internet. Which distribution method would be appropriate if a distribution server exists?

❍ a. Multiple floppies

❍ b. CD-ROM

❍ c. Single floppy

❍ d. All of the above

The correct answer is c. In ISP mode, the most effective choice for distributing Internet Explorer 4.01 is to use the single-floppy method. Note that in this question, a distribution server is available. If a distribution server were not available, the custom build would have to be distributed on either CD-ROM or multiple floppies.

Question 5

As an ISP, you have made the decision to offer Internet Explorer 4.01 to all your customers. Some of your customers are concerned that they will lose their Favorites list of Web sites. Which of the following users will need to manually reconstruct their Favorites list in IE4?

❍ a. Netscape users

❍ b. IE3 users

❍ c. All users

❍ d. All users who were not using Netscape or Internet Explorer

The correct answer is d. Internet Explorer 4.01 will automatically convert Netscape and IE bookmarks or Favorites. Other packages have no conversion option.

Need To Know More?

Microsoft Press: *Microsoft Internet Explorer Resource Kit.* Redmond, WA, 1998. ISBN 1-57231-842-2. Chapter 27 discusses Security Zones; Part 9 discusses creating custom builds.

Search the TechNet CD-ROM using keywords within the IE and IEAK areas, both of which provide detailed information on Webcasting and the Windows Desktop Update.

The Microsoft Knowledge Base provides detailed information on all products, including IE and IEAK. It also provides detailed information on both Webcasting and the Windows Desktop Update. Search for the keywords *Webcasting*, *desktop update*, and *CDF* for detailed information. The Microsoft Knowledge Base is located at **http://support.microsoft.com/support/a.asp?M=S**.

9

Optimization And Troubleshooting

Terms you'll need to understand:

- √ Caching
- √ Troubleshooting
- √ TCP/IP (Transmission Control Protocol/Internet Protocol)
- √ IPCONFIG
- √ WINIPCFG
- √ PING
- √ TRACERT
- √ ARP (Address Resolution Protocol)
- √ Network Monitor
- √ NSLOOKUP

Techniques you'll need to master:

- √ Understanding the troubleshooting process
- √ Optimizing network resources
- √ Troubleshooting the IE4 deployment process
- √ Identifying common network connection failures
- √ Diagnosing and resolving common TCP/IP connectivity problems

Optimizing resources and troubleshooting problems with IE4 are key to a successful IE deployment. In this chapter, you'll take a look at the available methods for optimizing network and system resources. You'll also learn about the tools and methods available to troubleshoot a variety of connection and deployment problems.

Optimizing Resources

IE4 has extremely powerful capabilities. That is great for the end user, but not so great for network resources. Preventative measures are crucial to making sure that the use of these capabilities does not get out of hand. Following are some strategies for optimizing network resources:

- Phased deployment
- Managed Webcasting
- Multicasting
- Caching

Phased Deployment

Administrators may want to consider doing a phased rollout of IE4, providing users with additional functionality with each phase. When users receive all of IE4's functionality at once, it can seem overwhelming.

For example, a user might subscribe three levels deep to multiple Web sites and only view the downloaded information once or twice. The subscriptions would continue to download at every specified interval, even though the user has forgotten about them.

Introducing one piece of functionality at a time prevents misuse of IE4's functionality. During each phase, administrators can provide end-user education on site subscriptions, channels, and the Active Desktop.

Managed Webcasting

Managed Webcasting is a set of options used to control potentially network-hazardous functionality. Chapter 4 discusses these options in detail, but the following list highlights IEAK's Managed Webcasting options:

- **Predefine subscription and channel settings** Using the IEAK, you can set the maximum amount of data that is downloaded, the maximum number of subscriptions, the download time intervals, and the maximum depth level allowed for subscriptions.

- **Lock down the ability to download content** Perhaps the greatest benefit of using Webcasting is the ability to download information for offline viewing. Although this is beneficial to mobile users and ISP users, it might simply cause bandwidth issues for the average corporate network. Instead of downloading multiple levels of content, it might be more efficient to configure IE to send an email message when a site has been updated or to notify the user via the red gleam on the Favorites icon.
- **Completely disable the subscriptions and channels features** Within the Internet Restrictions section of the Profile Manager, administrators can choose to disable subscriptions and channels features in order to optimize network resources.
- **Configure users' browsers to update information only during off-peak hours** This reduces the daily network congestion caused by the increased Internet traffic.
- **Include a network-friendly Active Desktop and Active Channels** Using the IEAK Wizard, you can include preconfigured Active Desktop and Active Channels in your IE package. To reduce network traffic, you might want to install the Active Desktop file locally and include only channels that are deemed network-friendly.

Another option available for managing Webcasting on the network is to require Web site administrators to use a CDF file, which specifies how frequently a user can download the Web site and what content the user can download. A corporate intranet Web site policy that mandates a CDF for all intranet Web sites enables users to download the most important and worthwhile information, rather than an entire site.

Multicasting

Streaming audio and video with multimedia tools, such as Microsoft NetShow, use an enormous amount of network bandwidth. By implementing multicasting on the network, bandwidth overhead is dramatically reduced.

Currently, the two most popular types of multimedia traffic are unicast and broadcast:

- **Unicast** Separate copies of the data are sent to each client that requests it.
- **Broadcast** One copy of the data is sent to all clients on the network, regardless of whether the client requests it.

In a multicast environment, one copy of data is sent to only the clients requesting it. Therefore, multicasting minimizes the demand for bandwidth by not sending multiple copies of data unnecessarily and by not sending data to clients who do not want it.

Caching

Internet caching refers to the act of storing objects locally for later use. Caching helps minimize network congestion by enabling users to retrieve Web pages locally rather than having to fetch them from the Internet. There are two kinds of caching that affect how Internet Explorer retrieves content: local caching and proxy server caching.

Local Caching

When users browse the Internet, accessed files are placed in the \Windows\Temporary Internet Files directory. To view Internet Explorer's caching options, follow these steps:

1. From within IE, choose View|Internet Options.
2. In the General tab under Temporary Internet Files, click on the Settings button.

Three caching options are available to you (see Figure 9.1):

- **Every Visit To The Page** Internet Explorer will never retrieve Web pages from the local cache. Instead, it will retrieve content from the Internet without storing any pages locally. However, it will still store image files and other file types in the Temporary Internet Files folder.

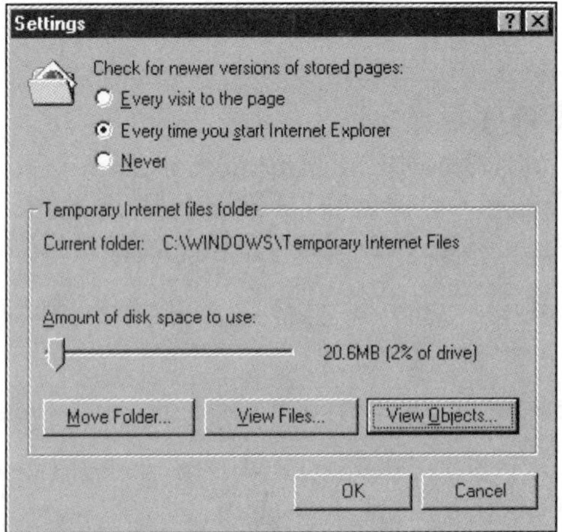

Figure 9.1 Temporary Internet Files Settings dialog box.

- **Every Time You Start Internet Explorer** Within one browser session, IE will check only for a newer version of the page during the first visit. Upon subsequent requests for the page, the page will be retrieved from the local cache. When IE is closed and restarted, the process repeats.
- **Never** Internet Explorer will always retrieve Web pages from its cache whenever possible, even when Internet Explorer is restarted.

The second option—Every Time You Start Internet Explorer—is the default. Although the Never option seems the most network friendly, it is not always the smartest choice, because choosing this option keeps users from obtaining pages that have been updated on the server.

Proxy Server Caching

Although a proxy server's main objective is to shield users on a corporate network from the Internet, its caching functionality has an added benefit of preventing heavy usage of the WAN connection bandwidth. Proxy servers, such as Microsoft Proxy 2, store accessed pages within its caching structure. You can also choose to manually download Web content into its cache.

When a user browses the Internet through a proxy server and the file resides in the proxy's cache, the file will be retrieved from the proxy's cache. This provides the following benefits:

- **Minimizes network traffic** After an object has been downloaded from the Internet, subsequent users will retrieve that object from the cache instead of requesting the same object across a remote network connection.
- **Provides faster access** Typically, a proxy cache resides much closer to an end user than the remote Web server, so the access speed is noticeably faster.

If the file does not exist in the proxy's cache, the proxy uses HTTP to request the file from the Internet.

Troubleshooting Deployment Failures

When installing IE4, two log files are created in the \Windows directory: IE4 Setup Log.txt and Active Setup Log.txt. If a problem occurs in the first stage of Setup, view the IE4 Setup Log file. It contains details on the first phase of Setup when the IE core files are installed.

The Active Setup Log provides an overview of the Setup process, including the download and installation of IE and other components. Search for the word *error* or *fail* in the Active Setup Log.txt file to find setup errors. Look for the following common active setup errors:

- **Failure to access a file** Make sure that the file exists and is accessible on the Web server.
- **CAB signing failure** If you see *TestSigned* in the log file, it means that a test certificate was used to sign the CAB files. Use SETREG.EXE to set the users' systems to accept test certificates.
- **CIF/CAB file size discrepancy** If the file sizes do not match, installation might fail.

Common Installation Errors

Some installation errors can almost be expected when deploying new technology. A proactive approach to troubleshooting and resolving the problems is very important.

IE4.txt contains information about known issues with IE4. To view the most updated version of this document, you can access it via the Web at **http://www.microsoft.com/iesupport/content/readme/iew95.htm**.

Also, Microsoft commonly provides Service Releases, which are sets of patches and updates for Internet Explorer. Service Releases are provided no more than once per quarter.

Common installation errors include:

- Wininet.dll and Run.dll errors
- Cannot access download site
- Red X marks next to components
- The Uninstall feature is disabled

Wininet.dll And Run.dll Errors

When users delete the Wininet.dll and Run.dll shared DLL files or the files are corrupted, the IE4 installation process will fail. If this happens, there is nothing wrong with the IE4 package—the operating system itself is corrupt. Reinstalling the operating system is usually the best way to fix this problem.

Cannot Access Download Site

The following error message occurs when the download site is too busy to service the download request:

Setup Was Unable to Download Information About Available Installation Sites

To correct this situation, first verify that the user is connected to the Internet and can access the URL. Then, depending on whether multiple download sites are set up, try downloading IE from a different download site or having the user try at a less busy time.

Red X Marks

Red X marks might appear next to each of the items listed in the IE4 Setup Install list. The following error might also occur:

Could Not Open... or Could Not Load... File_Name

Table 9.1 shows the possible causes and resolutions for this error.

Uninstall Feature Disabled

When users already have IE4 on their systems and the Uninstall feature is grayed out, the users will see the following message when attempting to reinstall IE4:

You are upgrading a version of Internet Explorer 4.0 in which the uninstall feature has been disabled.

This message does not actually stop the installation process; however, the Uninstall feature within Add/Remove Programs will remain disabled. This problem is usually caused by missing or corrupt Setup files. In some cases, IE must be removed using the ieremove.exe utility. Otherwise, the operating system must be installed in a different directory in order to reinstall the appropriate files.

Table 9.1 Resolving errors displaying as red X marks.

Possible Cause	Resolution
There is not enough free disk space.	Increase the amount of free disk space.
Another program is using a file that IE is attempting to copy to the hard drive.	Close all other programs before running Setup again.
One or more of the installation files is corrupt.	Re-download the Setup files into the \IE4.0 Setup Files folder.
The machine has lost its connection to the download site.	Reconnect to the Internet and check your proxy settings or verify that the download site is still available.

Other Installation Failures

In addition to the common error messages just covered, there are two additional common problems—Active Desktop Disabled and Failure of the Floppy Distribution Method—that can affect users.

Active Desktop Disabled

If users install IE preconfigured with Active Desktop, but Active Desktop is disabled, there could be a conflicting language issue. This problem occurs when users install a different language version of IE than the language version of their operating system. For example, if you deployed an English version of IE4 to users who have a non-English version of Windows 95, they will not be able to view the Active Desktop. The only way to correct this problem is to uninstall IE4, then reinstall a version of IE in which the language matches the operating system language.

Failure Of Floppy Distribution Method

The IE4Site directory specified in the download site URL should automatically have appended itself to that URL. A common mistake when building an IE package is to manually place the IE4Site directory there before the IEAK Configuration Wizard completes. Doing this will cause the installation to fail as soon as Setup searches for the download site URL. To correct this, you must run the wizard again to create a new build.

Troubleshooting Network Connection Failures

TCP/IP (Transmission Control Protocol/Internet Protocol) is a suite of protocols that define how machines on the Internet talk to one another. All Internet users must be TCP/IP-enabled and each machine on the Internet must have a unique IP address. Fortunately, Microsoft provides some tools and tips to help troubleshoot connection failures.

Tools For Troubleshooting Network Connection Failures

Windows 95 and Windows NT come with several built-in tools that help diagnose network connection failures. The most common tools used for TCP/IP-related troubleshooting are:

- PING
- IPCONFIG and WINIPCFG

- TRACERT
- Network Monitor
- ARP
- NSLOOKUP
- Telnet

PING

PING is a command-line utility that tests to see if a host on a TCP/IP network is reachable. You can use PING to test network, as well as host, connectivity.

To use PING, at the command prompt, type

```
PING IP_address
```

where **IP_address** is the IP address of the host you want to reach.

A set of replies from the IP address should reveal that you are connected to the Internet and the host is reachable. However, PING can also respond with one of the following error messages:

- **Request Timed Out** The host is not reachable.
- **Destination Net Unreachable** You either are not connected to the Internet or a proxy server or firewall is prohibiting a successful PING.
- **Bad IP Address** Your DNS server could be down or configured improperly.

IPCONFIG And WINIPCFG

These utilities provide users with their own IP configuration information. To obtain your IP configuration information, go to a command prompt, then:

- Windows NT users should run IPCONFIG.EXE.
- Windows 95 users should run WINIPCFG.EXE.

To review advanced IP configuration, run the appropriate IP configuration utility with the **/ALL** switch. For example, Windows 95 users can run **WINIPCFG /ALL**. Among other benefits, using the IP configuration with the **/ALL** switch provides you with the following information, as shown in Figure 9.2:

- Host Name
- DNS Servers

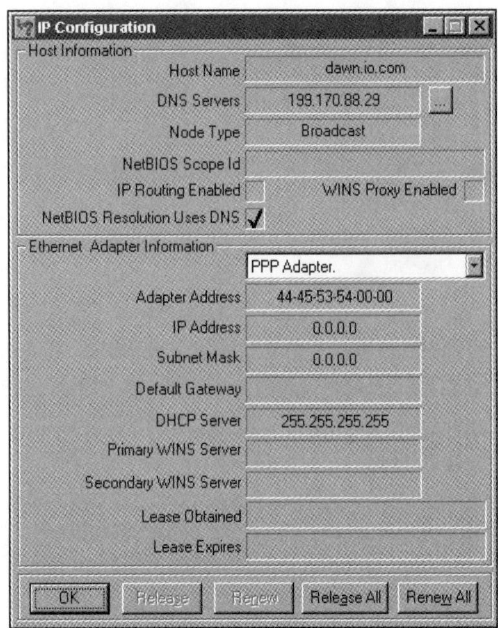

Figure 9.2 WINIPCFG is the TCP/IP configuration utility for Windows 95.

- IP Address
- Subnet Mask
- Default Gateway
- DHCP Server
- WINS Servers

This information can be extremely useful in the troubleshooting process.

TRACERT

The **TRACERT** (trace route) command is a utility used to determine the route a request takes to reach another computer. To use the **TRACERT** command to trace a route, go to a command prompt and type

```
TRACERT IP_address,
```

where **IP_address** is the IP address of the other computer.

> *Note: When using* **TRACERT***, you might receive a failing response when there is a proxy or a firewall between your computer and the computer you are trying to reach.*

Network Monitor

When a client has difficulty downloading a file from a server, you can configure a capture trigger in Network Monitor, which records the session and reveals the exact point of failure. Network Monitor is a built-in tool in Windows NT. To run it, choose Start|Programs|Administration Tools|Network Monitor.

ARP

The Address Resolution Protocol (ARP) cache is a list of recently resolved IP addresses mapped to their matching Media Access Control (MAC) addresses. The *MAC address* is the unique physical address embedded in each network adapter. To display all mappings currently in the ARP cache, go to a command prompt and type:

```
arp -a
```

To remove an incorrect entry in the ARP cache, type

```
arp -d IP_address,
```

where **IP_address** is the incorrect IP address of the destination. Use this command for each incorrect entry in the ARP cache until all incorrect entries have been deleted.

NSLOOKUP

The NSLOOKUP tool displays DNS server configuration information. It is available only for Windows NT.

Telnet

Telnet is a TCP/IP tool that enables users to interactively connect to a remote computer. To use Telnet, go to a command prompt and type

```
telnet IP_address,
```

where **IP_address** is the IP address of the other computer.

Troubleshooting Steps

This section describes how to troubleshoot some common network communication problems that you might experience when you use TCP/IP as your network protocol. These problems usually fall into one of the following two categories:

- **Basic connectivity problem** You are unable to connect to a specific IP address.

- **Domain name resolution problem** You are able to connect to an IP address, but you cannot access a site via its Fully Qualified Domain Name (FQDN).

Basic Connectivity Problem

Follow these steps when you are unable to connect to a specific IP address:

1. Check your IP configuration. Depending on your operating system, use either the **IPCONFIG** or **WINIPCFG** command to verify that the IP address and subnet mask specified for your computer are correct.
2. PING the loopback address. Use the **PING** command to verify that TCP/IP is working properly. To do so, PING the loopback address (127.0.0.1) by typing the following command at a command prompt (see Figure 9.3):

   ```
   PING 127.0.0.1
   ```

3. PING your IP address. Use the PING tool to see if there is a communication problem between your operating system and your network adapter.
4. Check the ARP cache. If an entry in the ARP cache is incorrect, your TCP/IP requests could be sent to the wrong computer. Clear the ARP cache to verify that this isn't the problem.
5. Check the default gateway. Use the **IPCONFIG** or **WINIPCFG** command to obtain the IP address defined for your default gateway. If it is correct, PING its IP address to verify that you can communicate with your default gateway.

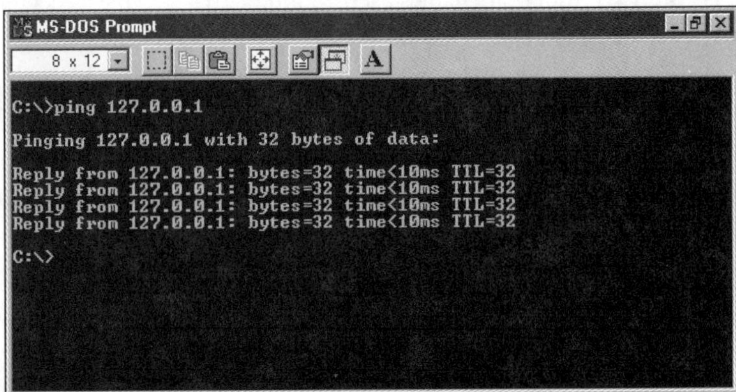

Figure 9.3 A successful loopback response.

6. PING the destination's IP address. Use the PING tool to see if there is either a problem with the target computer or an improperly configured router between you and the target computer. If the destination receives the PING but cannot respond, its subnet mask could be incorrect.
7. Trace the route. Use the **TRACERT** command to see if there is a configuration problem with one of the routers between you and the destination computer.
8. Check the services on the destination. Verify that the necessary services are running on the destination. For example, if you are attempting to use Internet Explorer to connect to a Web server, verify that a Web server service is configured and running on the destination.
9. Verify that the port number is correct. Using Telnet, try to connect to the server using the port number. Some standard port settings include:
    - HTTP—Port 80
    - FTP—Port 21
    - Telnet—Port 23
    - Gopher—Port 70

Domain Name Resolution Problem

If you are able to connect to the other computer using its IP address, but you are not able to connect using its domain name, there might be a name resolution problem. There are four main methods that can be used to accomplish name resolution on a network:

- **HOSTS file** A static text file that maps host names with IP addresses.
- **Domain Name Service (DNS)** A server that resolves host names to IP addresses.
- **LMHOSTS file** A static text file that maps NetBIOS names with IP addresses.
- **Windows Internet Name Service (WINS)** A server that dynamically resolves NetBIOS names to IP addresses.

Depending on your configurations, use the appropriate troubleshooting methods, as follows:

- Check your HOSTS file for an invalid entry. Search your HOSTS file for the host name of the other computer, verify that there is only one entry for it, and verify that the IP address and NetBIOS for the host name of the other computer are correct.

- Check your LMHOSTS file for an invalid entry. Search your LMHOSTS file for the NetBIOS name of the other computer, verify that there is only one entry per NetBIOS name, and verify that the IP address and NetBIOS name of the target computer are correct.
- Check your WINS configuration. To verify that you can communicate with your WINS server, PING your WINS server's IP address. If you can PING the IP address of your WINS server but cannot resolve the NetBIOS name of the other computer, your WINS server might not be resolving NetBIOS names properly. If your network contains multiple WINS servers, configure your computer to use a different WINS server.

Common Internet Connection Errors

Each of the following is a common Internet connection error:

- Cannot open Internet site.
- Slow Internet connection when using NetWare and a proxy server.
- Email notification is not sent for updated Web sites.
- NetMeeting connects to the incorrect ISP.
- NetMeeting cannot connect to a Directory Server.
- NetMeeting connection fails when using a firewall.

Cannot Open Internet Site

The following message might occur when attempting to access Web sites (see Figure 9.4):

Internet Explorer cannot open the Internet site <address>.

A connection with the server could not be established

Table 9.2 lists some possible reasons for this message and the resolutions.

Slow Internet Connection When Using NetWare And A Proxy Server

When you use IE with a proxy server and Novell NetWare 32-bit client software, you might experience the following:

- Slow connections
- Inconsistent downloads
- An inability to view non-Microsoft Web sites

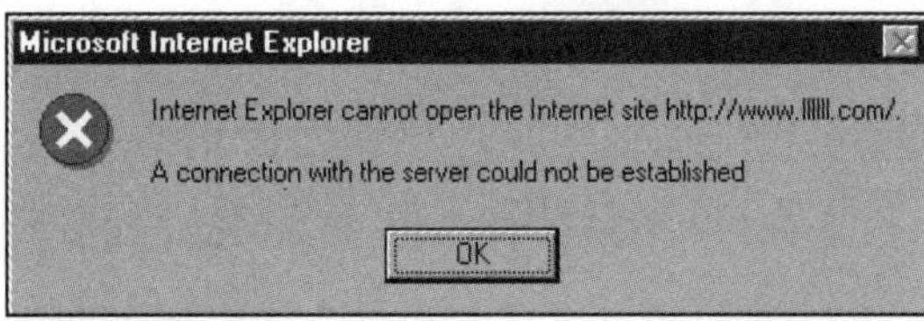

Figure 9.4 An Internet site connection error message.

To resolve these problems, follow these steps:

1. Open the Windows Registry.
2. Create a new binary value named *DontUseDNSLoadBalancing* under the following Registry key:

```
HKEY_CURRENT_USER\Software\Microsoft\Windows\CurrentVersion\
Internet Settings
```

3. Set the value to 01 00 00 00.
4. Restart your computer.

When a user has Microsoft Client For NetWare Networks installed and the IPX/SPX-compatible protocol bound to the Dial-Up Adapter, the user will receive the following message when trying to perform an unattended dial-up connection:

You are currently using NetWare servers, which will be inaccessible if you establish this connection.

Table 9.2 Possible causes and resolutions for Internet Explorer server connection errors.

Possible Cause	Resolution
You might have entered an incorrect URL.	Check the Internet address for typos.
You do not have a proper connection to the Internet.	If you are on a corporate network and a proxy server is set up as your connection to the Internet, you might have empty or inaccurate proxy server settings. Choose the Connection tab under View|Internet Options to modify your proxy server settings.
Your system has an incorrect version or multiple versions of the wsock32.dll file.	Multiple versions of this file should be removed from the system. Incorrect versions should be renamed and a new version, which can be extracted from your Windows CD, should be added back into the \Windows\System directory.

To disable the IPX/SPX protocol in the Dial-Up Adapter:

1. Double-click on the My Computer icon.
2. Double-click on the Dial-Up Networking icon.
3. Right-click on the connection you are using for the unattended dial-up, then click on Properties.
4. Click on Server Type, then click on the IPX/SPX Compatible checkbox to clear it.
5. Click on OK, then click on OK again.

Email Notification Is Not Sent For Updated Web Sites

For IE4 users to receive email notifications, all three of the following conditions must be met:

- The email feature must be enabled in the CDF file.
- The user must choose to be notified by email when subscribing to a site.
- When prompted for an email address, the user must enter the correct email address and SMTP server name.

NetMeeting Connects To The Incorrect ISP

By default, NetMeeting dials the ISP specified in the Internet Explorer Connection tab. If users wish to use different dial-up connections, they should connect to that ISP manually before using NetMeeting.

NetMeeting Cannot Connect To A Directory Server

Table 9.3 shows some possible causes and resolutions for a NetMeeting connection problem.

NetMeeting Connection Fails When Using A Firewall

As discussed in Chapter 5, several ports must be open in the corporate firewall to establish a NetMeeting connection across the Internet. NetMeeting uses several IP ports to communicate with other meeting participants. If you use a firewall to connect to the Internet, the firewall must be configured so that the ports used by NetMeeting are not blocked. NetMeeting uses the Internet Protocol (IP) ports shown in Table 9.4.

If NetMeeting connections can be made through the firewall, but you are unable to use NetMeeting's audio features, the dynamically assigned ports are not configured on the firewall. If you are able to connect to computers outside the

Table 9.3 Possible causes and resolutions for NetMeeting connection problems.

Possible Cause	Resolution
The Directory Server could be down.	Try to connect to the server at a later time or connect to a different Directory Server.
You are using a 16-bit WinSock connection.	Either establish the connection before starting NetMeeting or install a 32-bit WinSock.
You are connected to the Internet via a proxy server.	Port 389 on the proxy server must be opened to connect to an Internet Locator Server (ILS).
You have recently closed NetMeeting.	Wait a few minutes after you close NetMeeting before you reconnect so the Directory Server has time to remove your username from its list.

firewall, but outside NetMeeting users cannot connect to you, the most likely explanation is that the firewall cannot dynamically virtualize an optional number of internal IP addresses.

If you are having difficulty connecting to NetMeeting, try to connect to the NetMeeting server with Telnet over the various ports. If you cannot connect with Telnet, the problem most likely lies in one of the ports not being open.

Table 9.4 Vital statistics about NetMeeting ports.

Port	Purpose
389	Internet Locator Server (ILS)
522	User Location Server (ULS)
1503	T.120
1720	H.323 call setup
1731	Audio call control
Dynamic	H.323 call control
Dynamic	H.323 streaming

Exam Prep Questions

Question 1

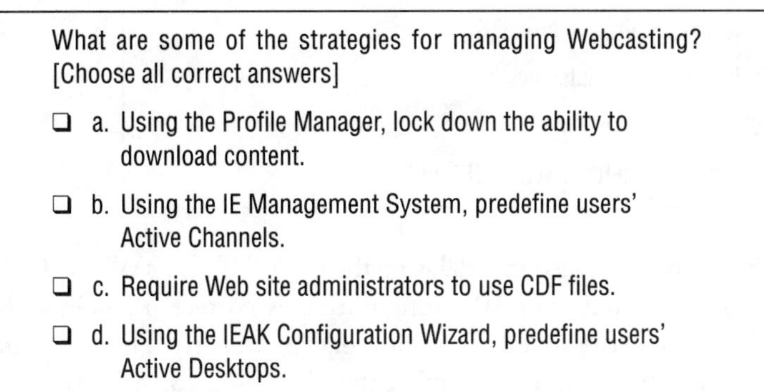

What are some of the strategies for managing Webcasting? [Choose all correct answers]

- ❑ a. Using the Profile Manager, lock down the ability to download content.
- ❑ b. Using the IE Management System, predefine users' Active Channels.
- ❑ c. Require Web site administrators to use CDF files.
- ❑ d. Using the IEAK Configuration Wizard, predefine users' Active Desktops.

The correct answers to this question are a, c, and d. Locking down the ability to download content, requiring the use of CDF files, and predefining users' Active Desktops are all strategies that can be used for managing Webcasting. The IE Management System is a fictitious application. Therefore, answer b is incorrect.

Question 2

Your network consists of five Windows NT 4 Workstations, five NT 4 Servers, and five Windows 95 machines. Which tools do you need to verify the DNS host names and MAC addresses of each of these machines? [Choose all correct answers]

- ❑ a. IPCONFIG
- ❑ b. TRACERT
- ❑ c. DNSLOOKUP
- ❑ d. WINIPCFG

The correct answers to this question are a and d. Windows NT 4 machines use IPCONFIG.EXE and Windows 95 machines use WINIPCFG.EXE to verify DNS host names and MAC addresses. Neither b nor c is a TCP/IP configuration utility; therefore, they are incorrect.

Question 3

You are having basic connectivity problems. How would you verify that your client machine is configured properly?

- ❍ a. PING the loopback address.
- ❍ b. PING the default gateway.
- ❍ c. PING the remote host.
- ❍ d. Use the IPCONFIG or WINIPCFG utility.

The correct answer to this question is d. Using the IPCONFIG or WINIPCFG utility, you can verify that your IP configuration is correct. PINGing the loopback address will verify that TCP/IP is working properly. Therefore, answer a is incorrect. PINGing the default gateway is used to verify that the default gateway is connected to the network and functioning properly. Therefore, answer b is incorrect. PINGing the remote host enables you to check if there is an improperly configured router between your computer and the other computer or to ascertain if the other computer is down. Therefore, answer c is incorrect.

Question 4

Which of the following dynamically maps NetBIOS names with IP addresses?

- ❍ a. WINS server
- ❍ b. DNS server
- ❍ c. LMHOSTS
- ❍ d. HOSTS

The correct answer to this question is a. WINS servers dynamically map NetBIOS names with IP addresses. DNS servers dynamically map host names with IP addresses. Therefore, answer b is incorrect. HOSTS and LMHOSTS files are used for static configuration only. Therefore, answers c and d are incorrect.

Question 5

Which of the following multimedia streaming protocols sends one copy of the data to only clients who request it?

- ❍ a. Unicast
- ❍ b. Multicast
- ❍ c. Broadcast
- ❍ d. Bicast

The correct answer to this question is b. Unicasts send separate copies of the data. Therefore, answer a is incorrect. Broadcasts send one copy to all clients, whether or not they request it. Therefore, answer c is incorrect. Bicast is a fictitious protocol. Therefore, answer d is incorrect.

Question 6

Which of the following tools will help you determine the number of hops taken to get to another computer on the Internet from your Windows 95 machine?

- ❍ a. WINIPCFG
- ❍ b. TRACERT
- ❍ c. ARP
- ❍ d. DNSLOOKUP
- ❍ e. All of the above
- ❍ f. None of the above

The correct answer to this question is b. TRACERT provides the number of hops from one computer to another. None of the other tools listed provide the required functionality. Therefore, answers a, c, and d are incorrect.

Question 7

Which of the following provides a static database of IP addresses mapped with host names?

❍ a. HOSTS file

❍ b. LMHOSTS file

❍ c. WINS server

❍ d. DNS server

The correct answer to this question is a. Only a HOSTS file provides a static database of IP addresses and host names. Therefore, answers b, c, and d are incorrect.

Question 8

You are attempting to browse **www.microsoft.com** from your Windows NT machine, and you receive a *Cannot open Internet site* error message. You enter the Microsoft Web site's IP address, and it resolves successfully. You use a DNS server to resolve host names. What should you do to diagnose the problem?

❍ a. Use IPCONFIG to determine the IP address of your DNS server. PING its IP address to make sure it is available.

❍ b. Verify that you have a connection to the Internet by trying to access a different Web site.

❍ c. PING the loopback IP address.

❍ d. Telnet to the server.

The correct answer is b. The first thing you should do when this error occurs is to verify that you have a connection to the Internet. Although PINGing your DNS server's IP address could help troubleshoot the problem, it is not the first step you should take in this situation. Therefore, answer a is incorrect. PINGing the loopback address and Telneting to the server are steps for troubleshooting problems when you cannot access the IP address. Therefore, answers c and d are incorrect.

Question 9

A user calls to report that her IE4 installation failed almost immediately after running ie4setup.exe. Which log file from her machine should you review to troubleshoot this problem?

- ❍ a. Active Setup Log.txt
- ❍ b. IE4 Setup Log.txt
- ❍ c. IE4 Install Log.txt
- ❍ d. IE4 Setup.log

The correct answer is b. Setup Log.txt is used to troubleshoot the first part of the installation process (copying files). Active Setup Log.txt is used to troubleshoot setup problems for each of the IE components. Therefore, answer a is incorrect. Answers c and d are incorrect because they are fictitious file names.

Need To Know More?

Tittel, Ed, Kurt Hudson, and J. Michael Stewart. *MCSE TCP/IP Exam Cram*. Certification Insider Press, Scottsdale, AZ, 1998. ISBN 1-57610-195-9. An excellent choice for TCP/IP information. See Chapter 16 for information on specific IP troubleshooting techniques.

Microsoft TechNet. Search using the keyword *troubleshooting* to find detailed information on troubleshooting TCP/IP connections.

For additional detailed information on troubleshooting Internet Explorer problems, refer to Microsoft's support site at **http://support.microsoft.com**. Search using the keyword *troubleshooting* in the Internet Explorer 4 category.

Sample Test

The following sections provide a number of pointers for developing a successful test-taking strategy, including how to choose proper answers, decode ambiguity, work within the Microsoft framework, decide what to memorize, and prepare for the test. At the end of this chapter, we provide a practice test that covers subject matter pertinent to the Implementing and Supporting Microsoft Internet Explorer 4.0 by Using the Internet Explorer Administration Kit exam. Good luck!

Questions, Questions, Questions

There should be no doubt in your mind that you are facing a test full of questions. The IEAK exam is comprised of 70 questions, and you are allotted 90 minutes to complete the exam. Remember, questions are of four basic types:

- Multiple choice with a single answer
- Multiple choice with multiple answers
- Multipart with a single answer
- Picking the spot on the graphic

Always take the time to read a question twice before selecting an answer and be sure to look for an Exhibit button. The Exhibit button brings up graphics and charts used to help explain the question, provide additional data, or illustrate layout. You'll find it difficult to answer this type of question without looking at the exhibits.

Not every question has a single answer. There are lots of questions that require more than one answer. In fact, there are some questions for which all the answers should be marked. Read each question carefully so you know how many answers are necessary and look for additional instructions for marking your answers. Additional instructions usually appear in brackets.

Picking Proper Answers

Obviously, the only way to pass any exam is to select the correct answers. But the Microsoft exams are not standardized like SAT and GRE exams—they are more diabolical and convoluted. In some cases, questions are so poorly worded that deciphering them is nearly impossible. In those cases, you may need to rely on answer-elimination skills. There is almost always at least one answer out of the possible choices that can be immediately eliminated because:

- The answer doesn't apply to the situation.
- The answer describes a nonexistent issue.
- The answer is already eliminated by the question text.

After eliminating obviously wrong answers, you must rely on your retained knowledge to eliminate further answers. Look for items that sound correct but refer to actions, commands, or features not present or unavailable in the described situation.

If after these phases of elimination you still are faced with a blind guess between two or more answers, reread the question. Try to picture in your mind's eye the situation and how each of the possible remaining answers would alter the situation.

If you have exhausted your ability to eliminate answers and are still unclear about which of the remaining possible answers is the correct one—guess! An unanswered question offers you no points, but guessing gives you a chance of getting a question right. Just don't be too hasty in making a blind guess. Wait until the last round of reviewing marked questions before you start to guess. Guessing should be a last resort.

Decoding Ambiguity

Microsoft exams have a reputation for including questions that are at times difficult to interpret, confusing, and ambiguous. In our experience with numerous exams, we consider this reputation to be completely justified. The Microsoft exams are difficult. They are designed specifically to limit the number of passing grades to around 30 percent of all who take the test. In other words, Microsoft wants 70 percent of test takers to fail.

The only way to beat Microsoft at its own game is to be prepared. You'll discover that many exam questions test your knowledge of things that are not directly related to the issue raised by the question. This means that the answers offered to you, even the incorrect ones, are just as much part of the skill assessment as the question itself. If you don't know about all aspects of Internet Explorer and the Administration Kit cold, you might not be able to eliminate obviously wrong answers because they relate to a different area of IE4 or IEAK than the one being addressed by the question.

Questions often give away the answer, but you have to be better than Sherlock Holmes to see the clues. Often, subtle hints are included in the text in such a way that they seem like irrelevant information. You must realize that each question is a test in and of itself, and you need to inspect and successfully navigate each question to pass the exam. Look for small clues, such as the mention of times, group names, configuration settings, and even local or remote access methods. Little items such as these can point out the right answer; if missed, they can leave you facing a blind guess.

Another common difficulty with the certification exams is that of vocabulary. Microsoft has an uncanny knack of naming utilities and features very obviously on some occasions and completely inanely in others. This is especially so in the area of System Policies And Restrictions. Be sure to brush up on the options presented in those chapters that discuss this topic. You may also want to review the Glossary before approaching the test.

Working Within The Framework

The test questions are presented to you in a random order and many of the elements or issues are repeated in multiple questions. It is not uncommon to find that the correct answer to one question is the wrong answer to another. Take the time to read each answer, even if you know the correct one immediately. The incorrect answers might spark a memory that helps you on another question.

You can revisit any question as many times as you like. If you are uncertain of the answer to a question, make a mark in the box provided so that you can return to it later. You should also mark questions you think might offer data you can use to solve other questions. We've marked 25 to 50 percent of the questions on exams we've taken. The testing software is designed to help you mark as many questions as you want, so use its framework to your advantage. Everything you want to see again should be marked—the software will help you return to marked items.

Deciding What To Memorize

The amount of memorization you must do for the exams depends on how well you remember what you've read. If you are a visual learner and can see the drop-down menus and the dialog boxes in your head, you won't need to memorize as much as someone who is less visually oriented. The tests will stretch your recollection of commands and functions of IE4 and the IEAK.

The important types of information to memorize are:

- The media options available for each build type
- How to get customization codes
- The protocols supported by each component
- The role of AVS and what the icons mean

If you work your way through this book while sitting at a machine with IE4 and the IEAK, you should have little or no problem interacting with most of these important items.

Preparing For The Test

The best way to prepare for the test—after you've studied—is to take at least one practice exam. We've included a practice exam in this chapter; the test questions are located in the following pages. You should give yourself 90 minutes to take the test. Keep yourself on the honor system, and don't cheat by looking at the text earlier in the book. After your time is up or you finish, you can check your answers in the next chapter, which is an answer key to this sample test.

If you want additional practice exams, visit the Microsoft Training and Certification site (**http://www.microsoft.com/train_cert**) and download the Self-Assessment Practice Exam utility.

Taking The Test

Relax. Once you are sitting in front of the testing computer, there is nothing more you can do to increase your knowledge or preparation. Take a deep breath, stretch, and attack the first question.

Don't rush. There is plenty of time to complete each question and to return to skipped questions. If you read a question twice and are clueless, mark it and move on. Both easy and difficult questions are dispersed throughout the test in a random order. Don't cheat yourself by spending so much time on a difficult question early on that it prevents you from answering numerous easy questions positioned near the end. Move through the entire test and before returning to the skipped questions, evaluate your time in light of the number of skipped questions. As you answer each question, remove the mark. Continue to review the remaining marked questions until your time expires or you complete the test.

That's it for pointers. Here are some practice questions for you.

Sample Test

Question 1

In Stage 3 of the IEAK Wizard, you specify that the installation directory should be D:\MSIE. A user has IE3 installed in their C:\Program Files\Internet Explorer directory. When they upgrade their browser with the package built with the IEAK, where will IE4 be installed?

❍ a. C:\MSIE

❍ b. D:\MSIE

❍ c. C:\Program Files\Internet Explorer

❍ d. D:\Program Files\Internet Explorer

Question 2

Which protocol in the TCP/IP protocol suite can resolve an IP address into a network adapter MAC address?

❍ a. ARP

❍ b. SNMP

❍ c. TCP

❍ d. DHCP

Question 3

Which file can be used instead of WINS to resolve NetBIOS names to IP addresses?

❍ a. HOSTS

❍ b. LMHOSTS

❍ c. HOSTS.TXT

❍ d. LMHOSTS.TXT

Question 4

Which commands can be used to view the local MAC address?

- ❑ a. WINIPCFG /ALL
- ❑ b. ARP -A
- ❑ c. IPCONFIG /ALL
- ❑ d. IPCONFIG /Release

Question 5

In the Systems Policies And Restrictions area of the IEAK, which objects can be modified by an Internet Content Provider?

- ❑ a. Microsoft Chat
- ❑ b. Microsoft NetMeeting
- ❑ c. Outlook Express
- ❑ d. Internet settings
- ❑ e. Internet restrictions
- ❑ f. Subscriptions

Question 6

A user running the IEAK Configuration Wizard in Corporate Administrator mode did not set the user's browsers to use an Auto-configuration URL. Now, the only way to enable a client's Auto-configuration URL setting is to create a new build of Internet Explorer with the new configuration, then redistribute the browser.

- ❍ a. True
- ❍ b. False

Question 7

If an Auto-configuration time interval is not set in the IEAK, how often does IE check for updates?

❍ a. Every 10 minutes

❍ b. Every 60 minutes

❍ c. Every time the user reboots

❍ d. Every time the user invokes IE

Question 8

You have been asked to create an IE channel for your organization. Which tools will help you with this task?

❑ a. IEAK

❑ b. FrontPage

❑ c. ActiveX Control Pad

❑ d. Internet Client SDK

Question 9

When installing IE4 on a Windows NT 4 machine, the user must be logged in as a member of which of the following groups?

❍ a. Power Users

❍ b. Server Operators

❍ c. Administrators

❍ d. Backup Operators

Question 10

When a user runs the IEAK Configuration Wizard in ISP mode, he can choose to force everyone to use the Active Desktop.

❍ a. True

❍ b. False

Question 11

Which of the following files would you use to modify an IE4 build's configuration?

❍ a. Install.ins

❍ b. Autoconfig.ins

❍ c. Install.inf

❍ d. Setup.adm

Question 12

When using the IEAK, for which operating systems can IE4 be built?

❑ a. Windows 3.x

❑ b. Windows For Workgroups

❑ c. Macintosh

❑ d. Unix

❑ e. Windows NT Server 4

Question 13

When installing IE4 over IE 3.x, which of the following settings are preserved?

❑ a. Default home page

❑ b. Proxy settings

❑ c. Favorites

❑ d. Security Zone settings

❑ e. ActiveX controls

Question 14

What entry would you enter in a user's proxy exceptions list to bypass the Gopher site at **www.acmesite.com**, which has the IP address 244.111.111.111?

- ❍ a. http://www.acmesite.com
- ❍ b. *.acmesite.com
- ❍ c. gopher://www.acmesite.com
- ❍ d. 244.111.111.111
- ❍ e. www.acmesite.com

Question 15

Which of the following file types can be updated using the IEAK Profile Manager?

- ❑ a. TXT
- ❑ b. INS
- ❑ c. ADM
- ❑ d. CAB
- ❑ e. INF

Question 16

You want to access a Web server named Queen on the acmesite.com domain. Which format would you use?

- ❍ a. http://www.acmesite.com/queen
- ❍ b. http://www.queen.acmesite.com
- ❍ c. http://www.queen.com/acmesite.com
- ❍ d. http://queen.acmesite.com

Question 17

An IEAK 3.x INS file can be manipulated with the IEAK 4 Profile Manager.

❍ a. True

❍ b. False

Question 18

What is the difference between IE4's history and cache?

❍ a. History is a collection of shortcuts to recently visited Web sites; cache is a collection of shortcuts storing data that is used by IE's AutoComplete feature.

❍ b. History is a collection of shortcuts to recently visited Web sites; cache is a collection of Web pages, Office documents, images, and other recently downloaded items.

❍ c. History is a set of recently viewed HTML pages; cache is a collection of non-HTML files and images.

❍ d. History is kept in the C:\History directory; cache is kept in the C:\Windows\Occache directory.

Question 19

What is the default number of days that IE history is held?

❍ a. 5 days

❍ b. 10 days

❍ c. 15 days

❍ d. 20 days

Question 20

Which of the following items is a component of Internet Explorer that provides Web page editing functionality?

- ❍ a. Microsoft FrontPage 98
- ❍ b. Microsoft Content Publisher
- ❍ c. Microsoft FrontPage Express
- ❍ d. Microsoft NotePad Express

Question 21

A client's installation of Internet Explorer has failed. Upon inspecting the Active Setup Log.txt file, you find CAB signing failures. You had used test certificates to sign your CAB files. What should you do to resolve the problem on the client?

- ❍ a. Run SETREG.EXE to set the clients to accept TestSigned files.
- ❍ b. Have the user run setup in silent mode to bypass the need to have signed CAB files.
- ❍ c. Download the CAB files to the user's local machine first before running setup again.
- ❍ d. All of the above.
- ❍ e. None of the above.

Question 22

When installing IE4 on a machine with Netscape, which of the following Netscape items is migrated successfully to IE4?

- ❍ a. Temporary Internet Files
- ❍ b. Plug-ins
- ❍ c. Favorites
- ❍ d. Security settings
- ❍ e. History files
- ❍ f. Cookies

Question 23

Which Security Zone settings are configurable through the File menu in IE4?

- ❑ a. Local Intranet Zone
- ❑ b. Trusted Intranet Zone
- ❑ c. Restricted Sites Zone
- ❑ d. Trusted Sites Zone
- ❑ e. Internet Zone
- ❑ f. Local PC

Question 24

Which protocol is the ILS dynamic directory based on?

- ❍ a. RNPG
- ❍ b. NNTP
- ❍ c. LDAP
- ❍ d. SMTP

Question 25

Which of the following mail protocols does Outlook Express use as an outgoing transport protocol?

- ❍ a. LDAP
- ❍ b. IMAP4
- ❍ c. S/MIME
- ❍ d. SMTP
- ❍ e. POP3

Question 26

How many custom components can be added to a build of Internet Explorer using the IEAK Configuration Wizard?

❍ a. 5

❍ b. 10

❍ c. Unlimited

❍ d. Depends on the mode you choose in Stage 1

Question 27

A user is running the IEAK Configuration Wizard in ISP mode and has created an IE4 package that is now ready for distribution. As long as she has already set up Auto-configuration within the browsers and has placed the INS files on a central Web server, she will be able to update users' browser settings automatically using the Profile Manager.

❍ a. True

❍ b. False

Question 28

Outlook Express can import mail from which of the following clients?

❑ a. Eudora Light or Pro

❑ b. Internet Mail And News

❑ c. CSV

❑ d. Microsoft Exchange

❑ e. Microsoft Outlook

❑ f. Microsoft Windows Messaging

Question 29

Outlook Express can import addresses from which of the following clients?

- ❑ a. Microsoft Exchange Personal Address Book
- ❑ b. Internet Mail And News
- ❑ c. CSVs
- ❑ d. Netscape Communicator
- ❑ e. Microsoft Internet Mail for Windows 3.1
- ❑ f. Eudora Light or Pro

Question 30

What is the most efficient method of migrating Netscape client's Bookmarks?

- ❍ a. Download and use a Favorites migration utility from the Web.
- ❍ b. Check the Import Bookmarks option in the IEAK.
- ❍ c. Include a batch file in the package that copies the Netscape Bookmarks folder to IE4's Favorites folder.
- ❍ d. IE4 Setup automatically imports Netscape Bookmarks into Internet Explorer.

Question 31

Which of the following accurately describes the difference between NetMeeting and NetShow?

- ❍ a. NetMeeting is for one-to-many broadcasts. NetShow is for one-to-one collaboration.
- ❍ b. NetMeeting works for one-to-many collaboration. NetShow is for one-to-one collaboration.
- ❍ c. NetMeeting is for one-to-many broadcasts. NetShow is for one-to-many or one-to-one collaboration.
- ❍ d. NetMeeting is for one-to-one broadcasts or one-to-many collaboration. NetShow is for one-to-many broadcasts.
- ❍ e. None of the above.

Question 32

Which of the following is the location of IE4 ActiveX controls?

❍ a. C:\Windows\Downloaded Program Files

❍ b. C:\Windows\Temporary Internet Files

❍ c. C:\Windows\History

❍ d. C:\Windows\Occache

Question 33

Which of the following settings can be imported from a CompuServe browser?

❍ a. Proxy settings

❍ b. Favorites

❍ c. Default home page

❍ d. Plug-ins

❍ e. All of the above

❍ f. None of the above

Question 34

Which of the following applications provides an online directory service for finding users on the Internet?

❍ a. Internet Directory Server

❍ b. Internet Explorer

❍ c. Internet Locator Service

❍ d. NetMeeting

Question 35

Which of the following restrictions can be set using the Profile Manager?

- ❑ a. Disable Shut Down
- ❑ b. Disable adding a printer
- ❑ c. Hide all items on the desktop
- ❑ d. Remove the Programs group from the Start menu on Windows 95 machines
- ❑ e. Remove Find from the Start menu
- ❑ f. Disable the File menu in shell folders

Question 36

Running the IEAK Wizard in ISP mode, a user can add only one custom desktop component and one software distribution channel.

- ❍ a. True
- ❍ b. False

Question 37

Which of the following features of Outlook Express allows a user to define a rule to forward, move, or copy messages automatically based on user-defined criteria?

- ❍ a. InfoPane
- ❍ b. Inbox Assistant
- ❍ c. Rule Creator
- ❍ d. vCards

Question 38

Using the IEAK Wizard, you have specified a URL on the intranet as a user's Outlook Express InfoPane. When a user is offline with the configuration, what will Outlook Express do?

- ❍ a. Immediately attempt to connect to the Internet to retrieve the page.
- ❍ b. Prompt the user with a message indicating that the InfoPane is not available.
- ❍ c. Present the user with a cached version of the InfoPane page.
- ❍ d. Present the user with a blank page.

Question 39

Which of the following features of NetMeeting can be completely disabled from the IEAK Profile Manager?

- ❑ a. Application sharing
- ❑ b. Receiving audio
- ❑ c. Receiving video
- ❑ d. Directory services
- ❑ e. My Information Options page
- ❑ f. Sending video

Question 40

Suppose you notice a red circle with an X next to FrontPage Express while attempting to create your first custom build of IE4 using the IEAK Wizard. What would this mean?

- ❍ a. You have not yet downloaded FrontPage Express.
- ❍ b. There is no need to download this component. You have the most current version of FrontPage Express.
- ❍ c. FrontPage Express is no longer a supported IE component.
- ❍ d. You need to upgrade your version of FrontPage Express.

Question 41

Users in your organization have already installed Outlook Express as their email program. When you create the IE 4.01 build, you choose not to include Outlook Express in the package. However, you can still choose to make Outlook Express the default mail client used with Internet Explorer.

❍ a. True

❍ b. False

Question 42

In general, how many download sites can be specified in the IEAK Configuration Wizard?

❍ a. 1

❍ b. 5

❍ c. 10

❍ d. Unlimited

Question 43

When creating a custom build of IE4 using the IEAK in Corporate mode, which of the following distribution methods can you use?

❑ a. CD

❑ b. Single floppy

❑ c. Multiple floppies

❑ d. Web site download

Question 44

You have just created your build of IE4 and have chosen to use the Download installation option only. The next step is to place the setup files onto the defined Web server, where users can then download the files.

❍ a. True

❍ b. False

Question 45

You are attempting to browse **www.microsoft.com** from your Windows NT machine, and you receive a "Cannot open Internet site" error message. You enter the Microsoft Web site's IP address, and it resolves successfully. You use a DNS server to resolve host names. What should you do to diagnose the problem?

❍ a. Use IPCONFIG to determine the IP address of your DNS server. PING its IP address to make sure it is available.

❍ b. Verify that you have a connection to the Internet by trying to access a different Web site.

❍ c. PING the loopback IP address.

❍ d. Telnet to the server.

Question 46

When creating a customized version of IE4 using the IEAK in Corporate Administrator mode, which of the following options is available?

❑ a. Configure FrontPage Express settings

❑ b. Configure Security Zones

❑ c. Configure proxy settings

❑ d. Choose whether to install Active Desktop

Question 47

You have created a custom build of IE4, and your boss installs it. As he installs it, he sees that the company name is spelled incorrectly during the installation process. He removes IE immediately after the installation process and asks you to rebuild a package with the company name spelled correctly. What is the easiest, quickest way of making this change to the build?

❍ a. Modify the Install.inf file in the IEAK Profile Manager

❍ b. Modify the Setup.ins file in the IEAK Profile Manager

❍ c. Rerun the IEAK Wizard, making the appropriate change

❍ d. Modify the Install.ins file in the IEAK Profile Manager

Question 48

What are the main components of a channel?

- ❑ a. A Web page
- ❑ b. A CDF file
- ❑ c. JavaScript
- ❑ d. Images

Question 49

What is the primary function of WINS?

- ❍ a. To assign IP addresses to clients
- ❍ b. To resolve host names to IP addresses
- ❍ c. To resolve NetBIOS names to IP addresses
- ❍ d. To map IP addresses to Fully Qualified Domain Names

Question 50

What is the difference between a HOST file and an LMHOSTS file?

- ❍ a. A HOST file maps NetBIOS names to host names; an LMHOSTS file maps DNS names to NetBIOS names.
- ❍ b. A HOST file maps host names to IP addresses; an LMHOSTS file maps NetBIOS names to IP addresses.
- ❍ c. A HOST file maps NetBIOS names to IP addresses; an LMHOSTS file maps DNS names to IP addresses.
- ❍ d. A HOST file maps host names to NetBIOS names; an LMHOSTS file maps DNS names to NetBIOS names.

Question 51

Which of the following protocols does NetMeeting support?

- ❑ a. H.323
- ❑ b. RTP/RTCP
- ❑ c. LDAP
- ❑ d. T.120

Question 52

A user in your organization would like to have a NetMeeting session with one of the company's vendors through the firewall. She will be connecting to an ILS server and only wishes to use the chat, file transfer, and whiteboard features of NetMeeting. Which ports must be open on the firewall to allow this connection?

- ❑ a. 389
- ❑ b. 522
- ❑ c. 1720
- ❑ d. 1503
- ❑ e. 1731

Question 53

Which of the following file extensions are valid Auto-proxy file extensions?

- ❑ a. .JCT
- ❑ b. .JS
- ❑ c. .PAS
- ❑ d. .PCT
- ❑ e. .JVS
- ❑ f. .PAC

Question 54

The **PING** command can perform which of the following functions?

- ❑ a. Display local TCP/IP configuration values, such as the subnet mask and WINS and DNS configuration
- ❑ b. Provide the client's local IP address
- ❑ c. Display the address translation tables
- ❑ d. Verify the existence of a remote host

Question 55

What additional capabilities does a client receive if the Active Desktop is installed with Internet Explorer?

- ❑ a. A single Explorer
- ❑ b. AutoComplete on the Run menu of the Start menu
- ❑ c. AutoComplete on the Address bar of Internet Explorer
- ❑ d. A channel bar

Question 56

A user is not able to download a file on the Internet, even if she tries to refresh the page from within IE. What should she do next?

- ❍ a. Open Windows Explorer and delete all files under C:\Windows\History.
- ❍ b. Open Windows Explorer and delete all files under C:\Windows\Temporary Internet Files.
- ❍ c. Open Internet Explorer, choose View|Internet Options, then choose Clear History under the History section.
- ❍ d. Open Internet Explorer, choose View|Internet Options, then choose Delete Files under the Temporary Internet Files section.

Question 57

On a Windows 95 computer, what are the minimum specifications necessary to install Internet Explorer (browser only) without the Active Desktop?

- ❍ a. 486/66 processor, 8MB RAM, and 43MB free disk space
- ❍ b. Pentium/66, 12MB RAM, and 32MB free disk space
- ❍ c. Pentium/150, 16MB RAM, and 48MB free disk space
- ❍ d. Pentium/66, 12MB RAM, and 43MB free disk space

Question 58

In what stage of the IEAK Configuration Wizard is Automatic Version Synchronization?

❍ a. 1

❍ b. 2

❍ c. 3

❍ d. 4

❍ e. 5

Question 59

You want to create five packages of IE4: an English Windows 95 version, an English Unix version, a Korean Windows 95 version, a Korean Unix version, and Korean Windows For Workgroups version. How many times must you run the IEAK Configuration Wizard to create all of these builds?

❍ a. 1

❍ b. 2

❍ c. 3

❍ d. 5

Question 60

Which step must a user perform to make Netscape helper applications work with IE4?

❍ a. Copy the applications to the C:\Windows\Downloaded Program Files directory.

❍ b. Add the applications' file extensions to the Windows file type associations.

❍ c. Netscape helper applications are not compatible with IE4.

❍ d. Choose Start|Run and type "Regsvr32 <filepath\filename>".

Question 61

Which is the protocol used to transport newsgroup messages?

❍ a. Usenet

❍ b. Outlook Express

❍ c. NNTP

❍ d. IMAP4

Question 62

Lorraine has created an email message using HTML stationery and embedded animated GIFs. She wants to send this great-looking email message to her friend, Richard, but she is concerned about how it will look to him. Richard's email client supports MIME, but it does not support MIME HTML. How will Lorraine's HTML message be presented?

❑ a. It will be converted to text, and Richard will not see the HTML version.

❑ b. Richard will be able to view the translated Web Content within the email message.

❑ c. The HTML content will be included as an attachment.

❑ d. The HTML content will be presented as raw HTML.

Question 63

You are creating a custom browser package in the Corporate Administrator mode. Users need to be configured to where they do not use the proxy server when accessing the **www.acmesite.com** Web site, and this site needs to be included in the Trusted Internet Zone of the browser. This configuration may change in the near future. Which of the following Auto-configuration URL extensions should you use?

❍ a. An Auto-configuration URL with an .INS extension

❍ b. An Auto-configuration URL with a .JVS extension

❍ c. An Auto-configuration URL with a .JS extension

❍ d. An Auto-configuration URL with a .PAC extension

Question 64

You would like the Acme Web site's signed ActiveX controls to download automatically and safe scripting to run without prompting you. In which zone(s) could the Acme Web site belong to accomplish this?

- ❑ a. Local Intranet Zone
- ❑ b. Trusted Sites Zone
- ❑ c. Internet Zone
- ❑ d. Restricted Sites Zone

Question 65

You have an intranet that includes a component download server and an installation server. The components have moved to a different server. What change must you make on the installation server?

- ❍ a. Update the IE4Sites.dat file
- ❍ b. Update the Install.ins file
- ❍ c. Delete the IE4Site\En folder
- ❍ d. Update the IE4Setup.exe file

Question 66

How do you release a DHCP lease on a Windows 95 machine?

- ❍ a. Run the DHCP /Release command.
- ❍ b. Run IPCONFIG and choose to release the IP address.
- ❍ c. Run WINIPCFG and choose to release the IP address.
- ❍ d. Run the IPCONFIG /Release command.

Question 67

You have just added **www.microsoft.com** to your Favorites list, and you have chosen to make it a subscription. By default, how many layers deep will IE download for offline viewing?

❍ a. 0

❍ b. 1

❍ c. 2

❍ d. 3

Question 68

Which of the following Microsoft products are available for download via the IEAK Automatic Version Synchronization (AVS) stage?

❑ a. FrontPage

❑ b. VB Runtime

❑ c. Internet Explorer Sound Pack

❑ d. Wallet

❑ e. Content Advisor

Question 69

What is the term used for basic Webcasting (where a user subscribes to a site, and IE periodically checks for updated content)?

❍ a. Smart Pull

❍ b. Programmed Pull

❍ c. Smart Push

❍ d. Programmed Push

Question 70

A CDF file defines Webcasting information for which of the following IE features?

- ❑ a. Site subscriptions
- ❑ b. Active Desktop items
- ❑ c. Channel screen savers
- ❑ d. Software Distribution Channels

11

Answer Key

1. c
2. a
3. b
4. a, c
5. a, d
6. b
7. d
8. b, d
9. c
10. b
11. a
12. a, b, c, d, e
13. b, c
14. c
15. b, d, e
16. d
17. a
18. b
19. d
20. c
21. a
22. c
23. a, c, d, e
24. c
25. d
26. b
27. b
28. a, b, d, e, f
29. a, b, c, d, e, f
30. d
31. d
32. a
33. f
34. c
35. a, b, c, e, f
36. b
37. b
38. d
39. a, b, c, d, e, f
40. a
41. b
42. c
43. a, c, d
44. b
45. b
46. b, c, d
47. d
48. a, b, d
49. c
50. b
51. a, b, c, d
52. a, c, d
53. b, e, f
54. b, d
55. a, b
56. d
57. a
58. b
59. b
60. b
61. c
62. a, c
63. a
64. a, b, c
65. a
66. c
67. a
68. b, c, d
69. a
70. b, c, d

Question 1

The correct answer is c. Despite the installation directory specification in the IEAK, Internet Explorer will be installed in the same directory as IE3, because it acts as an upgrade. Therefore, answers a, b, and d are incorrect.

Question 2

The correct answer is a. ARP is the protocol used to resolve an IP address into a MAC (Media Access Control) address. Therefore, answers b, c, and d are incorrect.

Question 3

The correct answer is b. The LMHOSTS file located in the C:\Windows\System32\Drivers\Etc directory is a static file that can be used to resolve NetBIOS names to IP addresses. The HOSTS file can be used in place of a DNS server. Therefore, answer a is incorrect. Neither of these files has a file name extension. Therefore, answers c and d are incorrect.

Question 4

The correct answers are a and c. Running WINIPCFG with an /ALL switch on a Windows 95 computer and IPCONFIG with an /ALL switch on a Windows NT 4 computer will provide the client's local MAC address. Running ARP -A will provide the MAC addresses of computers to which you have connected. Therefore, answer b is incorrect. IPCONFIG /Release will only release an NT 4 client's DHCP lease. Therefore, answer d is incorrect.

Question 5

The correct answers are a and d. Internet Content Providers can only specify settings for Microsoft Chat and Internet settings. Only Corporate Administrators and Internet Service Providers can specify settings for NetMeeting and Outlook Express. Therefore, answers b and c are incorrect. Only Corporate Administrators can specify settings for Internet restrictions and subscriptions. Therefore, answers e and f are incorrect.

Question 6

The correct answer is b, False. Users can manually add the Auto-configuration URL to their browser through the Internet Explorer File menu.

Question 7

The correct answer is d. By default, Internet Explorer checks for newer versions of Auto-configuration files every time the browser is invoked.

Question 8

The correct answers are b and d. Microsoft provides SDKs (Software Development Kits) that provide sample code and a complete reference for all objects. The Internet Client SDK is very helpful when creating Internet applications and content. FrontPage also provides a GUI (graphical user interface) for channel creation. The IEAK and ActiveX Control Pad cannot be used to create IE channels. Therefore, answers a and c are incorrect.

Question 9

The correct answer is c. Only administrators can complete an installation of IE4 on a Windows NT machine.

Question 10

The correct answer is b, False. End users who are installing an ISP IE4 package will always be prompted. The ability to choose whether to force the installation of the Active Desktop is only available to Corporate Administrators.

Question 11

The correct answer is a. Install.ins is the default Internet settings file used with an IE4 build. Autoconfig.ins, Install.inf, and Setup.adm are fictitious file names. Therefore, answers b, c, and d are incorrect.

Question 12

The correct answers are a, b, c, d, and e. Internet Explorer supports the following platforms: Windows 3.x (including Windows For Workgroups), Mac, Unix, NT 4, and Windows 95.

Question 13

The correct answers are b and c. Proxy settings and Favorites are preserved when upgrading Internet Explorer. The default home page is not preserved. Therefore, answer a is incorrect. Because the security settings have a completely new structure in IE4, the security settings in IE3 are not imported into IE4's security settings. Therefore, answer d is incorrect. ActiveX controls must be re-downloaded after an upgrade of Internet Explorer. Therefore, answer e is incorrect.

Question 14

The correct answer is c. You are only interested in excluding the Gopher site, so entering the gopher:// protocol before the domain name would do the trick. Entering www.acmesite.com, http://www.acmesite.com, or the IP address of the server would exclude the entire Web server of that domain. Therefore, answers a, d, and e are incorrect. Specifying *.acme.com would exclude all protocols and all servers in the acmesite.com domain. Therefore, answer b is incorrect.

Question 15

The correct answers are b, d, and e. The Profile Manager updates INS files and their accompanying INF files, which are then packaged into updated CAB files. TXT files are not used with the Profile Manager, and ADM files are only used as templates—they are not updated with the Profile Manager. Therefore, answers a and c are incorrect.

Question 16

The correct answer is d. The correct DNS syntax is <server_name>.<domain_name>. In this case, that would be http://queen.acmesite.com. All other answers are incorrect.

Question 17

The correct answer is a, True. The INS files are backward compatible. Saving an IEAK 3 INS file using the Profile Manager would use the same settings, plus add more entries to the file.

Question 18

The correct answer is b. History is a collection of shortcuts to recently visited Web sites, whereas cache is a collection of recently downloaded items, such as Web pages and images. Therefore, answers a and c are incorrect. Answer d is also incorrect, because history is kept in the C:\Windows\History folder and IE4 cache is kept in the C:\Windows\Temporary Internet Files folder.

Question 19

The correct answer is d. This setting is adjustable to any of the listed options, but 20 days is the default number of days that history is held. Therefore, answers a, b, and c are incorrect.

Question 20

The correct answer is c. The IEAK Configuration Wizard has an option to include FrontPage Express, which provides Web page editing functionality. FrontPage 98 is not included as a component of IE4. Therefore, answer a is incorrect. Microsoft Content Publisher and Microsoft NotePad Express are fictitious applications. Therefore, answers b and d are incorrect.

Question 21

The correct answer is a. To complete the installation process via a Web site download, the files should either be signed with real certificates or the users should be able to accept TestSigned CAB files via the SETREG.EXE utility. Having the user run setup in silent mode or download the CAB files to his local machine would not resolve the problem. Therefore, answers b and c are incorrect.

Question 22

The correct answer is c. From the list provided, only Favorites are migrated to IE4. Temporary Internet Files, Plug-ins, security settings, and history files are not migrated. Therefore, answers a, b, d, and e are incorrect.

Question 23

The correct answers are a, c, d, and e. The settings for the Local Intranet Zone, Trusted Sites Zone, Internet Zone, and Restricted Sites Zone can be modified using Internet Explorer. A Trusted Intranet Zone does not exist. Therefore, answer b is incorrect. The Local PC is only configurable through Profiles. Therefore, answer f is incorrect.

Question 24

The correct answer is c. The Lightweight Directory Access Protocol (LDAP) is used to create an online directory of users. RNPG is a fictitious protocol. Therefore, answer a is incorrect. NNTP is the newsgroup transport protocol. Therefore, answer b is incorrect. SMTP is an outgoing mail transport protocol. Therefore, answer d is incorrect.

Question 25

The correct answer is d. SMTP (Simple Mail Transfer Protocol) is used for outgoing mail. The other mail protocols are not used for the transport of outgoing mail. Therefore, answers a, b, c, and e are incorrect.

Question 26

The correct answer is b. No matter which mode you are in, you can add up to 10 components to your IE package. Therefore, answers a, c, and d are incorrect.

Question 27

The correct answer is b, False. The Auto-configuration feature of the IEAK is not available in ISP mode.

Question 28

The correct answers are a, b, d, e, and f. Outlook Express can import mail from Eudora, Internet Mail and News, Exchange, Windows Messaging, and Outlook. CSVs (Comma Separated Values) are text files that can contain address lists—they are not email clients. Therefore, answer c is incorrect.

Question 29

The correct answers are a, b, c, d, e, and f. Address books from all the clients mentioned can be imported to Outlook Express.

Question 30

The correct answer is d. Bookmarks are automatically imported into the Imported Bookmarks folder during the IE4 installation process. Downloading migration tools from the Web and including a batch file in the IE package are possible but unnecessary steps. Therefore, answers a and c are incorrect. An Import Bookmarks option does not exist in the IEAK. Therefore, answer b is incorrect.

Question 31

The correct answer is d. NetMeeting multipoint collaboration can be one-to-many; however, for audio or video conferencing, it can only handle one-to-one broadcasts. NetShow, on the other hand, is used for one-to-many broadcasts. All other answers are incorrect.

Question 32

The correct answer is a. IE4 ActiveX controls are installed in the C:\Windows\Downloaded Program Files directory. C:\Windows\Temporary Internet Files is the directory where the IE4 cache is stored. Therefore, answer b is incorrect. C:\Windows\History is where history files are kept. Therefore, answer c is incorrect. IE3, not IE4, stores its ActiveX controls in the C:\Windows\Occache directory. Therefore, answer d is incorrect.

Question 33

The correct answer is f. When you install IE4 over a browser program other than Netscape Navigator or Internet Explorer 3.x, no settings are automatically imported into IE4. Therefore, answers a, b, c, d, and e are all incorrect.

Question 34

The correct answer is c. An ILS (Internet Locator Service) maintains a list of Internet users and can be used as an online version of a phone book. Internet Explorer and NetMeeting merely provide the media for accessing an ILS. Therefore, answers b and d are incorrect. An Internet Directory Server is a fictitious application. Therefore, answer a is also incorrect.

Question 35

The correct answers are a, b, c, e, and f. All the listed restrictions can be set with the Profile Manager, except the Programs group, which can only be deleted from the Start menu on Windows NT 4 machines. Therefore, answer d is incorrect.

Question 36

The correct answer is b, False. ISP mode allows you to add one custom desktop component and one channel. However, that channel cannot be a software distribution channel. Only Corporate Administrators can add software distribution channels.

Question 37

The correct answer is b. The Inbox Assistant allows users to create rules for incoming email. An InfoPane is a default or customized Web page that links to mail and news items or other URLs. Therefore, answer a is incorrect. The Rule Creator is a fictitious feature. Therefore, answer c is incorrect. vCards are electronic business cards often used as AutoSignature files for outgoing mail. Therefore, answer d is incorrect.

Question 38

The correct answer is d. When offline viewers open Outlook Express and the InfoPane contains online content, a blank page will be supplied as a replacement for the online content. All other answers are invalid. Therefore, answers a, b, and c are incorrect.

Question 39

The correct answers are a, b, c, d, e, and f. The IEAK Profile Manager provides a way to lock down all of these NetMeeting features.

Question 40

The correct answer is a. The red symbol means that the component has not yet been downloaded to your local drive. A yellow symbol means that you do not have the most current version, and a green symbol means that you have the most current version. Therefore, answers b and d are incorrect. Answer c is also incorrect, because if FrontPage Express were no longer a supported application, it simply would not be listed in the set of components in the AVS (Automatic Version Synchronization) stage.

Question 41

The correct answer is b, False. If the administrator chooses not to include the Outlook Express component, then the Internet Mail Customization section of the wizard, which contains the option to make Outlook Express the default mail client, will not be presented.

Question 42

The correct answer is c. Unless you choose the silent mode option, you can specify up to 10 IE download sites. Therefore, answers a, b, and d are incorrect.

Question 43

The correct answers are a, c, and d. By default, files are copied to a specified URL available for download. Therefore, answer d is correct. Corporate Administrators also have the ability to create CD and multiple floppy media. Therefore, answers a and c are also correct. However, the single floppy distribution method is only available in ISP mode of the IEAK, making answer b incorrect.

Question 44

The correct answer is b, False. The files are automatically placed on the defined Web server.

Question 45

The correct answer is b. The first thing you should do when this error occurs is to verify that you have a connection to the Internet. Although PINGing your DNS server's IP address may help troubleshoot the problem, it is not the first step you should take in this situation. Therefore, answer a is incorrect. PINGing the loopback address and Telneting to the server are steps for troubleshooting problems when you cannot access the IP address. Therefore, answers c and d are incorrect.

Question 46

The correct answers are b, c, and d. Unlike ISVs and ISPs, Corporate Administrators can choose whether to install the Active Desktop and can configure Security Zones and proxy settings. However, FrontPage Express settings cannot be configured using the IEAK Configuration Wizard. Therefore, answer a is incorrect.

Question 47

The correct answer is d. The most efficient method of making a setting change after creating an IE package is to simply modify the Install.ins file with the IEAK Profile Manager. Install.inf and Setup.ins are fictitious file names in this case. Therefore, answers a and b are incorrect. Creating a brand new build by running the IEAK Wizard again would resolve the problem, but it is not the easiest, quickest method of making the change. Therefore, answer c is incorrect.

Question 48

The correct answers are a, b, and d. The components of a channel are a mail Web page, a CDF (Channel Definition Format) file, and two images—an 80×32 pixel logo and a 16×16 pixel icon. JavaScript is not a main component of a channel. Therefore, answer c is incorrect.

Question 49

The correct answer is c. The primary function of WINS is to resolve NetBIOS names to IP addresses. DHCP assigns IP addresses to clients. Therefore, answer a is incorrect. DNS resolves host names and Fully Qualified Domain Names to IP addresses. Therefore, answers b and d are incorrect.

Question 50

The correct answer is b. A HOST file maps host names to IP addresses, whereas an LMHOSTS file maps NetBIOS names to IP addresses. Therefore, answers a, c, and d are invalid.

Question 51

The correct answers are a, b, c, and d. H.323 is a set of protocols for multipoint data over TCP/IP. RTP/RTCP (Real-time Protocol/Real-time Control Protocol) provides a standard format for TCP/IP packets sent in realtime. LDAP (Lightweight Directory Access Protocol) is a set of protocols for directory access. T.120 is a set of protocols for multipoint data conferencing. All of these protocols are supported in Microsoft NetMeeting.

Question 52

The correct answers are a, c, and d. Port 389 must be open to connect to an ILS (Internet Locator Server). Port 1503 must be open to use NetMeeting's multipoint data conferencing features, such as chat, file transfer, and whiteboard. Port 1720 must be open to establish a NetMeeting call. Port 522 would need to be opened only if the user was connecting to a ULS server. Therefore, answer b is incorrect. Port 1731 would need to be open if the user planned on using the audio features of NetMeeting. Therefore, answer e is incorrect.

Question 53

The correct answers are b, e, and f. .JS, .JVS, and .PAC are all valid Auto-proxy extensions. Choices a, c, and d are incorrect, because they are all fictitious file extensions in this context.

Question 54

The correct answers are b and d. **PING** can be used to view the local IP address or to verify the existence of a remote host. The IP configuration utilities—IPCONFIG and WINIPCFG—display the subnet mask and WINS and DNS configuration. Therefore, answer a is incorrect. ARP is the tool that displays the address translation tables. Therefore, answer c is incorrect.

Question 55

The correct answers are a and b. A single Explorer and the AutoComplete feature at the Start|Run command are additional capabilities a client receives if the Active Desktop is installed. The channel bar and Internet Explorer AutoComplete feature can be enabled without having to install the Active Desktop. Therefore, answers c and d are incorrect.

Question 56

The correct answer is d. The user should clear her cache. To do that, she should choose to delete the Temporary Internet Files within IE. Manually deleting cached files deletes cookies and other pertinent files. Therefore, answer b is incorrect. IE history is merely a collection of shortcuts, so clearing these files would not help with troubleshooting. Therefore, answers a and c are incorrect.

Question 57

The correct answer is a. At a minimum, a Windows 95 machine should have a 486/66 processor, 8MB RAM, and 43MB free disk space.

Question 58

The correct answer is b. Stage 2 is for specifying Active Setup information, where you download and specify the components to be included in your package. Therefore, automatic synchronization occurs in this stage. Stage 1 is for gathering information, such as your company information, your role, and what distribution media you want to use. Therefore, answer a is incorrect. Stage 3 is for customizing Active Setup, where you define the way Setup appears and works. Therefore, answer c is incorrect. Stage 4 is where you customize Internet Explorer settings. Therefore, answer d is incorrect. Stage 5 is where you customize IE components and set policies and restrictions. Therefore, answer e is incorrect.

Question 59

The correct answer is b. You need to run the IEAK for each language package you wish to build. However, each package can contain different configurations.

Question 60

The correct answer is b. Internet Explorer uses the file type associations set in Windows. For Netscape's file type associations to be recognized in IE, the user should add the associations to Windows using the Windows Explorer File menu. Simply copying the files over to a different directory will not enable them to work with IE4. Therefore, answer a is incorrect. Although there are some helper applications that only work with Netscape, for the most part they are not browser-specific. Therefore, answer c is incorrect. Running the regsvr32 utility will register controls. Therefore, answer d is incorrect.

Question 61

The correct answer is c. NNTP (Network News Transfer Protocol) is the transport protocol used for public and private newsgroups. Usenet is a newsgroup communication medium, and Outlook Express is the client front-end for newsgroups. Therefore, answers a and b are incorrect. IMAP4 is a mail message handling protocol. Therefore, answer d is incorrect.

Question 62

The correct answers are a and c. If the client does not support MIME (Multipurpose Internet Mail Extensions), text-based information is presented first, and the raw HTML shows up at the bottom of the message. If the client supports MIME only, the user will see the text-based information, and the HTML version will be included as an attachment. Because Richard's mail client supports MIME, answer d is incorrect. The untouched HTML message would only be viewable in an email client that supports MIME HTML. Therefore, answer b is incorrect.

Question 63

The correct answer is a. Only INS files can be used to change Internet settings, such as Security Zone settings, as well as proxy settings. Auto-proxy files (JS, PAC, and JVS) can be used only to configure users' proxy settings. Therefore, answers b, c, and d are incorrect.

Question 64

The correct answers are a, b, and c. By default, the Local Intranet Zone, Trusted Sites Zone, and Internet Zone are all set to use the low security level, in which users are not warned when signed controls are downloaded and scripting is run. The Restricted Sites Zone, on the other hand, is set to a high security level, in which users are either prompted or denied the ability when trying to run active content. Therefore, answer d is incorrect.

Question 65

The correct answer is a. The IE4Sites.dat file on the installation server has pointers to the location where the components reside. Changes must be made in this file to reflect the new location. All other answers are incorrect.

Question 66

The correct answer is c. To release a DHCP lease on a Windows 95 machine, run WINIPCFG and choose to release the IP address. IPCONFIG is a Windows NT 4 utility. Therefore, answers b and d are incorrect. DHCP is a server that assigns IP addresses; it is not a Windows 95 command. Therefore, answer a is incorrect.

Question 67

The correct answer is a. By default, IE will only download the initial page. By clicking on the Customize button, a user can specify to download content up to three layers deep.

Question 68

The correct answers are b, c, and d. Microsoft VB Runtime, Internet Explorer Sound Pack, and Microsoft Wallet are all components listed in the AVS stage of the IEAK Configuration Wizard. FrontPage is not included as an IE component. It is FrontPage Express, which provides a subset of FrontPage's functionality, that is included. Therefore, choice a is incorrect. Content Advisor is a feature of IE, not a component. Therefore, answer e is incorrect.

Question 69

The correct answer is a. Basic Webcasting is often referred to as *Smart Pull* because the user requests the information, but the browser controls the information flow. *Programmed Pull* is the term sometimes used for Managed Webcasting, where there is more control over what and when content is downloaded. Therefore, answer b is incorrect. The terms *Smart Push* and *Programmed Push* do not exist in the Microsoft model of Webcasting. Therefore, answers c and d are incorrect.

Question 70

The correct answers are b, c, and d. CDF (Channel Definition Format) files are used to define channels, Active Desktop items, and channel screen savers. Site subscriptions generally do not have CDF files associated with them. Therefore, answer a is incorrect.

Appendix

Custom Build Checklist

The lists in this appendix are provided to assist you in preparing custom builds for the Internet Explorer Administration Kit (IEAK) Configuration Wizard. These lists present all the configuration options that will be available to you when creating a custom build. You can use this information as a handy guide while you generate your custom build.

The lists are organized under headings that correspond to the stages of the build. The lists within each stage represent the dialog boxes that stage contains. Within each dialog box listed, we present each of the options that are available to you and, when necessary, we've divided this information into sections similar to those seen in the dialog box. Following each option is an icon; the icons and what they represent are as follows:

- Button Button
- Drop-down list drop-down list
- List box select from list
- Radio button
- Scrolling list
- Text box enter text here
- Yes or no checkbox

Options or dialog boxes that are only available through a particular build mode are noted in italics. Radio buttons indicate a choice between the options on the screen. For example, consider the following dialog box options:

Windows 95/NT 4.0	○
Windows 3.11/WFW/NT 3.51	○

The radio buttons indicate that you can choose either the Windows 95/NT 4.0 option or the Windows 3.11/WFW/NT 3.51 option.

Stage 1—Gathering Information

Enter Company Name and Customization Keycode

Name of Company	enter text here
Internet Explorer Administration Kit Keycode	enter text here
Automatic Version Synchronization Support	☐

Select a Platform

Windows 95/NT 4.0	○
Windows 3.11/WFW/NT 3.51	○
UNIX	○

Select a Language

Target Language	drop-down list

Media Type to Distribute the Browser

Destination Folder for your Custom Build	enter text here
Single Floppy *(ISP mode)*	☐
Multiple Floppies	☐
CD-ROM	☐

Stage 2—Specifying Active Setup Parameters

Select a Download Location

Downloading Site	drop-down list

Automatic Version Synchronization (AVS) *(Choose to synchronize one or all)*

Internet Explorer 4.01 Web Browser

Internet Explorer Core fonts

Microsoft NetMeeting

Microsoft Outlook Express

Microsoft Chat V.2.0

Microsoft NetShow

Indeo 5 (Intel)

VDOLive Player

Microsoft Interactive Music Control

Microsoft IE Sound Pack

Shockwave Director (Macromedia)

Shockwave Flash (Macromedia)

Real Player (Progressive Networks)

Microsoft Front Page Express

Microsoft Web Publishing Wizard

Microsoft Visual Basic Runtime

Microsoft Wallet

Microsoft Task Scheduler

Internet Explorer Supplemental Fonts

Active Setup components (select up to 10) *(Define custom components)*

Components	enter text here
Location	enter text here
Commands	enter text here
Global Universal IDs (GUIDs)	enter text here
Parameters	enter text here
Versions	enter text here
File Size	enter text here
Uninstall keys	enter text here

Specify Trusted Publishers

Trusted Publishers	select from list

Stage 3—Customizing Active Setup

Autorun Screen for CD-ROM installs *(if previously selected)*

Title bar text	enter text here
Custom Bitmap locations for Backgrounds	enter text here
Text Color	enter text here
Button Styles	*Standard/3-D/Custom*

Customize Active Setup Wizard

Active Setup Title Bar Text	enter text here
Active Setup Bitmap path	enter text here

Customize Internet Connection Manager *(ISP mode)*

Use custom profile for ICM	☐
Path of connection profile	enter text here

Custom Component Install *(if defined)*

Custom Component Install Title	enter text here

Silent Install *(Corporate Administrator Mode)*

Select Silent Install	☐

Select Install Options

Option Names	*Minimum/Standard/Full/Custom*
Option Description	enter text here
Component Combinations	select from list

Specify Download URLs

Site Names enter text here

Site URLs enter text here

Site Region enter text here

Choose Version Number

Version Number enter text here

Configuration ID enter text here

Product Update URL enter text here

Browser Install Location *(Corporate Administrator mode)*

Within the Windows folder ◯

Within the Program Files folder ◯

In a custom folder ◯ enter text here

Integrating Web Desktop Update *(Corporate Administrator mode)*

Yes ◯

No ◯

User Preference ◯

Stage 4—Customizing The Browser

Customize the Window Title and Toolbar Background

Customize Title Bar ☐

Title Bar Text *(if yes)* enter text here

Toolbar Background Bitmap location *(if yes)* enter text here

Customize the Start & Search Pages

Start Page URL enter text here

Search Page URL enter text here

Specify an Online Support Page for the Browser

Online Support page URL	enter text here

Favorites Folder and Links Customization

Add URLs	Button enter text here
Test URLs	Button enter text here
Import URLs	Button enter text here

Customize the Welcome Message and Desktop Wallpaper

Display Default Welcome Page	○
Do not Display Welcome Page	○
Display Custom Welcome Page	○ enter text here
Disable IE 4.01 Welcome Window	☐
Path to Custom Desktop Wallpaper file	enter text here

Customize the Active Channel Bar

Launch Channel Guide *(Corporate Administrator mode)*	Button
Delete Channels through IE	
Add Channels through IE	
Import Channels through IE	
Don't Customize Channels	○
Import Current Channel Configuration	○
Delete Existing Internet Explorer 4 Channels *(if importing)*	☐
Show Channel Bar by default *(NT only)*	☐

Delete Competing Channels *(Content Provider and ISP modes)*

Delete competing channels	select from list

Customize Software Update Channels *(Corporate Administrator and ISP modes)*

Don't Customize Software Distribution Channels	◯
Import the Current Software Distribution Channel Configuration	◯
Schedule (None/Auto/Daily/Weekly/Monthly)	drop-down list

Add a Custom Desktop Component *(Content Provider and ISP modes)*

Desktop component URL or file path	enter text here

Specify Active Desktop Components *(Corporate Administrator mode)*

Don't Customize Active Desktop	◯
Import the Current Active Desktop Components	◯ Button
Background HTML Settings through dialog box	
Web (Desktop Settings) through dialog box	

Customize Desktop Toolbars *(Corporate Administrator mode)*

Don't Customize	◯
Import Current Desktop Toolbar Settings	◯

My Computer and Control Panel Web View Customization *(Corporate Administrator mode)*

Path of My Computer	enter text here
Path of Control Panel	enter text here

User Agent String Customization

Custom String to Be Appended to User Agent	enter text here

Automatic Browser Configuration *(Corporate Administrator mode)*

Enable automatic browser configuration	☐
Auto-configure URL *(if yes)*	enter text here
Auto-proxy URL (.JS/.PAC files)*(if yes)*	enter text here
Auto-configure at n Minutes *(if yes)*	enter text here

Specify Proxy Settings *(Corporate Administrator and ISP modes)*

Enable Proxy Settings	☐
HTTP *(if yes)*	enter text here
Secure *(if yes)*	enter text here
FTP *(if yes)*	enter text here
Gopher *(if yes)*	enter text here
Socks *(if yes)*	enter text here
Same proxy settings for all addresses?	☐
Exceptions to proxy server	enter text here
Don't use proxy server for local (intranet) addresses	☐

Select a Sign-up Method *(ISP mode)*

Internet Sign-up Server	○
Serverless sign-up	○
No sign-up	○

Specify Custom Sign-up Files *(if Internet or Serverless selected in previous dialog box) (ISP mode)*

Path or folder that contains your sign-up files	enter text here

Certificate Settings *(Corporate Administrator mode)*

Do not customize Certificate Authorities	
Import Certificate Authorities	Button
Do not customize Authenticode settings	
Import Authenticode Security	Button

Security Zones and Content Ratings Customization *(Corporate Administrator mode)*

Do not modify Security Zones	
Customize Security Zone settings	Button

Security Zone Modifications

Zones	drop-down list
Local Intranet Zone Setting (High/Medium/Low/Custom)	Button
Trusted Sites Zone Setting (High/Medium/Low/Custom)	Button
Internet Zone Setting (High/Medium/Low/Custom)	
Restricted Sites Zone Setting (High/Medium/Low/Custom)	Button
Custom Settings	
ActiveX Controls and Plug-ins	
Download unsigned ActiveX controls (Prompt/Enable/Disable)	
Script ActiveX controls marked for safe scripting (Prompt/Enable/Disable)	
Initialize and script ActiveX controls not marked as safe (Prompt/Enable/Disable)	
Download signed ActiveX controls (Prompt/Enable/Disable)	
Run ActiveX controls and plug-ins (Prompt/Enable/Disable)	
User Authentication	
Logon (Automatic logon with current username and password/Automatic logon only in intranet zone/Prompt for username and password/Anonymous logon)	
Downloads	
Font download (Prompt/Enable/Disable)	
File download (Prompt/Enable/Disable)	

Setting	Control
Java	
Java permissions (Medium Safety/Low Safety/High Safety/Disable Java/Custom)	◯
Miscellaneous	
Software channel permissions (Medium Safety/Low Safety/High Safety)	◯
Launching applications and files in an IFRAME (Prompt/Enable/Disable)	◯
Installation of desktop items (Prompt/Enable/Disable)	◯
Submit non-encrypted form data (Prompt/Enable/Disable)	◯
Drag and drop or copy and paste files (Prompt/Enable/Disable)	◯
Scripting	
Scripting of Java applets (Prompt/Enable/Disable)	◯
Active scripting (Prompt/Enable/Disable)	◯
Do not customize content ratings	◯
Import the current content ratings settings	◯ Button
Ratings Tab	
Language	*0—4 (none—explicit)*
Nudity	*0—4 (none—explicit)*
Sex	*0—4 (none—explicit)*
Violence	*0—4 (none—explicit)*
General Tab	
User Options	
Users Can See Sites That Have No Rating	☐
Supervisor Override For User Access to Restricted Content	☐
Supervisor Password	Button
Advanced Tab	
Rating Systems	Button
Ratings Bureau	drop-down list

Stage 5—Component Customization

Specify Internet Mail Servers, Domain, and News Server *(Corporate Administrator and ISP modes)*

Incoming Server (POP3 or IMAP)	drop-down list
Incoming Server	enter text here
Outgoing Mail Server (SMTP)	enter text here
Internet News Server	enter text here
Outlook Express is the Default Mail Client	☐
Outlook Express is the Default News Client	☐
Secure Password Authentication	☐

Specify LDAP Server Settings *(Corporate Administrator and ISP modes)*

Friendly Name	enter text here
Directory Service	enter text here
Home Page	enter text here
Search Base	enter text here
Service Bitmap	enter text here
Check Names Against This Server When Sending Mail	☐
Authentication Type (Anonymous/Password/Secure Password)	○

Outlook Express Customizations *(Corporate Administrator and ISP modes)*

Customize InfoPane

URL	○ enter text here
Local File Path	○ enter text here

Custom Welcome Message

HTML Path	enter text here
Sender	enter text here
Reply-to	enter text here

Include a Signature *(Corporate Administrator mode)*

Append to Mail Messages	☐ enter text here
Append to News Postings	☐ enter text here

Stage 6—System Policies And Restrictions *(All are available in Corporate Administrator mode)*

Microsoft NetMeeting Settings *(ISP mode)*

Restrict the Use of File Transfer

Prevent the User from Sending Files	☐
Prevent the User from Receiving Files	☐

Restrict the Use of Application Sharing

Disable All Application Sharing Features	☐
Prevent the User from Sharing the Clipboard	☐
Prevent the User from Sharing MS-DOS windows	☐
Prevent the User from Sharing Explorer windows	☐
Prevent the User from Collaborating	☐

Restrict the Use of the Options Dialog

Disable the General Options Page	☐
Disable the My Information Options Page	☐
Disable the Calling Options Page	☐
Disable the Audio Options Page	☐
Disable the Video Options Page	☐

Disable the Protocols Options Page ☐

Prevent the User from Answering Calls ☐

Prevent the User from Using Audio Features ☐

Restrict the Use of Video

Prevent the User from Sending Video ☐

Prevent the User from Receiving Video ☐

Prevent the User from Using Directory Services ☐

Set the Default Directory Server [enter text here]

Set Exchange Server Property for NetMeeting Address [enter text here]

Preset User Information Category [enter text here]

Set NetMeeting Home Page *(Corporate Administrator mode)* [enter text here]

Set Limit for NetMeeting Throughput *(Corporate Administrator mode)* [enter text here]

Microsoft NetMeeting Protocols

Disable TCP/IP ☐

Null modem Disabled ☐

Web Desktop Settings

Desktop

Desktop

- Disable Active Desktop ☐
- Don't allow changes to Active Desktop ☐
- Hide Internet Explorer icon ☐
- Hide Network Neighborhood icon ☐
- Hide all items on Active Desktop ☐

Active Desktop Items

- Disable All Desktop Items ☐
- Disable Adding Desktop Items ☐
- Disable Deleting Desktop Items ☐
- Disable Editing Desktop Items ☐
- Disable Closing Any Desktop Items ☐

Desktop Wallpaper

- No HTML Wallpaper ☐
- Disable Change of Wallpaper ☐

Desktop Toolbars Settings

- Disable Dragging, Dropping, Closing All Toolbars ☐
- Disable Resizing All Toolbars ☐

Start Menu

Start Menu

- Remove Favorites from Start Menu ☐
- Remove Find from Start Menu ☐
- Remove Run from Start Menu ☐
- Remove Documents from Start Menu ☐
- Don't Keep History of Recently Opened Documents ☐
- Clear History of Recently Opened Documents ☐
- Disable Logoff ☐
- Disable Shut Down ☐
- Disable Changes to Control Panel/Printers Settings ☐
- Disable Changes to Taskbar/Start Menu Settings ☐
- Disable Context Menu for Taskbar ☐
- Hide Custom Programs Folders ☐
- Hide Common Program Groups in Start Menu *(NT only)* ☐

Shell Settings

- Enable Classic Shell ☐
- Disable File Menu in Shell Folders ☐
- Don't Allow Customization of Folders in Web View ☐
- Disable Context Menu in Shell Folders ☐
- Only Allow Approved Shell Extensions ☐
- Don't Track Shell Shortcuts During Roaming ☐
- Hide Floppy Drives @ My Computer ☐
- Disable Net Connections/Disconnections ☐

Printer Settings

Hide General and Details Tabs in Printer Properties	☐
Disable Deletion of Printers	☐
Disable Addition of Printers	☐

System

Run only specified Windows applications	Button
Don't allow computer to restart in MS-DOS mode	☐

Internet Settings *(Content Provider and ISP modes)*

Colors

General Colors	
Background Color (0,0,0 - 255,255,255)	enter text here
Text Color (0,0,0 - 255,255,255)	enter text here
Use Windows Colors	☐
Link Colors	
Link Color (0,0,0 - 255,255,255)	enter text here
Visited Link Color (0,0,0 - 255,255,255)	enter text here
Use Hover Color	☐
Hover Color (0,0,0 - 255,255,255)	enter text here

Fonts

Western Proportional Font	enter text here
Western Fixed Font	enter text here

Languages

Choose the Default Language Preferences	enter text here

Modem Settings

Connection Type	drop-down list
Enable Autodialing	☐
Number of Times to Attempt Connection	⬍

Number of Seconds to Wait Between Attempts	⬍
Connect Without User Intervention	☐
Disconnect If Idle After Specified Number of Minutes	☐
Minutes to Wait Before Disconnecting	⬍
Perform System Security Check Before Dialing	☐

Programs

Program to use for Calendar	enter text here
Program to use for Contacts	enter text here
Program to use for Internet Call	enter text here

Advanced Settings

Browsing	
Disable Script Debugger	☐
Launch Channels in Full Screen Mode	☐
Launch Browser in Full Screen Mode	☐
Use Autocomplete	☐
Show Friendly URLs in Status Bar	☐
Enable Smooth Scrolling	☐
Enable Page Transitions	☐
Browse in a New Process	☐
Enable Page Hit Counting	☐
Enable Scheduled Subscription Updates	☐
Underline Links (Always/Never/Hover)	drop-down list
Multimedia	
Show Pictures	☐
Play Animations	☐
Play Videos	☐
Play Sounds	☐
Smart Image Dithering	☐
Security	
Enable Profile Assistant	☐
Delete Saved Pages When Browser Is Closed	☐
Don't Save Encrypted Pages to Disk	☐

Warn If Forms Submit is being Redirected	☐
Warn If Changing Between Secure and Insecure Mode	☐
Cookies (Accept/Prompt/Disable)	drop-down list
Java VM	
JIT Compiler Enabled	☐
Java Logging Enabled	☐
Printing	
Print Background Colors and Images	☐
Searching	
Autoscan Common Root Domains	☐
Search When URL Fails (Search/Always Ask/Never Search)	drop-down list
Toolbars	
Show Font Button	☐
Small Icons	☐
HTTP 1.1 Settings	
Use HTTP 1.1	☐
Use HTTP 1.1 Through Proxy Connections	☐

Outlook Express Settings *(ISP mode)*

General Settings

Mail and News Security Zones	
Mail and News in the Restricted Sites Zone (Not the Internet Zone)	☐
HTML Mail and News Composition Settings	
Mail: Plain Text Composition for Mail Messages (instead of HTML mail)	☐
News: HTML Message Composition the Default (instead of plain text)	☐

View Customization

Folder and Message Navigational Elements	
Turn On Outlook Bar	☐
Turn Off Folder List (use a tree view of folders)	☐
Turn On Folder Bar (horizontal line for folder names)	☐
Turn Off the Tip of the Day	☐

Channels and Subscriptions Settings

Maximum KB of Site Subscriptions (zero disables restriction)

Maximum KB of Channel Subscriptions (zero disables restriction)

Maximum Number of Site Subscriptions That Can Be Installed (zero disables restriction)

Minimum Number of Minutes Between Scheduled Subscription Updates (zero disables restriction)

Beginning of Range in Which to Exclude Scheduled Subscription Updates. Minutes from Midnight (zero disables restriction)

End of Range in Which to Exclude Scheduled Subscription Updates. Minutes from Midnight (zero disables restriction)

Maximum Site Subscription Crawl Depth — drop-down list

Internet Restrictions

General Tab Settings

Disable Change of Home Page Settings

Disable Change of Cache Settings

Disable Change of History Settings

Disable Change of Color Settings

Disable Change of Link Color Settings

Disable Change of Font Settings

Disable Change of Language Settings

Disable Change of Accessiblity Settings

Security Tab Settings

Use Only Machine Settings for Security Zones

Don't Allow Users to Change Policies for Any Security Zone

Don't Allow Users to Add/Delete Sites from a Security Zone

Content Tab Settings

Disable Change of Ratings Settings

Disable Change of Certificate Settings

Disable Change of Profile Assistant Settings

Disable Change of Microsoft Wallet Settings

Connection Tab Settings

- Disable Calling Connection Wizard ☐
- Disable Change of Connection Settings ☐
- Disable Change of Proxy Settings ☐
- Disable Change of Automatic Configuration Settings ☐

Programs Tab Settings

- Disable Change of Messaging Settings ☐
- Disable Change of Calendar and Contact Settings ☐
- Disable Change of Internet Explorer Default Browser Settings ☐

Advanced Tab Settings

- Disable Change of Settings on Advanced Tab ☐

Code Download

Path

Channels Settings

- Disable Channel User Interface ☐
- Disable Add and Subscribe to Channels ☐
- Disable Edit of Channel Properties and Channel Subscriptions ☐
- Disable ability to Remove Channels and Subscriptions to Channels ☐
- Disable Add Site Subscriptions ☐
- Disable Edit Site Subscriptions ☐
- Disable Remove Site Subscriptions ☐
- Disable Channel Logging ☐
- Disable Update Now and Update All for Channels and Subscriptions ☐
- Disable All Scheduled Channel and Site Subscriptions ☐
- Disable Unattended Dialing by Subscriptions ☐
- Disable password caching for all channel or site subscriptions ☐
- Disable Download of Channel Subscription Content ☐
- Disable Download of Site Subscription Content ☐
- Disable Editing and Creating of Schedule Groups ☐

Microsoft Chat Settings *(Content Provider and ISP modes)*

Chat Server List (semicolons to separate)	
Default Chat Server	enter text here
Default Chat Room	
Default Character	
Default Backdrop	enter text here
User Profile String	
Show Only Registered Rooms in Room List	☐

Glossary

Active Channel—Microsoft technology that uses server push to deliver Web-based information on a particular topic to users who subscribe to the channel.

Active Desktop—A component of IE that enables a user to have the more advanced features of IE4 (e.g., Active Channels) displayed on the desktop. It is more or less a Web page layered on top of the desktop.

Active Server—A Web server or similar application that supports server-side scripting. Also known as Active Server Pages.

Active Setup—A new program in IE4 that checks the system for installed components to prevent you from downloading unneeded files.

ActiveX—A suite of technologies that you can use to deliver business solutions over the Internet and the intranet.

ActiveX controls—A stripped-down version of OLE controls that optimizes the size and speed of the controls for use over the Internet. They are used to add special functions, such as animation, to Web pages, desktop applications, and software development tools.

ADM (policy template file)—A file used as a template for user and system policy (POL) files.

alias—A short name for a directory that is easy to use and remember.

applet—The designation for a Java-based application that runs within the context of an HTML document, as opposed to a full-blown Java application that runs by itself outside any Web context.

ARP (Address Resolution Protocol)—The ARP cache is a list of recently resolved IP addresses mapped to their matching Media Access Control (MAC) addresses.

ASP (Active Server Pages)—A Web-programming technique that enriches commerce and business communications by improving script management. ASP can execute with a transaction. Therefore, if the script fails, the transaction is aborted.

assessment exam—Similar to the certification exam, this type of exam gives you the opportunity to answer questions at your own pace. This type of exam also uses the same tools as the certification exam.

Authorized Academic Training Program (AATP)—A program that authorizes accredited academic institutions of higher learning to offer Microsoft Certified Professional testing and training to their students. The institutions are allowed to use the Microsoft Education course materials and Microsoft Certified Trainers.

Authorized Technical Education Center (ATEC)—The location where you can take a Microsoft Official Curriculum course taught by Microsoft Certified Trainers.

AutoComplete—An IE feature that compares user input in the IE Address box to its existing History and Favorites lists of URLs and completes strings that it can recognize from this internal store of URLs.

Auto-configure URL—This URL points to the Auto-configuration (INS) file for this custom package.

Auto-proxy file—As an alternative to setting users' proxy settings with an INS file, IE can be configured to use this file to set the address of the proxy server to use for several protocols, including HTTP, FTP, and Gopher. Auto-proxy files can dynamically define the hosts that are exceptions to using the proxy server.

AVS (Automatic Version Synchronization)—A deployment feature of the IE Administration Kit that automatically informs you whether the browser and its components are up to date with the latest versions.

bandwidth—The range of frequencies that a communications medium can carry. For baseband networking media, the bandwidth also indicates the theoretical maximum amount of data that the medium can transfer. For broadband networking media, the bandwidth is measured by the variations that any single carrier frequency can carry.

basic Webcasting—A type of Webcasting in which the user subscribes to a Web site that is periodically checked for new content by the browser. Also known as smart pull technology.

beta exam—A trial exam that is given to participants at a Sylvan Prometric Testing Center before the development of the Microsoft Certified Professional certification exam is finalized. The final exam questions are selected on the basis of the results of the beta exam. For example, if all beta exam participants get certain answers correct or wrong, those questions usually will not appear in the final version.

BINHEX—A process used to convert nontextual data into an encoded form that uses plain text characters only.

CAB (cabinet file)—Storage files for all components of IE and other Microsoft products.

cache—A temporary storage area that holds current information and is able to provide that information faster than other methods.

caching—The act of storing objects locally for later use.

CDF (Channel Definition Format)—An implementation of the Extensible Markup Language (XML) used to create Active Channels, Active Desktop items, and channel-based screen savers.

certificate—A digital signature issued by a third party (called a Certificate Authority, or CA) that claims to have verified the identity of a server or an individual for security purposes.

Certificate Authority (CA)—A third party that issues certificates and that claims to have verified the identity of a server or an individual for security purposes.

channel screen saver—Similar to Active Desktop items but activated as screen savers on the user's computer.

client—A computer that initiates requests and subscribes to the services that the server provides within the realm of a network.

COM (Component Object Model)—Microsoft's groundwork of the ActiveX platform that is used to support interprocess communications and that was designed to promote software interoperability.

cookie—A marker downloaded to a PC that identifies a specific user to a Web site.

cut score—The lowest score a person can receive on the Microsoft Certified Professional exam and still pass.

database—A collection of information arranged and stored so that data can be accessed quickly and accurately.

digital certificate—An electronic identification and verification tool used to secure online commerce and other transactions.

DirectX 5—A new technology that complements the new NetMeeting features. It allows communication with video cameras with Universal Serial Bus (USB) and the new video device driver model.

domain name—A text identifier of a specific Internet host. When you first install Windows NT, the installation program prompts you to assign a domain name to the Internet host on which you are installing NT.

Domain Name System (DNS)—A distributed database that provides a hierarchical naming system for identifying systems on the Internet or on intranets.

Dynamic HTML—A combination of standard HTML and scripting used to create Web pages that react on the fly to user interactions.

ERD (Emergency Repair Disk)—The diskette, built with the rdisk /s command, that contains files and other resources that can be used to repair the system partition for a Windows NT computer.

Exam Preparation Guides—Guides that provide information specific to the material covered on Microsoft Certified Professional exams to help students prepare for these exams.

Exam Study Guide—Short for Microsoft Certified Professional Program Exam Study Guide, this guide contains information about the topics covered on more than one of the Microsoft Certified Professional exams.

firewall—A hardware or software networking component used to secure an Internet connection.

FrontPage Express—A wizard-based method for creating Web sites. The program is a scaled-down version of Microsoft's FrontPage HTML editor.

Fully Qualified Domain Name (FQDN)—The full Domain Name System (DNS) path of an Internet host.

gateway—An address tool within a subnet. A gateway address is one of several ports of a router or multihomed server. A gateway router has the ability to transfer packets from one subnet to another.

gleam—The red dot that appears on a site's Favorites icon when IE discovers that a site has been updated.

Gopher—A large database that provides search capabilities and presents Internet material in textual format.

GUID (globally unique identifier)—An option in the Specify Custom Active Setup Components dialog box that is the globally unique identifier for the application.

H.323—A standard for multimedia communications for networks lacking in guaranteed Quality Of Service (QOS) that is based on the efforts of the Internet Engineering Task Force (IETF) created by the ITU (International Telecommunications Union).

Hypertext Markup Language (HTML)—The language used to create static Web pages.

Hypertext Transfer Protocol (HTTP)—The protocol used to communicate between a Web browser and a Web server (uses HTML).

IEAK Configuration Wizard—A component of IE that allows administrators to create customized builds of IE.

IEAK Profile Manager—The utility that provides an interface for the options available in configuration files. It allows an Administrator to easily manage large numbers of IE implementations.

IMAP4 (Internet Message Access Protocol version 4)—A new message-handling protocol that permits incoming mail to be collected and held at your mail server.

Inbox Assistant—A component of Outlook Express that allows users to create rules that forward, move, or copy messages automatically on the basis of predefined criteria for each email account.

INF file—A policy and restriction information file.

InfoPane—The start page of Outlook Express that allows users to jump quickly to the task of their choice.

INS (configuration file)—Text-based files that contain cross-platform IE configuration information.

Integrated Services Digital Network (ISDN)—A form of digital communication that has a bandwidth of 128Kbps.

Internet—The collection of TCP/IP-based networks around the world. Information on nearly every subject is available in some form somewhere on the Internet.

Internet Information Server (IIS)—Web server software by Microsoft that is included and implemented with Windows NT Server.

Internet Locator Server (ILS)—A service offered by NetMeeting that offers standard-based dynamic directory solutions to the user's location problem on the Internet. ILS enables NetMeeting users to locate one another on the Internet or a corporate network.

Internet Packet Exchange/Sequenced Packet Exchange (IPX/SPX)—Novell's NetWare protocol, reinvented by Microsoft and implemented in Windows NT under the name NWLink. It is fully compatible with Novell's version and, in many cases, is a better implementation than the original.

Internet Service Provider (ISP)—A service company that sells network access to the Internet. It purchases bandwidth in bulk and, in turn, resells it in smaller packages.

intranet—An internal, private network that uses the same protocols and standards as the Internet.

IP address—Four sets of numbers, separated by decimal points, that represent the numeric address of a computer attached to a TCP/IP network, such as the Internet.

IPCONFIG—In the Windows NT version of TCP/IP, a command-line utility that displays IP configuration details.

ITU (International Telecommunications Union)—A professional union group that governments and organizations use to coordinate global telecom networks and services.

JavaScript (JScript)—A standard text-based scripting language that can be included within HTML documents to support interactivity, invoke external programs, and perform basic tasks on behalf of the document in which it appears. (It is known as JScript in Microsoft terminology.)

job function expert—A person with extensive knowledge about a particular job function and the software products and technologies related to that job. Typically, a job function expert is currently performing the job, has recently performed the job, or is training people to do this job.

JS—The identifier given to Auto-proxy setting files that are created with a configuration file for a user group.

JScript—See **JavaScript**.

LDAP (Lightweight Directory Access Protocol)—An Internet protocol that allows access to directory information.

link crawl—The process used to determine whether new content exists on a particular Web site. Also known as Web crawl.

local area network (LAN)—A network that is confined to a single building or geographic area and that is made up of servers, workstations, peripheral devices, a network operating system, and a communications link.

MAC (Media Access Control)—The unique physical address embedded in each network adapter.

managed Webcasting—A type of Webcasting in which users subscribe to a particular Web site, but the site has been configured to participate as an Active Channel.

Microsoft Certification Exam—A test created by Microsoft to verify a test taker's mastery of a software product, a technology, or a computing topic.

Microsoft Certified Professional (MCP)—An individual who has taken and passed at least one of the Microsoft certification exams.

Microsoft Certified Professional Certification Update—A newsletter for Microsoft Certified Professional candidates and Microsoft Certified Professionals.

Microsoft Certified Solution Developer (MCSD)—An individual with this certification has passed the four necessary exams and is qualified to create and develop solutions for businesses using the Microsoft development tools, technologies, and platforms.

Microsoft Certified Systems Engineer (MCSE)—An individual with this certification has passed the six necessary exams and is an expert on Windows NT and the Microsoft BackOffice integrated family of server software. This individual can plan, implement, maintain, and support information systems associated with these products.

Microsoft Certified Systems Engineer + Internet (MCSE+I)—An individual with this certification has passed the nine necessary exams and is an expert not just on Microsoft operating systems, but also on Microsoft's Internet servers and TCP/IP.

Microsoft Certified Trainer (MCT)—An individual who is qualified by Microsoft to teach Microsoft education courses at sites authorized by Microsoft.

Microsoft Developer Network (MSDN)—The official source for Software Development Kits (SDKs), Device Driver Kits (DDKs), operating systems, and programming information associated with creating applications for Microsoft Windows and Windows NT.

Microsoft official curriculum—Microsoft education courses that support the certification exam process and are created by the Microsoft product groups.

Microsoft Online Institute (MOLI)—An organization that offers training materials, online forums and user groups, and online classes.

Microsoft Roadmap to Education and Certification—An application, based on Microsoft Windows, that takes you through the process of determining your certification goals and suggests the best way to achieve them.

Microsoft Sales Fax Service—A service through which you can obtain exam preparation guides, fact sheets, and additional information about the Microsoft Certified Professional program.

Microsoft Solution Provider—An organization, not directly related to Microsoft, that provides integration, consulting, technical support, and other services related to Microsoft products.

Microsoft Technical Information Network (TechNet)—A service provided by Microsoft that provides helpful information through a monthly CD-ROM. TechNet is the primary source of technical information for people who support and/or educate end users, create automated solutions, or administer networks and/or databases.

MIME (Multipurpose Internet Mail Extensions)—A protocol that allows multiple file types to be transmitted across TCP/IP networks.

multiple-rating item (MRI)—An item that gives you a task and a proposed solution. Every time the task is set, an alternate solution is given, and the candidate must choose the answer that gives the best results produced by one solution.

name resolution—The main function of the Domain Name System (DNS) that resolves Fully Qualified Domain Names (FQDNs) to IP addresses and IP addresses to FQDNs.

NetBEUI—A simple Network layer transport protocol developed to support NetBIOS networks.

NetMeeting—Software used to enable conferencing in realtime over the Internet or an intranet.

Netscape Navigator—A Web browser developed by Netscape used to access Internet- or intranet-based materials.

NetShow—A component of IE4 that is similar to NetMeeting; however, it is designed for a one-to-many broadcast of information.

NetWare—A network operating system from Novell.

network—A collection of server and client computers that communicate over wire-based media to share resources.

Network Monitor—A built-in Windows NT tool that records a session and reveals the exact point of failure.

Network News Transfer Protocol (NNTP)—The protocol used to distribute, retrieve, inquire about, and post Network News articles.

nondisclosure agreement (NDA)—A legal agreement, signed both by Microsoft and by a vendor, that renders certain rights and limitations.

NSLOOKUP—A Windows NT tool that displays DNS server configuration information.

operating system (OS)—A software program that controls the operations on a computer system.

Outlook bar—A navigational tool provided by Outlook Express that allows easy navigation of folders and modules.

Outlook Express—The IE messaging tool used for email messaging and newsgroup communications.

PAC—The identifier given to Auto-proxy setting files that are created with a configuration file for a user group.

permissions—A level of access assigned to files or folders. Permissions determine who has access rights to those files or folders.

PICS (Platform for Internet Content Selection)—The most common Web site rating standard that can be used by IE to determine whether a user has access to a particular site on the basis of its content rating.

PING—A command-line utility that tests whether a host on a TCP/IP network is reachable.

POL file—A collection of elements that define a user's desktop and computing environment.

policies—The evaluation of requests and issuing of new certificates is governed through the use of policies. Policies are installed by an administrator and instruct the Certificate Server to accept, deny, or delay a request on the basis of the contents of the request. Policies are written in Java, Visual Basic, or C/C++.

POP3 (Post Office Protocol version 3)—The most common protocol used to retrieve incoming email from a server.

preview pane—A command in Outlook 98 that allows you to view the contents of your messages without opening them in a separate window.

proxy server—A software product that acts as a moderator or go-between for a client and a remote host. Most proxy servers also offer content caching and firewall capabilities.

pull technology—A technology that allows the Web browser (e.g., IE) to automatically request information from a Web site.

push technology—A technology that sends information automatically from the server, without client browser intervention.

Registry—A database that stores all the configuration information for Windows operating systems.

Resource Kit—The additional documentation and software utilities distributed by Microsoft to provide information and instruction on the proper operation and modification of its software products.

scripting—A type of programming language used to write custom code for Web pages.

Secure Sockets Layer (SSL)—A protocol that creates secure communications using public key cryptography and bulk data encryption.

security—The protection of data by restricting access only to authorized users.

Security Zones—An area of trust enabled by IE4 to protect your computer from unknown or undesirable sites on the Internet. They also provide a high level of protection for your privacy and your computer.

server—A computer dedicated to servicing requests from other computers within a network.

Service Pack—A patch or fix distributed by Microsoft after the final release of a product to repair errors, bugs, and security breaches.

silent install—A setting available through Corporate Administrator mode that completes an installation of IE and its components without end-user interaction.

site subscription—A process that enables users to connect to the Internet, automatically download new information from a number of sites, and then disconnect and view the information.

Smart Recovery—A feature of the IE installation program that picks up where it left off in the event that the installation is interrupted.

S/MIME (Secure MIME)—An email security technology that uses digital signatures and encryption.

SMTP (Simple Mail Transfer Protocol)—A protocol typically used to communicate with an email server for outgoing mail.

SoftBoot—A process that takes note of which programs are open and then closes them, updates the Registry, and reopens the programs that were open. Currently available only in Windows 95 and Windows 98.

stationery—A particular group of settings that define how a user's messages are displayed.

subnet—A portion or segment of a network.

subnet mask—A 32-bit address that indicates how many bits in an address are being used for the network ID.

System Policies And Restrictions—The various settings in the IEAK Configuration Wizard and the IEAK Profile Manager that control how IE and its components function.

T.120—A suite of communication and application protocols developed and approved by the international telecom groups. The protocols enable developers to create products and services for realtime, multipoint data connections, and conferencing.

TCP/IP (Transmission Control Protocol/Internet Protocol)—The most commonly used network protocol and the central protocol of the Internet.

TRACERT—A utility used to determine the route that a request takes to reach another computer.

troubleshooting—A systematic approach to identifying, categorizing, and solving computer system problems that relies on establishing a list of likely hypotheses, testing those hypotheses in their order of greatest likelihood, and eliminating incorrect hypotheses until a solution is found.

true Webcasting—A type of Webcasting in which the information is pushed to a user's desktop without user or browser intervention.

Unicode—A 16-bit system used to encode characters and letters from many different languages.

Unix—An interactive time-sharing operating system developed in 1969 by a hacker to play games. This system developed into the most widely used industrial-strength computer operating system in the world and ultimately supported the birth of the Internet.

URL (Universal Resource Locator)—The addressing scheme used to identify resources on the Internet.

USB (Universal Serial Bus)—A fairly new serial interface that allows peripheral devices, such as game controllers and mice, to be dynamically configured when attached to or detached from the system.

UUENCODE—A process used to convert nontextual data into an encoded form that uses plain text characters only.

VBScript (Visual Basic, Scripting Edition)—A version of Microsoft's popular Visual Basic programming environment that is designed for use within a variety of applications, including Web documents, to add basic programming and interactive capabilities.

Visual Basic—A version of the Basic programming language written by Microsoft for rapid programming of Windows applications by plugging together components in a visual designer environment.

Web crawl—The process used to determine whether new content on a particular Web site exists. Also known as link crawl.

Web server—A network application that fulfills requests from Web clients (Web browsers) for Web documents from a Web site.

Web site—A collection of Web documents, all of which are focused around a single purpose or content topic linked together to form a cohesive whole. A Web server can host multiple Web sites; a Web site can be composed of several Web documents; a Web document can be composed of several Web objects or components.

Web view—When Windows Desktop Update allows folders and the desktop to be viewed in Web format (HTML).

Webcasting—The term used to describe the technologies used to automatically deliver information to a client's desktop using push and pull technologies.

wide area network (WAN)—A network that spans geographically distant segments. Often, a distance of two miles or more is used to define a WAN; however, Microsoft equates any Remote Access Service (RAS) connection as establishing a WAN.

Windows Desktop Update—A feature of IE that creates one common view of the local machine or network and the Internet.

Windows NT—A network operating system from Microsoft.

Windows NT Server 4.0—The latest version of the network operating system developed by Microsoft. This software product boasts several key features, including security, fault tolerance, high performance, central administration, scalability, and auditing.

WINIPCFG—A Windows 95 service that allows a client to display its IP configuration and lease information.

XML (Extensible Markup Language)—A complementary format to HTML that is used to define, validate, and share document formats in a rich and structured manner.

Index

Bold page numbers indicate sample exam questions.

B

G

H

I

N

O

T

U

V

Certification Insider™ Press

Exam Cram Series

Designed especially for the busy, working professional, Coriolis's Exam Cram guides go right to the core of certification. Each guide is jam-packed with hundreds of test-taking tips, insights, and strategies that simply cannot be found anyplace else. What makes the Exam Cram series different from other certification study guides is that each book is organized and linked to a specific exam. Each chapter is divided into three parts. The first part reviews and analyzes a specific section of a certification test and discusses important test-taking terminology. The second part contains review questions and discusses the wrong answers as well as the right ones. The third part contains resources and very valuable online pointers. Each book has a sample test with answers and a special chapter on test-taking strategies.

Test and perfect your skills using the interactive study center CD-ROM

ISBN: 1-57610-198-3
$99.99 U.S. $139.99 CAN

ISBN: 1-57610-285-8
$99.99 U.S. $139.99 CAN

ISBN: 1-57610-191-6
464 PAGES $29.99 U.S.
$41.99 CAN

ISBN: 1-57610-190-8
416 PAGES $29.99 U.S.
$41.99 CAN

ISBN: 1-57610-192-4
352 PAGES $29.99 U.S.
$41.99 CAN

ISBN: 1-57610-193-2
480 PAGES $29.99 U.S.
$41.99 CAN

ISBN: 1-57610-195-9
416 PAGES $29.99 U.S.
$41.99 CAN

ISBN: 1-57610-287-4
446 PAGES $29.99 U.S.
$41.99 CAN

ISBN: 1-57610-236-X
480 PAGES $29.99 U.S.
$41.99 CAN

ISBN: 1-57610-194-0
300 PAGES $29.99 U.S.
$41.99 CAN

ISBN: 1-57610-229-7
300 PAGES $29.99 U.S.
$41.99 CAN

ISBN: 1-57610-230-0
300 PAGES $29.99 U.S.
$41.99 CAN

ISBN: 1-57610-286-6
300 PAGES $29.99 U.S.
$41.99 CAN

Available Soon

ISBN: 1-57610-221-1
300 PAGES $26.99 U.S.
$37.99 CAN

Available Soon

ISBN: 1-57610-222-X
300 PAGES $26.99 U.S.
$37.99 CAN

Available Soon

ISBN: 1-57610-223-8
300 PAGES $26.99 U.S.
$37.99 CAN

Prices and availability are subject to change.

www.certificationinsider.com